WARREN HASTINGS

and

British India

is one of the volumes
in the

TEACH YOURSELF HISTORY
LIBRARY

Edited by A. L. ROWSE

Teach Yourself History

VOLUMES READY OR IN PREPARATION

The Use of History, by A. L. Rowse
Pericles and the Athenian Tragedy, by A. R. Burn
Alexander the Great and the Hellenistic Empire, by A. R. Burn
Julius Cæsar and the Fall of the Roman Republic,
   by M. I. Henderson
Augustus and the Roman Empire, by M. P. Charlesworth
Constantine and the Conversion of Europe, by A. H. M. Jones
Marco Polo and the Discovery of China, by G. F. Hudson
Innocent III and the Mediaeval Papacy, by A. Hamilton Thompson
John Wycliffe and the Lollards, by K. B. McFarlane
Henry V and the Invasion of France, by E. F. Jacob
Joan of Arc and the Recovery of France, by Alice Buchan
Erasmus and the Renaissance, by Margaret Mann Phillips
Cranmer and the English Reformation, by F. E. Hutchinson
Queen Elizabeth and Her Age, by A. L. Rowse
Raleigh and the British Empire, by D. B. Quinn
Laud and the English Church, by Norman Sykes
Cromwell and the Puritan Revolution, by Mary Coate
Gustavus Adolphus and the Thirty Years' War, by Raymond Carr
Richelieu and the French Monarchy, by C. V. Wedgwood
Milton and the English Mind, by F. E. Hutchinson
Louis XIV and the Greatness of France, by Maurice Ashley
Wesley and the Methodist Movement, by Norman Sykes
Chatham and the British Empire, by Sir Charles Grant Robertson
Cook and the Opening of the Pacific, by James A. Williamson
Catherine the Great and the Expansion of Russia,
   by Gladys Scott Thomson
Bolivar and the Independence of Spanish America, by J. B. Trend
Jefferson and American Democracy, by Max Beloff
Pushkin and Russian Literature, by Janko Lavrin
Livingstone and Central Africa, by Jack Simmons
Gladstone and Modern Liberalism, by J. L. Hammond
Abraham Lincoln and the United States, by K. C. Wheare
Bismarck and the German Empire, by Con O'Neill
Parnell and the Irish Nation, by Nicholas Mansergh
Clemenceau and the Third Republic, by J. Hampden Jackson
Woodrow Wilson and American Liberalism, by E. M. Hugh-Jones
Venizelos and Modern Greece, by J. Mavrogordato
Lenin and the Russian Revolution, by Christopher Hill
Botha, Smuts and South Africa, by Basil Williams

WARREN HASTINGS
(*from the portrait by Tilly Kettle in the National Portrait Gallery*)

WARREN HASTINGS

and

British India

by

PENDEREL MOON

(SOMETIME FELLOW OF ALL SOULS COLLEGE, OXFORD)

Published by

HODDER & STOUGHTON LIMITED

for THE ENGLISH UNIVERSITIES PRESS

AT SAINT PAUL'S HOUSE

IN THE CITY OF LONDON

FIRST PRINTED OCTOBER 1947

PRINTED IN GREAT BRITAIN FOR THE ENGLISH UNIVERSITIES PRESS, LTD.
LONDON, BY HAZELL, WATSON AND VINEY, LTD., LONDON AND AYLESBURY

A General Introduction to the Series

THIS series has been undertaken in the conviction that there can be no subject of study more important than history. Great as have been the conquests of natural science in our time —such that many think of ours as a scientific age *par excellence*—it is even more urgent and necessary that advances should be made in the social sciences, if we are to gain control of the forces of nature loosed upon us. The bed out of which all the social sciences spring is history; there they find, in greater or lesser degree, subject-matter and material, verification or contradiction.

There is no end to what we can learn from history, if only we will, for it is coterminous with life. Its special field is the life of man in society, and at every point we can learn vicariously from the experience of others before us in history.

To take one point only—the understanding of politics: how can we hope to understand the world of affairs around us if we do not know how it came to be what it is? How to understand Germany, or Soviet Russia, or the United States —or ourselves, without knowing something of their history?

There is no subject that is more useful, or indeed indispensable.

Some evidence of the growing awareness of this may be seen in the immense increase in the interest of the reading public in history, and the much larger place the subject has come to take in education in our time.

This series has been planned to meet the needs and demands of a very wide public and of education—they are indeed the same. I am convinced that the most congenial, as well as the most concrete and practical, approach to history is the biographical, through the lives of the great men whose actions have been so much part of history, and whose careers in turn have been so moulded and formed by events.

The key idea of this series, and what distinguishes it from any other that has appeared, is the intention by way of a biography of a great man to open up a significant historical theme; for example, Cromwell and the Puritan Revolution, or Lenin and the Russian Revolution.

My hope is, in the end, as the series fills out and completes itself, by a sufficient number of biographies to cover whole periods and subjects in that way. To give you the history of the United States, for example, or the British Empire or France, via a number of biographies of their leading historical figures.

That should be something new, as well as convenient and practical, in education.

GENERAL INTRODUCTION

I need hardly say that I am a strong believer in people with good academic standards writing once more for the general reading public, and in the public being given the best that the universities can provide. From this point of view this series is intended to bring the university into the homes of the people.

A. L. Rowse.

All Souls College,
Oxford.

Contents

CHAPTER		PAGE
	A GENERAL INTRODUCTION TO THE SERIES	V
I.	INTRODUCTION	I
II.	BIRTH AND EDUCATION . . .	7
III.	CLERK IN THE EAST INDIA COMPANY	12
IV.	MEMBER OF VANSITTART'S COUNCIL	36
V.	ENGLAND AND MADRAS . . .	58
VI.	THE SITUATION IN BENGAL . .	70
VII.	HASTINGS, GOVERNOR OF BENGAL .	85
VIII.	THE ROHILLA WAR	117
IX.	THE NEW COUNCILLORS . . .	134
X.	DISCOMFITURE OF NANDAKUMAR .	151
XI.	HASTINGS RECOVERS POWER . .	168
XII.	HASTINGS AND FRANCIS . . .	187
XIII.	HASTINGS PRESERVES BRITISH DOMINION IN INDIA . . .	201
XIV.	INTERNAL DISSENSIONS . . .	235
XV.	THE BENARES OUTBREAK AND THE BEGUMS OF OUDH . . .	255
XVI.	LAST YEARS IN BENGAL . . .	284
XVII.	IMPEACHMENT AND RETIREMENT .	308
XVIII.	HASTINGS' CHARACTER AND OPINIONS	328
	NOTE ON BOOKS.	355

Chapter One

Introduction

WARREN HASTINGS was our first Governor-General in India. Lord Mountbatten is to be the last. We live at the close of an episode of which he witnessed the very first beginnings. In some ways we are perhaps better qualified to understand him than those who lived in the heyday of the British Raj and attributed to him all their own confident assumptions.

When he first landed in India, the English still bore what he called "the humble and undreaded character of trading adventurers." Their extraordinary metamorphosis into rulers of a mighty empire he experienced in his own person; for he himself lived for seven years as a humble trader in the country which he subsequently governed. Merely by following his career we can trace the ultimate origins of the British dominion.

It is often said that British dominion did not originate in aggression and was not prompted by 'imperialism.' Such statements are at best half-truths. They are not borne out by Hastings' testimony. He never ceased to deplore "our encroaching spirit and the insolence with which it has been exerted;" nor did he imagine that Plassey and Buxar, the two decisive battles which made the East India Company masters of Bengal, were fought by the Company in self-defence. The truth is that the instincts and motives which, when harnessed to the organised power of a modern State and consciously directed, produce 'imperialism,' gave birth also to the British dominion in India. It was unplanned, but it was not unpurposed. It originated in British aggression, but it was the instinctive aggression of individuals seeking their own fortunes rather than the planned aggression of a State or Corporation. Plassey and Buxar were neither planned nor willed by the Company's Directorate at home, still less by the British Government. They were just the natural consequences of the actions of the Company's servants on the spot, pursuing their own personal interests as much as those of the Company or the nation.

These adventurous freebooters did not profess or pretend to act for noble ends or from altruistic motives. They risked their lives in a distant country and unhealthy climate simply for gain. Fortunes for themselves, dividends for the Company, wealth rather than glory, plunder rather than power—these were their objects. In pursuit of them they discovered a new technique which even the planned neo-imperialisms of our own day have not despised. We have heard much of puppet governments; but the first puppet governments of the modern world were those of eighteenth-century India, under cover of which the servants of the East India Company amassed their fortunes. In Bengal, in the Carnatic, in Oudh, and, in a later generation, in Hyderabad, it was the same story. The predatory designs of individuals sheltered under the name, yet exploited the impotence, of puppet rulers. Hastings witnessed the system and grew to detest it. In Bengal he ended it, and by openly substituting British rule for the sham rule of a puppet Nawab, laid the foundations of something better.

It must not, however, be supposed that Hastings was an enthusiast for British rule or wished to extend it to other parts of India. On the contrary, such was his dislike of it and his anxiety to preserve native Governments in their full integrity, that in the Carnatic and in Oudh he unwittingly preserved or promoted that very type of sham régime which he detested. Unlike Englishmen a century later, he never imagined that for a people to be conquered and ruled by foreigners was anything other than a grave misfortune—a misfortune which might be mitigated but could hardly be converted into a blessing in disguise. The idea of 'trusteeship' as applied to subject peoples had not yet been born, and he could not escape the influence of obvious facts falling within his own observation. After Plassey he saw the gentle, submissive Bengali terrorised by overbearing Englishmen: he saw the trade of the country ruined, the government disorganised, and immense wealth drained away in the remittance of private fortunes without return of any kind. It never occurred to him that such indisputable loss could be offset by the advantages of British rule—if indeed it possessed any. In his view, British rule suffered from "many radical and incurable defects," could not be lasting, and was of questionable benefit even to Britain herself. The most that wise policy could achieve was to minimise its evils, to make the best of such temporary advantages as it offered and "to protract that decay which sooner or later must end it."

The end that is now coming is totally different from anything that Hastings could have foreseen; but he might justly claim that he contributed as much as any man to its postponement; indeed, if it had not been for him, the British Raj must have collapsed almost before it had begun. He steered it at its very start through greater perils than it ever again encountered till 1941–42. Philip Francis, Hastings' colleague and enemy, bears witness to these perils. Even before the crisis caused by the disastrous War of American Independence, he was saying that he fancied himself "on Board a

4

great leaky vessel, driving towards a Lee Shore and Shipwreck not to be avoided, but by a Miracle." The miracle occurred. Through sheer industry and administrative ability Hastings brought order into the chaotic government of Bengal and then, with indomitable courage, fought off all enemies, both external and internal. Though in 1780 the Company was faced with a combination of all the strongest powers in India, supported by the French; though temporarily Britain lost command of the sea; and though elsewhere in the world British arms were suffering reverses, Hastings never wavered, never cried out for peace. His dogged refusal to give in and his active boldness even in the midst of adversity gave the Rulers and Peoples of India a deeper impression of British strength and character than any famous victories.

The story of Hastings' career in India has been overlaid with controversy regarding certain relatively unimportant episodes. Some discussion of these old matters of controversy—the Rohilla war, the trial of Nandakumar, the treatment of Chait Singh of Benares, the spoliation of the Begums of Oudh—cannot be avoided. Whatever their interest may be to the political moralist, historically their significance is small; and they are perhaps mainly valuable to-day simply as illustrations of the ways in which power tends to operate in India. They must not be thought of just as episodes from a vanished age, but as characteristic also of the India of our own times. Hastings' tyrannical behaviour towards Chait Singh is only a conspicuous instance of a tyranny still frequently practised on a small scale by district officers in India. The forced extraction of money from the miserly eunuchs of the Begums of Oudh has its modern analogy in the collection of war funds during the last two wars. Nor is the dramatic and seemingly fortuitous discomfiture of Hastings' accuser Nandakumar without its modern parallels. Those in authority in India still sometimes see disaster overtake their enemies by what seems to be an inexplicable stroke of fate, but is really the result of the subterranean working of their friends.

Chapter Two

Birth and Education

AMONG the immediate ancestors of a great man it is usually possible to detect some traces of the genius which has raised him above the common level. This is not so with Hastings. Nothing that is known of his parents or near relatives affords the slightest indication whence he derived his remarkable qualities of mind and character.

He came of a family which had once owned large estates, but had been ruined during the Civil War owing to its devotion to the King. In 1715 even the family seat, the Manor at Daylesford, had to be sold, and Hastings' grandfather, who had taken Orders and become rector of Daylesford, moved with his family to a small house in the neighbouring village of Churchill.

Here Hastings was born in December 1732. His mother, Hester Warren, the daughter of a Gloucestershire farmer, died a few days after his birth. He was her second child—the first had been a daughter—and was called Warren after her. His father, Penyston Hastings, who, like the grandfather, took Orders, remarried shortly after her death and went away to the

Barbadoes, where he became rector of Christchurch and died about ten years later.

Warren Hastings was thus left, for all practical purposes, an orphan. He was brought up by his grandfather at Churchill, and from his earliest childhood heard from him stories of the former wealth and greatness of the family. These made a deep impression on his mind, and he has himself left a record of his childish dream that one day he might restore the family's fallen fortunes and recover Daylesford Manor, the home of his ancestors. "One bright summer's day," musing beside the village brook, "when I was scarcely seven years old, I well remember that I first formed the determination to purchase Daylesford. I was then literally dependent upon those whose condition scarcely raised them above the pressure of absolute want; yet somehow or other the child's dream, as it did not appear unreasonable at the moment, so in after years it never faded away."

Hastings' grandfather sent him to the village school at Churchill; but when he was eight years old, an uncle, Howard Hastings, who held a post in the Customs and was comparatively well-to-do, assumed responsibility for his education. Realising perhaps that young Warren was a decidedly clever boy and would profit from a proper education, he brought him to London and sent him to a school at Newington. There he was well taught but badly fed. He himself always attributed—doubtless erroneously—his small frame and stature to under-nourishment at this time. After rather more than two years of this Spartan discipline he went on to Westminster which then ranked with Eton as the leading school in the country.

Education in the eighteenth century meant education in the classics. Other subjects were scarcely taught at all. From study of the classics a boy was expected to acquire noble and generous sentiments and to learn to prefer virtue to vice. Homer and Virgil, Chatham told his nephew, "are not only the two greatest poets, but they contain the finest lessons for your age to imbibe: lessons of honour, courage, disinterestedness, love of truth, command of temper, gentleness of behaviour, humanity, and in one word, virtue in its true significance." The classical education which Hastings received at Westminster certainly influenced him profoundly. In his case the mere fact that he received and appreciated it was to be of considerable significance. It meant that this orphan, brought up in a village by an impoverished clergyman and packed off to India at the age of seventeen as a clerk in a trading company, possessed, nevertheless, a cultivated and enlightened mind; and it meant that this trading company, when suddenly called upon to govern a distant empire, found among its servants a man who was a scholar and a states-

man, not a mere merchant or fortune-hunter—
a man who brought to the task of government
a mind enlarged and a character strengthened
by the wisdom, the warnings and the examples
of classical antiquity.

Hastings was a good scholar and a favourite
pupil of Dr. Nicholls, the headmaster. When
only fourteen he gained first place in the
examination for the King's Scholarship. His
life-long friend, Elijah Impey, was placed
fourth.

Another contemporary at Westminster, Cowper, the poet, has left a hint of his character at school. Forty years later at the time
of the impeachment, Cowper remembered him
as such a pleasant, good-natured boy, that he
could not believe that he had been guilty of the
oppressions attributed to him. This good
nature, though it has been obscured by the con-
troversies in which his public life became involved, remained an essential feature of his
character and explains in part the popularity
which he later enjoyed as Governor-General.
His easy affability and natural friendliness of
disposition, contrasting so markedly with the
overbearing manners of his rival, Clavering, and
many other Englishmen, appealed strongly to
the people of Bengal.

When Hastings was fifteen, his career at Westminster was abruptly terminated. His uncle
died, leaving him to the care of a friend

and distant relative, named Creswicke. Mr. Creswicke had some influence with the East India Company (of which he later became a Director), and was in a position to secure for Hastings a post as writer or clerk in the Company's service. Hastings had nothing to tie him to England and no certain means of livelihood. The post in the Company's service in India offered immediate employment and the ultimate prospect of a fair fortune. Mr. Creswicke decided that Hastings should leave Westminster and take this opening; and Hastings himself seems to have agreed that this was the best course. Dr. Nicholls vainly remonstrated at the loss of his most promising scholar; he even offered to pay for the completion of his school education. If this offer had been accepted, Hastings would have proceeded in due course to a studentship at Christchurch, and might finally have distinguished himself as a scholar or a bishop or as both. But from these possibilities he was saved or debarred by the sound good sense of Mr. Creswicke, who firmly took him away from Westminster, and procured for him a writership in the East India Company. He spent a few months at a commercial academy learning accounts and book-keeping, and in January 1750, when he was only just seventeen, sailed for Calcutta.

Chapter Three

Clerk in the East India Company

WHEN Hastings reached India, the great Mogul empire, whose riches and splendour had dazzled the early European settlers, was already on the point of dissolution. Aurangzeb, the last effective emperor, though he had extended its boundaries to their farthest limits, had shaken its solidarity by his persecuting zeal; and the campaigns which he had conducted in his old age against the Maratha [1] powers of Central India had strained its resources without effectively crushing them. He had died in 1707 in his eighty-ninth year in a mood of doubt and anxiety. "All the soldiers," he wrote in a farewell letter to one of his sons, "are helpless, bewildered and perturbed, like me. I brought nothing with me into the world, and I am taking from it but the fruit of my sins. I know not what punishment will befall me. Though I have a firm hope in God's grace, yet for my deeds anxiety ever remains with me." He had some cause for apprehension. Fifty years earlier, in order to gain the throne, he had imprisoned his father and caused two of his brothers to be put

[1] See below, Chapter Eight, page 123.

to death. These crimes, even if they brought no retribution in another world, formed in this one a bad precedent. His death was the signal for an outbreak of fratricidal strife among his sons, followed a few years later by a similar struggle among his grandsons. From these disastrous conflicts there emerged no one of sufficient character and ability to hold the empire together. A succession of merely nominal sovereigns occupied the imperial throne. The Governors of distant provinces disregarded orders from Delhi and became virtually independent. The Marathas, ranging unchecked through Central India, appropriated the provinces of Malwa, Gujarat and Berar; and in 1739 the impotence of the Great Mogul was nakedly revealed when Nadir Shah of Persia invaded India, sacked Delhi and carried off the imperial treasures.

But though rotten at the centre, the empire still preserved in its outlying parts an appearance of order and majesty. Confusion was by no means universal. There were still large provinces, more extensive and populous than most countries of Europe, where Muslim Governors carried on uninterruptedly the Mogul system of administration and where the life of the people continued in peace and prosperity. Such was the case in Bengal. A Governor or Subahdar, known as the Nawab of Bengal, nominally a servant of the emperor but no longer effectively controlled from Delhi, ruled the province in the emperor's name with deputies in Bihar and Orissa. When Hastings first arrived in Bengal, Allahvardi Khan, a strong and capable man, had for ten years occupied the position of Nawab. During this time Maratha armies had made several incursions into his western territories and had once even caused alarm in Calcutta. But by a judicious combination of force and bribery he had succeeded in getting rid of them and in keeping Bengal itself free from serious commotion. The province was tranquil and flourishing.

The servants of the Company were accustomed to behave towards the Nawab with the humility and respect due to so great a potentate. Compared with him they were very small fry. They addressed him "with the humblest submission," conscious how much the success of their trade depended on his good-will. Hastings himself described them as being at this time "subject to the most slavish dependence on the Government." It had not yet occurred to them that the ruler of a large province and representative of the Great Mogul might really be only a man of straw whose power could easily be broken.

In Southern India the position was not very dissimilar. Here too there still ruled a Muslim Governor, the Nawab of the Carnatic, ostensibly deriving his authority from the Mogul emperor. To him the Company owed fealty for its

14

settlements at Madras (Fort St. George) and Fort St. David. But he was a lesser figure than the Nawab of Bengal. He ruled over a smaller territory and was subordinate to another official, the Subahdar of the Deccan, who controlled all the imperial dominions south of the river Nerbudda. From 1724 to 1748 this post of Subahdar was held by Asaf Jah,[1] one of the ablest of the Great Mogul officers of his time. He paid no tribute and gave scant recognition to the emperor at Delhi. His main concern was to keep his own territories free from the Marathas, and with this in view he did not hesitate to deflect them into the imperial provinces of Malwa and Gujarat. He succeeded by this means in keeping Southern India fairly free from tumult and disorder, and, so long as he lived, he constituted in these regions a lawful and recognised authority, seemingly powerful and reasonably effective.

Rulers such as Asaf Jah and Allahvardi Khan, by preserving within their great provinces something of the tradition and prestige of the Mogul empire, masked its precarious condition. When, therefore, Hastings landed in India, the imminence of its dissolution was not necessarily apparent to contemporary observers, least of all to the Company's servants in Bengal, living under Allahvardi Khan's steady and peaceful

[1] He enjoyed the title Nizam ul Mulk (Regulator of the State), by which his descendant, who rules to-day in Hyderabad, is still known.

15

sway. They could hardly guess that the whole vast structure was about to collapse in all its parts in utter and irretrievable ruin, still less could they guess that the Company was to take its place.

The English East India Company had by this date already taken the lead over other European organisations in the purely Indian trade, outdistancing its early rivals, the Dutch, who were increasingly concentrating their attention on the Malayan Archipelago. Its most active and dangerous competitors were now the French, who, though late in the field, had established themselves at Pondicherry, Chandernagore, and Mahé on the Malabar Coast. The English Company's main establishments were at Bombay, Madras and Calcutta. Each was at this time governed independently of the others by a President (or Governor) and Council who were responsible only to the Directors of the Company in England. Madras, the Company's oldest possession, had been acquired in 1639 from a Hindu ruler, who gave the Company permission to fortify and administer it in return for an annual quit-rent—an arrangement confirmed later by the Mogul authorities. Bombay had come into the possession of the British Crown as part of Catherine of Braganza's dowry, and no Indian authority had any claim to jurisdiction there. Since 1668 it had been held and administered by the Company on the Crown's behalf on payment of an annual rent of £10. In Bengal the Company had established a few trading stations by the middle of the seventeenth century; but it was not till nearly fifty years later that it acquired by purchase from the Nawab of Bengal the rights of 'zemindar' [1] in three villages which became the site of Fort William and the town of Calcutta. As 'zemindar,' the Company was responsible within its 'zemindari' for most functions of government, including the administration of justice.

In addition to powers derived from Indian authorities, the Company possessed jurisdiction over English subjects by virtue of charters granted from time to time by the Crown. These also authorised it to coin money and to keep armed men and vessels of war.

Thus at all three Presidencies the Governor and Council were charged with considerable administrative duties in addition to the management of the Company's mercantile business; and these multiplied as more and more Indian merchants came to settle in areas protected by the Company's fortresses. Consequently to fill adequately the Company's highest offices in India rather more was required than mere familiarity with the intricacies of trade. It was necessary, in the Directors' opinion, to be "a man of parts and education, a statesman as well as a merchant." The correctness of this opinion

[1] In this context may be roughly translated 'landlord.'

was soon to be proved in a manner which the Directors had hardly expected. Unfortunately, men of parts and education were not very readily to be found among the Company's servants.

Hastings at first had no concern with these administrative functions. He was set down to assist in the keeping of the accounts and in the superintendence of the warehousing of goods for export. These goods consisted principally of silks from Kasimbazar, muslins and textiles from Dacca and saltpetre from Patna, at all of which places the Company maintained factories. In exchange for these goods the Company sent out from England woollens, broadcloth, hardware, metals and guns. The Company's Bengal trade had been increasing steadily for some years, but it could at any moment be brought to a standstill if the Mogul authorities chose to be obstructive; for the principal markets were not near the coast but far inland, and goods moving between them and Calcutta had to pass through a whole network of inland customs posts at any one of which they might be held up. The Company had always been at pains to obtain for its trade exemption from these customs dues, and had from time to time persuaded the Mogul authorities to issue 'farmans,' granting it this privilege in return for lump-sum payments. The latest of these 'farmans' had been extracted in 1715 from the Emperor Farakhsiyar,

after the Company's emissary, John Surman, had
spent two years humbly waiting upon him. Its
terms were somewhat ambiguous and the
Emperor's authority over his nominal subordinate in Bengal was uncertain. But the 'farman' proved to be of some real value, and on the
strength of it successive Nawabs of Bengal
generally permitted the Company's own trade,
as well as the private trade of its European servants, to be carried on free of duty. During
Allahvardi Khan's time there were no serious
disputes or difficulties.

Little is known of Hastings' life at Calcutta
at this time. It may be surmised that his
official duties, though uninteresting, were
not arduous, and that, like other servants
of the Company, he devoted a good part of his
time to private trading on his own account.
Though at an earlier date forbidden, private
trade was now not only permitted but recognised
by the Company as the chief method by which
its servants might enrich themselves. Their official salaries were absurdly small. Hastings as a
writer drew only £5 per annum, and even the
Governor of Fort William received only £200.
The salaries were augmented, no doubt, by
various perquisites and allowances which in the
aggregate might amount to a very large sum;
but even so the emoluments would not have
been sufficient compensation for years of exile
in a trying climate unless supplemented by the

profits of private trade. These were often considerable. With good management a man might
hope to return to England after about fifteen
years with quite a substantial fortune—if he
survived the climate and the voyage. Trade with
Europe was not allowed, as this interfered with
the Company's own monopoly; but the Company's servants engaged in trade from port to
port in India, e.g. between Calcutta and Madras, and also exported Indian goods to far-
eastern countries.

After three years in Calcutta, Hastings was
sent up-country to the Company's factory at
Kasimbazar where a capable man named Watts
was in charge. Kasimbazar was a thriving commercial town only two miles from Murshidabad,
the capital of Bengal and the Nawab's place of
residence. Watts soon recognised Hastings'
abilities, and deputed him to organise an
'aurang' or sub-factory for the collection and
winding of raw silk at some little distance from
Kasimbazar. The life there was lonely, and
Hastings depended for society mainly on the
natives of the country. It must have been at this
time that, living "among the country people in
a very inferior station," as he himself describes
it, he acquired much of his knowledge of their
habits and customs and developed that regard
and respect for them which later distinguished
him from so many of his contemporaries. As
might be expected of a scholar of Westminster,

he took the trouble to study the languages of the country. He became fluent in Bengali, acquired a good knowledge of Urdu, and a useful knowledge—he himself denied that it was profound—of Persian, the language of the Muhammadan Court.

While Hastings was settling down to his humdrum duties in Bengal, events had been in progress in the Carnatic destined to produce a revolution in the political situation in India. In 1746, as a result of war in Europe between Britain and France, hostilities had broken out between the English at Madras and the rival French Settlement at Pondicherry. Anwar-uddin, the Nawab of the Carnatic, endeavoured to intervene and prevent fighting within his territories. He ordered the French to desist from attacking Madras and, when they persisted and captured the place, he sent forces to drive them out. These were routed with such ridiculous ease that the Nawab became more cautious. The French offered him presents and permission to fly his flag for one week at Pondicherry. Deciding that this was sufficient vindication of his honour and authority, he withdrew from the conflict, which was presently brought officially to an end by the Treaty of Aix-la-Chapelle, whereby Madras was restored to the English.

This result was not acceptable to Dupleix, Governor of Pondicherry. He had hoped to expel the English entirely from the Carnatic. He now revolved fresh plans for their discomfiture. The recent happenings, trivial in themselves, had revealed very strikingly the ineffectiveness of Anwar-ud-din; and in 1748 Asaf Jah, the Subahdar of the Deccan, Anwar-ud-din's patron and superior, died, leaving a disputed succession. This gave Dupleix his chance. He conceived the idea of using his handful of French troops to oust Anwar-ud-din and set up in his place a Nawab who would be entirely favourable to the French. A suitable candidate was available in the person of Chanda Sahib, a relation of a former Nawab who had been killed fighting the Marathas. Dupleix's plans were completely successful. With the aid of a few French troops Chanda Sahib defeated and killed Anwar-ud-din (1749), proclaimed himself Nawab, lavished gifts on Dupleix and his officers and made grants of territory to the French Company.

This was not the end of Dupleix's success. The same methods were employed to install a French nominee in the more important post of Subahdar of the Deccan. Dupleix supported the claims of Asaf Jah's grandson, and by means of intrigue and the use of French troops procured the murder of the rival candidate and the dispersal of his army. His own nominee, having shown his gratitude by the bestowal of the usual presents, was sent off at once to Hyderabad with a French detachment under Bussy to secure his position in the Deccan.

Dupleix was at the height of his power. Two Indian rulers were now his puppets. He had discovered a new technique—shortly to be copied with more lasting results—whereby a handful of European traders could, at immense profit to themselves, determine the rulers of great Indian provinces. Herein lies the importance of these events. They foreshadowed and indirectly gave the occasion for the English Company's subsequent mastery of Bengal.

Dupleix's success did not just spring from a sudden realisation that a small body of European troops could scatter a whole Indian army. The great superiority of European over Indian military technique had long been known; Anwar-ud-din's easy rout at Madras was merely a forcible reminder of it. But hitherto the European traders, far from home and uncertain of reinforcements, had seldom felt disposed to challenge a local ruler who had behind him the whole power of the Mogul empire. So long as that empire retained some semblance of cohesion their defiance and defeat of a local Nawab would only bring down on them some mightier servant of the Great Mogul, who by sheer overwhelming force of numbers would sweep them into the sea before help could come from distant Europe. What Dupleix realised was that with the decay of the Mogul power at the centre the old conditions no longer obtained. The local Nawabs, left without the support and authority of an organised system, were now entirely dependent on their own resources and exposed to the dangers of treachery and intrigue. European military superiority and internal Indian dissensions could now be exploited profitably to make and unmake Nawabs, to wring money and concessions from them and perhaps even to secure a continuous direction of their affairs.

When Dupleix first lent French troops to Chanda Sahib, he seems to have had no other purpose than to enrich himself and obtain for the French an advantage over the English. But the success of his plans, more especially the influence which Bussy gained at Hyderabad at the court of the Nizam, enlarged his ideas. He began to see the possibility of obtaining, through his control of Indian rulers, the real sovereignty over their territories.

It is not necessary to trace in detail how all his projects came to nothing. The English, confronted with what seemed a hopeless situation, rose to the occasion and under Clive's intrepid leadership rallied all the forces that were opposed to Chanda Sahib and the French. Dupleix, on the other hand, was fatally weakened by the absence at Hyderabad of his best officer, Bussy, and a considerable body of troops. Chanda Sahib was defeated and killed;

Muhammad Ali, a son of Anwar-ud-din, whose cause the English had espoused, became Nawab of the Carnatic; Clive returned in triumph to England and Dupleix was recalled to France in disgrace (1754); his grandiose schemes had brought little benefit to his employers; but they formed valuable precedents for the English.

It is not known whether Hastings and the Company's servants in Bengal grasped the full import of these happenings or whether they merely thought of them as incidents in a struggle against the rival French Company. Their significance was certainly not lost on Allahvardi Khan. The French and the English, who between them had overthrown and killed in quick succession three Muslim rulers in Southern India, both had settlements in Bengal and might be tempted to repeat the performance there. Some of his entourage advised him to expel the Europeans. But Allahvardi Khan was growing old and preferred to let sleeping dogs lie. Beyond threatening the French with seizure of their property, he did nothing. Possibly he had some inkling that the French and English, despite their insignificant numbers in India, had great reserves of strength across the sea. In 1756 he died.

He was succeeded by his grandson and adopted son, the notorious Siraj-ud-daula. Though not the monster of iniquity he has sometimes been painted, he was a treacherous

and somewhat despicable young man, altogether
wanting in firmness and judgment. But in view
of what had happened in the Carnatic, where,
according to Muslim reports, "the French and
English had divided the country and reduced
the Nawabs to mere shadows," he had good
reason to be nervous, especially as his own succession to Allahvardi Khan was none too secure.
Against the English he had also some special
grievances. A wealthy Hindu whom he wanted
to arrest had been given asylum at Calcutta and
was not surrendered when request was made.
There were also complaints that the English
were abusing their trade privileges. They were
said to be in the habit of selling to native merchants 'dustuks' or passes for trade duty-free—
a privilege which was meant to be confined to
the Company itself for its own goods. When
therefore the English, on rumours of the
imminent outbreak of war with France, began
increasing the fortifications of Calcutta, Siraj-
ud-daula sent peremptory orders that they
should desist and should demolish what they
had already constructed. Instead of complying,
the authorities at Calcutta replied that they
were merely repairing their batteries in case the
French should attack the place just as they had
previously attacked Madras. This was too much
for the Nawab. Here were the English, who had
already on several occasions given him cause
for annoyance, disputing his orders and calmly

suggesting that there might be a repetition in Bengal of the events in the Carnatic—the very thing he most dreaded. It was like a red rag to a bull. He wrote back in a fury saying that he was marching on Calcutta at once, and threatening to "expel them totally out of the country."

His first action was to seize the Company's factory at Kasimbazar. Watts, Hastings and the rest of the Company's servants there were all made prisoners and taken to Murshidabad. Hastings, however, who seems to have been popular with the native authorities, was quickly released and "permitted to go at large" on the security of Mr. Vynett, the chief of a Dutch factory near by. Similar security offered for the other prisoners was not accepted.

Meanwhile Siraj-ud-daula was marching on Calcutta. He appeared before it on June 16th with overwhelming numbers. The English took refuge in Fort William; but they only had a few hundred troops, and it was soon felt that resistance was hopeless. A decision to evacuate the place was followed by a panic rush for the ships. The Governor, Mr. Drake, was among those who abandoned the Fort "in this unaccountable manner." They made their way downstream to Fulta, a large village at which the Dutch had a factory. The small remnant left behind in the Fort surrendered the next day, and with few exceptions died of suffocation during the following night in the 'Black Hole'—the narrow

27

guard-room in which they were confined.[1] The
survivors were taken as prisoners to Murshidabad, where they were "not a little indebted to
the obliging and good-natured behaviour of Mr.
Hastings," who seems to have visited them as
often as he could.

Having captured Calcutta, Siraj-ud-daula
turned his attention to the suppression of a
rebellious relative. He probably had no idea of
the real strength of the English, and thought
that he could deal with the wretched fugitives
at Fulta at leisure and on his own terms.
Ordinarily his calculations would not, perhaps,
have been very wide of the mark. But, as it
happened, he had chosen a most inoppor-
tune moment to attack the English; for
owing to the recent activity of the French in
the Carnatic and the prospect of a fresh outbreak of war with France, they had assembled
at Madras "a greater naval and military force
than had ever before gathered together in
India." It was intended to use this force to
rescue the Nizam of Hyderabad from the control of Bussy and the French; but on receipt of
the news of the disaster in Bengal, plans were
altered, and an expedition was fitted out under
the command of Clive and Admiral Watson for
the recovery of Calcutta.

The expedition left Madras in October 1756,

[1] This gruesome incident has given Siraj-ud-daula a
dubious fame, but it is unlikely that he intended or was
responsible for it.

but was so greatly delayed by contrary winds that the first ships did not reach Fulta till the very end of the year. The refugees had meanwhile been in considerable distress for want of food, and Governor Drake, hoping to procure some relief from the Nawab, had got in touch with Hastings. To the correspondence which ensued between them Hastings "owed," he said, "his first consequence in the service." Drake wanted him to approach Siraj-ud-daula to make some arrangement for supplying them with food. Hastings thought it unwise to address the Nawab at this juncture and reveal to him the refugees' abject condition. However, on further pressure from Drake he did arrange through one of the Nawab's ministers for supplies to be made available at Fulta.

He also became the medium of further and more questionable correspondence which passed at this time between Fulta and certain influential Hindu bankers in Murshidabad. These wealthy Hindus had already been alienated by Siraj-ud-daula's violence and caprice and were meditating designs for his removal. It is not clear whether Hastings approved of this intrigue, and for the moment nothing came of it. But he seems to have decided that it was now dangerous for him to remain at Murshidabad. He left somewhat precipitately at night and made his way down to Fulta.

Here the refugees, in daily expectation of the

reinforcements from Madras, were engaged in drill and other martial exercises, in which Hastings joined; but the presence of a number of ladies afforded opportunity, during the intermissions of drill, for more congenial occupations, and Hastings quickly succumbed to the charms of a young widow whose husband, Captain Buchanan, of the Company's service, had died in the 'Black Hole.' Almost nothing is known of her. She became engaged to Hastings at Fulta, married him when Calcutta was recaptured, and died in 1759 at Kasimbazar. There were two children by the marriage, a boy and a girl. The latter died in infancy. The boy lived long enough to be sent to England to be educated, but died shortly before Hastings reached home in 1765. The marriage must have been productive of more sadness than happiness.

The forces under Clive and Watson, which reached Fulta in December, pushed on rapidly towards Calcutta, Hastings accompanying them as a volunteer. After a slight skirmish with a detachment of the Nawab's troops, the town was reoccupied. The Nawab himself now appeared with his main army, intending once again to storm the place. But a night attack on his camp (in which Hastings took part) thoroughly scared him. Realising that he was up against a power more formidable than he had bargained for, he made peace, agreeing to respect all the Company's former privileges and to pay compensation for the losses which he had caused.

Having thus completely recovered its position, the Company might well have rested content. But when Clive reached Bengal it was already known that war had again broken out with France. It was also known that there was disaffection at the Nawab's Court—Drake had already been privy to one abortive plot to remove him. Clive had been a witness of Dupleix's methods in the Carnatic. The situation which he found in Bengal offered a golden opportunity for their application. He was not slow to take it. Peace was made with the Nawab in February. By April Clive was engaged in a plot to depose him.

The lead seems to have come from the same Hindu bankers or Seths who had previously been in secret correspondence with Governor Drake. With Clive's active connivance they formed a plot to depose Siraj-ud-daula and replace him by one of his nobles, named Mir Jafar. The English were to supply the force and Mir Jafar the treachery. The Battle of Plassey was the result. Mir Jafar became the Nawab and the English the real masters of Bengal.

There is no evidence that Hastings had any part in the conspiracy. He was certainly too junior to share in its profits. These were handsome. Clive followed the Dupleix precedent in regard to the payment to be made by Mir Jafar for English services. The Company was granted 'zemindari' rights in about 900 square miles of land near Calcutta, and individual servants of the Company received presents in cash. Clive's own modest reward was over £200,000. Hastings' old chief, Watts, netted some £100,000, and others received sums ranging from £5,000 to £60,000. The advantages to be derived from staging a palace revolution were thus signally demonstrated.

Having set up a new Nawab, it was necessary for the English to support and direct him. Mir Jafar agreed to pay for the use of the Company's troops, whose numbers Clive, since his arrival in Bengal, had been rapidly increasing, and to receive a representative of the Company at his Court at Murshidabad. Mr. Scrafton was at first appointed to this important post, but Hastings, who had returned to the Kasimbazar factory at the end of 1757, was selected to succeed him in the following August. He probably owed his appointment, which he describes as "if not the most profitable, one of the most creditable employs in the service," partly to the recommendation of Watts; but Clive, who was *de facto* Governor—a position to which he was later regularly appointed—must have been really responsible for it, and Hastings in a letter to him says, "I look upon myself to be indebted principally to you for being elevated to this office."

He was at this time only twenty-five years old—a fairly early age at which to be given what in those days was the novel task of handling an elderly Indian prince. Clive instructed him, in his dealings with the Nawab, "to act on all occasions so as to avoid coming to extremities, and at the same time show as much spirit and resolution as will convince the Durbar that we always have it in our power to make ourselves respected." This demanded a good deal of discretion. Mir Jafar, old, lazy and rather incompetent, resented the interference of the English, chafed at his dependence on them and would gladly have been rid of them—he did indeed intrigue against them with the Dutch. His son Miran, who commanded the army, though not without vigour, was cruel and completely unreliable. "Sooner or later," Clive wrote to Hastings, "I am persuaded the worthless young dog will attempt his father's overthrow. How often have I advised the old fool against putting too much power in the hands of his nearest relative."

The 'old fool's' most serious difficulty was lack of money. The obligations which he had initially incurred towards the Company were more than he could readily afford. Then there were military operations which had to be undertaken to establish his position in Bihar, where the Shahzada (the Emperor's eldest son) suddenly appeared with an army of free lances, laid siege to Patna and only withdrew on Clive's approach. Added to all this were his own extravagances and incompetence against which Clive and Hastings vainly struggled. Mir Jafar's own solution of his difficulties would have been to plunder the Hindu Seths. But the Seths, having taken part in the plot against Siraj-ud-daula, were protected by the English; so this crude expedient afforded him no easy way out of his embarrassments.

A trivial episode during these early days at Murshidabad is worth mentioning, as it brought Hastings into collision with a man who was to figure prominently later in his life—the Brahman Nandakumar. The circumstances were as follows. Mir Jafar, in order to meet his pecuniary obligations to the English, assigned to them after Plassey the revenue of the districts of Burdwan, Nadya and Hugli. Finding that the revenue was not likely to be paid promptly, Clive and the Council at Calcutta appointed Nandakumar to collect it for them. But they omitted to inform Hastings of this arrangement. He was under the impression that, as Resident at Mir Jafar's Court, he was responsible for supervising these collections, and was therefore not a little put out to find Nandakumar unexpectedly interfering. At first he refused to recognise Nandakumar's authority, but later, when apprised by Clive of the true facts, he had to give way. It is evident that besides experiencing some personal mortification he formed a bad impression of Nandakumar at this time. Probably the Brahman used the power which English support gave him to collect the revenue with great rapacity and make a large profit for himself. Many years later Hastings wrote of him, "From the year 1759 to the time when I left Bengal in 1764, I was engaged in a continued opposition to the interests and designs of that man, because I judged him to be adverse to the welfare of my employers." Clive also came later to form an unfavourable opinion of him.

After he had been a year at Murshidabad, Hastings learnt that Clive was about to leave for England. Conscious of the utter instability of Mir Jafar's régime, which depended entirely on the support of Clive's commanding personality, he wrote to him urging him to remain in India; but without effect. Clive sailed for England in February 1760. With his departure there began one of the most disgraceful periods of our Indian history.

Chapter Four

Member of Vansittart's Council

CLIVE'S successor as President of the Calcutta Council was Vansittart, one of the Company's servants at Madras. He had impressed Clive there with his character and ability and owed his appointment to Clive's recommendation. Pending his arrival Holwell, a survivor from the 'Black Hole,' took charge. The state of affairs at this time was somewhat alarming. The Shahzada had reappeared with an army in Bihar. Eluding the forces sent against him, he entered Bengal and threatened Murshidabad. He was chased back towards Patna by Colonel Caillaud, but in the middle of the operations the Nawab's son and intended successor, Miran, was killed by a stroke of lightning. His death precipitated a crisis. The Nawab's troops began clamouring for pay. But Mir Jafar's treasury was empty, and the subsidies which he had promised to the Company, to defray the expenses of its military forces, were in arrears. The Company itself, though its servants were making large private fortunes, was in great want of money. The Directors at home, on the strength of Clive's misleading reports, had omitted to send out the usual exports from England. They imagined that all expenses in India, including the purchase of Indian goods for despatch to Europe and the cost of war with the French in the Carnatic, would now be met from the untold riches of Bengal! Hastings, pressed by Holwell to squeeze money out of the Nawab, but baffled by the Nawab's extravagance and mismanagement, painted a gloomy picture of the province. "The revenues of the country," he wrote, "have been dissipated in idle schemes of luxury and ill-timed vanity; misspent on useless alliances, and so scantily and injudiciously employed in the expenses of the war, that the sepoys are starving and dissatisfied with the service, the country left a prey to every invader, and the enemy, after continual losses and repeated disappointments, more powerful than ever. I need not observe how small a part of the province of Bahar is in the Nabob's possession. In this (i.e. Bengal proper) the Rajah of Beerboom has publicly thrown off his allegiance. . . . Private intrigues have been forming in the city; and, in a word, we may expect at the opening of the next campaign to see the whole country become a scene of war. The earliest and most vigorous measures are therefore required to obviate the impending dangers."

The step most immediately necessary was to

decide on a successor to Miran. There were two candidates, Mir Kasim Ali, the son-in-law of Mir Jafar, and a Hindu, named Raj Ballabh, who had been Miran's principal revenue officer. It fell to Hastings to advise on their respective merits. He unhesitatingly gave preference to Mir Kasim. Holwell agreed with him and supported Mir Kasim's candidature. He went further. He had reached the conclusion that Mir Jafar could no longer be tolerated and that there must be a radical change. He therefore suggested that Mir Jafar should be pensioned off, retaining only the rank and title of Nawab, and that all the real power of the administration should be transferred to Mir Kasim as his deputy. A barbarous atrocity which occurred about this time gave support to other arguments in favour of this course. Several ladies of rank, including two daughters of Allahvardi Khan, were murdered on the orders, so it was alleged, of Mir Jafar. On this even Hastings, who had generally been his advocate, turned against him.

Vansittart had by now arrived in Bengal. Quite new to the province and at a loss how to cope with the prevailing bankruptcy and confusion, he readily fell in with Holwell's suggestions. An agreement was drawn up with Mir Kasim, who, in return for being put in complete charge of the administration and guaranteed the support of the Company's forces, promised to pay up at once all arrears due to the Company and to cede to them the three districts of Burdwan, Midnapur and Chittagong.

Vansittart himself went up to Murshidabad to inform Mir Jafar of the proposed new arrangement. The old man was so humble and so apologetic for all his shortcomings that Vansittart seems to have felt sorry for him and at first merely brought Mir Kasim to his notice as a man who might help him to carry out reforms. But Mir Jafar would have none of Mir Kasim, and, convinced finally by Hastings that there was no alternative, he elected to abdicate altogether rather than accept Mir Kasim as his deputy. He retired therefore to Calcutta, and Mir Kasim became Nawab in his place (October 1760). Vansittart received from Mir Kasim £50,000 for his services, Holwell £27,000, and other members of Council sums ranging from £10,000 to £25,000. In fairness to Vansittart it must be said that he wished to dispense with these donations, but was compelled by his Council to ask for them.

Hastings had not initiated this revolution and he did not share in its pecuniary rewards; but there seems to be no doubt that he approved of it. He was weary of Mir Jafar. He had a high opinion of Mir Kasim. He believed that the change would be beneficial both to the Company and to the people of Bengal. And so it would have been if the English had behaved towards Mir Kasim after his accession with ordinary decency and justice.

To form a fair judgment of the sequel it is necessary to grasp what were the real implications of elevating an able man like Mir Kasim to the position of Nawab. Unlike Mir Jafar, he was quite capable of standing on his own legs. Efficient and patriotic, he was not disposed to be a mere puppet. He was ready to discharge faithfully all the obligations which he had incurred towards the Company; but he was not ready to comply with any and every demand however unreasonable and however injurious to himself or his subjects. Was the Company prepared to accept this position? Was it willing to let slip the virtual sovereignty that it had acquired after Plassey? Was it content to see a gradual reversion to something like the old order of things that had prevailed in the days of Allahvardi Khan? This, we can see now, was the issue necessarily raised by the substitution of a capable ruler like Mir Kasim for an ineffective one like Mir Jafar.

The Directors in England had neither the means of appreciating nor the opportunity of deciding this issue. It was decided, inevitably, by the Company's servants on the spot. Hastings undoubtedly favoured Mir Kasim just because he was capable. He considered that his desire to be Nawab in more than name was reasonable in itself and by no means incompatible with the

Company's essential interests. He refused to believe that he entertained treacherous designs against the English, and maintained that if the Company dealt fairly by him he would deal fairly by the Company. By the agreement made with him the Company had acquired land and revenues and the assurance of a favoured position which gave it an enormous advantage in trade over all European rivals. More than this was not required. Actual sovereignty, whether open or disguised, was not essential to the Company's interests. On several occasions we find him insisting on the point that Mir Kasim was a 'sovereign prince,' who should be allowed to exercise his rights as such, and that the Company should not usurp these rights, even though it might have the power to do so.

Very different was the outlook of most of Hastings' colleagues. Plassey had raised them from a position of "slavish dependence on Government" to one of dominance, enabling them to browbeat and bully the natives of Bengal (including the Nawab's own officials) and to make enormous private profits by the abuse of trade privileges. In no circumstances were they going to give up or endanger these inestimable advantages. On the contrary, the slightest disposition on the part of the Nawab to assert his authority or to curb their rapacity in the interests of his own people at once provoked a loud outcry and was speciously denounced as an attempt to infringe the rights of the Company and as clear evidence of hostile designs.

This being the prevailing temper of the Company's servants, there could be no accommodation with a Nawab like Mir Kasim. Between their determination to retain and exploit their dominance and his desire to be Nawab in more than name, there was an inescapable conflict. And so from the very instant of his advancement to the position of Nawab he was exposed, in Hastings' words, "to daily affronts such as a spirit superior to that of a worm when trodden on could not have brooked." In the end he was to be goaded into war and a violence bordering on insanity.

Vansittart, the new President of the Calcutta Council, though a better man than most of his contemporaries in India, had not a strong personality. His appointment was unpopular with the Company's servants in Bengal, many of whom felt that he had been brought in over their heads. The fact that almost immediately on arrival he collected £50,000 for making Mir Kasim Nawab did not diminish the prejudice against him; and his position was made more difficult by orders received from the Directors in the summer of 1761 for the reconstitution of his Council. Holwell had already gone home. Three other members who, like him, had shared in the spoils of the recent revolution were now recalled. To replace them the Directors appointed Hastings and three gentlemen, Messrs. Cartier, Hay and Johnstone, whose appetites were quite unsated and who were bitterly opposed to Vansittart and the whole Mir Kasim régime.

Vansittart, as President, had no power to override a majority of his Council. He was only *primus inter pares,* with the privilege of a casting vote in the event of a tie. He had none of Clive's prestige and was not a man, like Clive, who could dominate his Council by sheer force of personality. During the next three years Hastings was to witness him struggling helplessly against a hostile majority such as he himself was to be faced with twelve years later. Throughout this period he showed a loyalty to Vansittart and an honesty, moderation and fairness which deserve the highest admiration.

Before Hastings had even arrived from Murshidabad to take his place in Council, the new members had given evidence of their hostility and ill-will. An important post, that of Chief of the Company's factory at Patna, had fallen vacant. They insisted that it should be filled by a Mr. Ellis, a rude, overbearing man whose dislike of Vansittart was well known. He went off to Patna, ominously resolved to support what he called the interests of the Company and the honour of the English name. This meant, as it turned out, arrogating to himself the right to decide all disputes between employees of the Company and the Nawab's subjects, clapping even the Nawab's own servants into irons, sending a detachment of the Company's troops to search the Nawab's own fort for alleged deserters, and other such high-handed and ill-considered actions. The presence of Mr. Ellis at Patna was a continual source of trouble and irritation.

But even the bitterest opponent of the new Nawab could not deny that his vigour and efficiency produced remarkable results. While the Company's troops disposed of the Shahzada in Bihar, he himself suppressed the disaffected 'zemindars' who had been in semi-rebellion in Bengal. At the same time he rigorously curtailed expenditure with such success that, within eighteen months, he had paid off all the arrears due to the Company. He also began reorganising his army, which under Mir Jafar had been little more than a rabble, and after two years had a regiment of trained artillerymen and 25,000 infantry disciplined on the same lines as the Company's troops.

These military reforms of Mir Kasim, though very necessary, did not appeal to the English quite so much as the punctual payment of his debts. They appeared to indicate altogether too clearly his determination to be master in his own territories. He gave other unwelcome evidence of this determination. The Naib or

Deputy-Governor of Bihar was a rich and wily
Hindu named Ramnarain. Mir Jafar, doubtful
of his fidelity and covetous of his wealth, had
wanted to remove him; but Clive, who constantly intervened with the Nawab on behalf of
Hindu officials, had insisted that he should not
be disturbed, provided that he paid the revenue
and did not intrigue with foreign powers. Mir
Kasim decided to replace him. His wealth
and the very fact that he was looked upon as a
creature of the English doubtless influenced
the decision. But Mir Kasim had good reason for
distrusting him. During the Shahzada's incursions his conduct had at times been ambiguous;
and his wealth was ill-gotten. Mir Kasim demanded to see his accounts. Ramnarain evaded
compliance, representing that as he had regularly paid the stipulated revenue Mir Kasim had
no occasion to see his accounts. He was warmly
supported by the English. But Mir Kasim was
bent on having his own way, and despite English
protests Ramnarain was removed from his post
and imprisoned.

This was a resounding success for Mir Kasim
and a corresponding humiliation for the
English. It is hardly conceivable that Clive
would have permitted it. In Vansittart's Council
feeling was strong and there were acrimonious
debates. But Vansittart decided on a policy of
non-intervention and Hastings supported him.
It was not right, in Hastings' view, to encourage

Ramnarain, "an acknowledged servant of the Nabob," in an assumed independency.

Mir Kasim now proceeded to tread on more delicate ground—the Company's trade privileges. The Emperor Farakhsiyar's 'farman' had been couched in very wide terms, but the Nawabs of Bengal had rightly interpreted it as applying only to goods imported into the country or exported from it by the Company or its *bona fide* European servants. It was never intended that under cover of this privilege employees of the Company, whether European or Indian, should engage in the ordinary internal trade of the province, e.g. trade in grain, tobacco and betel, without paying duty; indeed, the Company's European servants were supposed to be debarred from this trade altogether. There were, however, complaints, even before Plassey, that the Company was abusing its privileges by selling its free 'passes' to native merchants, and this, it will be recalled, was one of the causes of Siraj-ud-daula's annoyance with the English. With his overthrow and the transference of substantial power to the Company, the privileges began to be abused more freely. The Company's servants saw that fortunes could rapidly be made by taking part in the internal trade of the province and using the Company's 'passes' to secure exemption from all the inland customs dues. Mir Jafar, who dared not oppose the all-powerful English,

was induced to issue general orders to his
subordinates that no dues were to be
charged on goods carried to or from the
Company's factories by the Company's agents.
This could be and was interpreted by the
Company's servants as conferring exemption
on any goods for which they cared to claim it.
Furthermore, Mir Jafar empowered the English
to punish any of his subordinates who contra-
vened his orders; so the Company's servants
were able, not only to carry on internal trade
free of all the duties which others had to pay,
but also to punish any official who interfered.
This, of course, gave them a totally unfair
advantage. It meant that they could monopolise
the trade of the country to the ruin of the
people whose livelihood depended on it. It also
opened the door wide to corruption. They
could now make easy money by corruptly selling to outsiders, whether Indian or European,
the right to use the Company's flag and passes.
The effect on the Nawab's revenues was
naturally disastrous.

So long as Clive remained in Bengal there
was some check on these abuses. But on his
departure "there was a general rush of the
Company's servants, and of Europeans of all
classes, towards the interior trade of the three
provinces." The Company's 'dustuks' (passes)
were freely made use of by persons with no
shadow of right to them, and if the Nawab's

47

officials attempted to intervene, a party of the Company's sepoys was summoned from the nearest factory to arrest them.

Mir Kasim, being an efficient ruler, was not prepared to tolerate this system, ruinous alike to his revenues and to his own subjects. He represented the matter to Vansittart, who was disposed to remedy his grievances. But the Majority in Vansittart's Council were indignant at the very suggestion that there should be any restriction on the rights and privileges of the Company. In other words, they were not going to give up their illegitimate profits. Hastings vainly reasoned with them. "The privileges claimed by the Company and allowed by the Government," he pointed out, "were originally designed by both for goods brought into the country, or purchased in it for exportation; in effect it was ever limited to that; nor can any difference of *power* convey to us a *right* which we confessedly wanted before." But the Majority were not amenable to reason. Their own interests were too deeply involved.

Owing to this dispute and the constant discourtesies of Mr. Ellis, relations between Mir Kasim and the Calcutta Council became severely strained. By the end of 1761 even the hostile Majority felt that some step should be taken to prevent an open rupture. Mir Kasim had withdrawn from Murshidabad and established his headquarters at Monghyr, on the borders of Bihar. At this distant capital, remote from Calcutta, he was reported to be busy remodelling his army with the help of foreign adventurers, and repairing and strengthening his fortresses. It was believed that he had concluded a close alliance with his neighbour, the Nawab of Oudh, and there were rumours that the latter intended to march into Bengal. In these circumstances it was decided that Hastings, who of all the members of Council was the most intimately acquainted with the politics and personalities of Mir Kasim's Court, should go up to Monghyr to see him and try to settle the various matters in dispute. He was also to report generally on Mir Kasim's activities and intentions.

As he journeyed up the country, Hastings was distressed to observe "the oppressions committed under the sanction of the English name." "This evil," he wrote, "is not confined to our dependants alone, but is practised all over the country by people falsely assuming the habits of our sepoys, or calling themselves our gomastahs (agents). . . . I have been surprised to meet with several English flags flying in places which I have passed; and on the river I do not believe that I passed a boat without one. By whatever title they have been assumed (for I could only trust to the information of my eyes, without stopping to ask questions), I am sure

49

their frequency can bode no good to the Nabob's revenues, to the quiet of the country, or the honour of our nation; but evidently tend to lessen each of them."

Hastings gained a most favourable impression of Mir Kasim's justice and vigour as an administrator. He reported that whatever his motive for remaining at Monghyr—he did not deny that this might be fear of the Company attempting to depose him—he had employed his time to the greatest advantage. As for his alliance with Shuja-ud-daula, the Nawab of Oudh, he pointed out that the two Nawabs had simply concluded an extradition treaty for the mutual surrender of refractory zemindars. He scouted the idea that there was any cause for alarm. Shuja-ud-daula, who had been appointed Wazir [1] or Prime Minister by the Shahzada (now Emperor under the name Shah Alam), was, he said, much more interested in establishing his nominal master at Delhi than in engaging in adventures in Bengal.

Hastings had hoped to see Mr. Ellis with a view to composing his numerous differences with the Nawab, but that explosive gentleman deliberately kept out of his way. As regards the trade dispute, he laid before the Nawab the following main proposals: (1) that the Nawab's officials should in future be clearly authorised to stop, by force if necessary, boats and con-

[1] Hence often referred to as the Vizier of Oudh.

veyances flying the English flag in order to satisfy themselves that the goods in them were properly covered by a Company's pass; and (2) that they should be empowered to take before a magistrate persons who resisted. The Nawab accepted these proposals, though they did not go so far as he would have wished. But when they were laid before the Council in Calcutta they aroused a storm of indignation. The Majority denounced them as insulting to the honour of the English name. It was intolerable, in their opinion, that the Nawab's officials should stop boats carrying the English flag, or that the Nawab's magistrates should punish persons purporting to be employees of the Company. They demanded that all the Company's servants and agents should be entirely exempt from control by the Nawab's Government. Hastings protested vigorously. "It is now proposed absolving every person in our service from the jurisdiction of the Government. This it is true will prevent their suffering any oppression; but it gives them a full licence of oppressing others, since, whatever crimes they may commit, the magistrate must patiently look on, nor dare even to defend the lives and properties of the subjects committed to his care, without a violation of our rights and privileges. Such a system of government cannot fail to create in the minds of the wretched inhabitants an abhorrence of the English name and authority, and how would it be possible for the Nawab, whilst he hears the cries of his people which he cannot redress, not to wish to free himself from an alliance which subjects him to such indignities?"

Hastings' attempt to effect a compromise having failed, Vansittart himself now went up to Monghyr, fully empowered, so he believed, by his Council, to reach a settlement with the Nawab. He put before him a fresh scheme, which he had devised with Hastings' help, and the Nawab agreed to give it a trial. A regular treaty was drawn up embodying it, and a copy signed by Vansittart was left with the Nawab, who immediately began to act on it. But when Vansittart got back to Calcutta, the Majority contended that he had not been empowered to conclude a treaty, condemned every article of it and flatly refused to confirm it.

On this Mir Kasim, driven to exasperation, took a decisive step: he abolished all inland customs throughout his territories (March 1763). Thus at one stroke, though with great loss to his own revenues, he deprived the English of the unfair advantage which they had been enjoying. The Majority and their supporters were furious. The Nawab's free-trade order, they declared, was a breach of all his engagements with the Company and must be withdrawn. Hastings replied: "The Nawab has granted a boon to his subjects, and there are no grounds for demanding that a sovereign prince should withdraw such a boon, or for threatening him with war in the event of refusal." But the Majority were determined to have their way even at the cost of war. Orders were issued to the military commanders to have the troops in readiness, and Mr. Ellis at the Patna factory was given discretion, despite Hastings' protests, to act as he might think fit, should the Nawab's conduct appear to imperil the Company's interests. He used this discretion to launch a sudden attack on Patna city.

Mir Kasim struck back with an appalling savagery. He captured Ellis and all his men, seized every other European on whom he could lay hands, held them at Patna as hostages, and when an English force from Calcutta advanced relentlessly against him, slaughtered them all in cold blood. Hindus suspected of sympathy with the English were executed and their bodies exposed. Ramnarain was thrown into the Ganges. "The hoarded resentment," wrote Hastings, "of all the injuries which he had sustained . . . now aggravated by his natural timidity and the prospect of an almost inevitable ruin before him, from this time took entire possession of his mind and drove from thence every principle, till it had satiated itself with the blood of every person within his reach, who had either contributed to his misfortunes or even by real or fancied connection with his

enemies become the objects of his revenge."
Such was the dreadful end of the measures
which Hastings had vainly opposed.

The Company's forces, brilliantly led by
Major Adams, advanced rapidly, capturing one
fortress after another. Mir Kasim, fancying that
he had been betrayed, put to death his
Armenian Commanders and retreated into
Oudh. His ally, Shuja-ud-daula, and the
Emperor Shah Alam decided to support him.
They could bring into the field a considerable
army, including 5,000 Afghans who had recently
sacked Delhi, and guns served by Europeans.
But it was all to no purpose. After a long campaign in Bihar, Major Munro, who had succeeded Major Adams, completely defeated them
at Buxar, in the biggest battle yet fought by the
Company in India (October 1764). The illusion
that the Nawab of Bengal might still be a ruler
in more than name was shattered for ever. The
Company was now indisputably and irrevocably
master in all his territories, the kingdom of
Oudh was at its mercy and the Mogul Emperor
a suppliant for its protection.

For every Englishman who knows of Plassey
and the Black Hole of Calcutta, how many can
tell who won the battle of Buxar or who perpetrated the massacre of Patna? Macaulay
doubted whether one in ten "even among
English gentlemen of highly cultivated minds"
could do so. Yet the Patna massacre was an

54

atrocity more costly in lives and far more deliberate than the Black Hole of Calcutta; and Buxar was a real battle costing the victors 847 casualties, whereas Plassey from a military point of view was a farce. Siraj-ud-daula's army was an antique, undisciplined rabble, its commanders were treacherous and he himself cowardly and hated. At Buxar, on the other hand, the Company was confronted by a force possessing at least the rudiments of modern training and representing all that still remained of the old Mogul power. Even if the Emperor himself was but a shadow, Mir Kasim and Shuja-ud-daula were both able Muslim rulers, exercising wide authority and animated by definite feelings of patriotism. Their combination was a real effort by the forces of the old order to withstand the Company's growing power; their defeat meant that the Company's sovereignty in Bengal, however disguised, could never again be called in question. The Nawab ceases to be an ally of the Company and a 'sovereign prince,' and becomes henceforth in fact and almost in theory a nonentity.

The course of action which led to Buxar and to these results was not determined by any profound considerations of policy, still less by any lofty motives; it was determined blindly by the natural operation of the ordinary desires of ordinary men, of whom Mr. Ellis was typical. Hastings, who steadily and strenuously opposed

55

it on grounds of reason and of justice, was over-
borne and overwhelmed by the passions of the
common man. Yet Hastings has been acclaimed
the second founder of our Indian empire, while
Mr. Ellis has been lost in obscurity.

There can be no doubt that Hastings felt
deeply at this time the defeat of all his aims and
the unpopularity which he had incurred among
his own colleagues and countrymen. There were
bitter recriminations in Council which reached
a climax a few days before the actual outbreak
of hostilities. One of the members, Batson,
accused Hastings and Vansittart of being Mir
Kasim's "hired solicitors" who had "defended
all his actions, however dishonourable and detrimental to the Company and nation." On
Hastings' denying the charge, Batson called him
a liar and hit him in the face.

Mir Kasim's subsequent conduct can hardly
have improved Hastings' spirits or sweetened
his relations with his colleagues. With the
murder of 200 Europeans at Patna, all that the
Majority had ever said against the man whom
he had defended must have appeared, on a super-
ficial view, as demonstrably justified. Dis-
heartened and disillusioned, he had already
decided to resign and go home, "being unwilling on the one hand to give authority to past
measures of which I disapprove . . . and apprehensive, on the other, that my continuance at
the Board might serve only to prejudice rather

than advance the good of the service, in keeping
alive by my presence the disputes which have so
long disturbed our councils." But war having
actually begun, he considered it "the duty of
every British subject to unite in support of the
common cause," and he therefore announced his
intention to remain at his post "not as long as
the war should last, but as long as the troubles
consequent from it may endanger the Company's affairs."

The various measures which the Council now
took he accepted as inevitable. Mir Kasim was
deposed and Mir Jafar was brought out again
from his retirement and installed once more as
Nawab. In his anxiety to resume the show of
power before he died, the poor old man promised everything that was wanted of him—to
reimpose the customs duties, to exempt there-
from the Company's servants, to contribute to
the cost of the war, and to pay compensation to
the Company for both corporate and individual
losses. Of the money that was extracted from
him at this time Hastings took no share. He
continued quietly discharging his duties as a
member of Council until Buxar had given decisive victory. Then, along with his superior,
Vansittart, he resigned office and sailed for
England (December 1764).

Chapter Five

England and Madras

HASTINGS spent four years in England, but almost all record of them has vanished. We know neither where he lived nor what he did. One of the few established facts of interest is that he met Dr. Johnson, and the acquaintance, though slight, led to Johnson sending him, when later he was Governor-General in Bengal, a copy of the *Journey to the Western Islands of Scotland* and of Jones's *Persian Grammar*. Hastings, it seems, tried to interest Johnson in a scheme for the establishment of a chair of Persian at Oxford; but nothing came of it.

Immediately on landing in England he learnt of the death of his boy, George. He was thus left without family as well as without employment, and he was soon to be without money. During his fifteen years in India he had accumulated by private trade a sum of about £30,000. Judged by the standards of contemporary 'Nabobs' this was not a large fortune; and it had been honestly come by. Though Hastings had witnessed several revolutions in Bengal, he had not, like others, made money out of them. His hands were clean.

His moderate fortune was not, however, sufficient for the realisation of his ambition to purchase and settle down at Daylesford; and in two
years most of it had disappeared. He was now, as
always, careless in his expenditure, and liberal
towards needy relatives. To his sister, Mrs.
Woodman, he made a present of £1,000 and he
purchased an annuity of £200 for an impoverished aunt. It did not therefore take him
long to run through the £5,000 which he had
actually brought home with him, and in 1767
he learnt that the balance, which he had left in
India, had all been lost, partly through default
of debtors and partly through his own
mismanagement.

He was thus quickly reduced to straitened
circumstances, and the Directors in power at
the India House were by no means disposed to
re-employ him. The dominant faction favoured
the greedy men in Bengal who had fought so
violently to retain their unfair trading privileges, and Hastings and Vansittart found themselves almost as unpopular in Leadenhall Street
as they had been in Calcutta. Clive, who at this
time wielded great influence in the Company,
was also ill-disposed towards them. Though
originally a friend of Vansittart, he had been
shocked at what he considered his weakness in
sacrificing Ramnarain to Mir Kasim, and was
disgusted at his inability to control his own
Council. He himself, in his own judgment, had

left the Company's affairs in Bengal in excellent order; Vansittart and Hastings had made a mess of them.

Vansittart, finding himself sadly discredited, set about trying to justify himself. This he could not do without indirectly casting reflections on Clive; for it was the evil legacy bequeathed to him by Clive which had been the principal cause of all his difficulties. When Clive left Bengal in 1760, the treasury had been empty and the Company's servants demoralised by a mad lust for money which his own example in calmly amassing a huge fortune had done nothing to check. Though Vansittart was at first careful not to attack Clive openly, the facts spoke for themselves. Clive's supporters quickly took up the challenge, and a heated controversy ensued in which Hastings, as Vansittart's principal supporter in Bengal, inevitably became involved. Now, as in Bengal, he remained faithful to Vansittart and helped him with his writings; but he thus became ranged in opposition to Clive, and for the time being found himself on the weaker side. His first requests for re-employment were refused by the Directors.

But the current of events and his friends' efforts on his behalf were already conspiring to assist him. The vast fortunes brought home from India by Clive and other servants of the Company had attracted attention and excited envy. There was a demand that the riches of Bengal should be enjoyed by the whole country instead of being monopolised by a few individuals. An enquiry—the first of many—was instituted by the House of Commons into the affairs of the Company and its newly acquired empire, and in the spring of 1767 Holwell, Hastings, Vansittart and others were called upon to give evidence at the bar of the House. There is unfortunately no record of their evidence, but Hastings is reported to have "attracted general notice by his prompt, masterly and intelligent expositions." Some of the Directors of the Company must have realised that in him they had had a very conscientious and able servant; and it was probably on this occasion that he first made an impression on Lord North and Lord Mansfield and other public men with whom he was brought into closer contact at a later date.

In the following year Francis Sykes, who had succeeded Hastings as Resident at Murshidabad and was on intimate terms both with him and with Clive, returned from Bengal to England. He was distressed to find Hastings in very reduced circumstances—"almost literally worth nothing," he wrote, "and must return to India or want bread." He begged Clive "if he could not consistently promote his re-appointment, at least, not to oppose it." Clive replied, "Mr. Hastings' connection with Vansittart subjects him to many inconveniences. . . . Indeed, he is so great a dupe to Vansittart's policies, that I

61

think it would be improper that he should go to Bengal in any station, and I am endeavouring to get him out to Madras, high in Council there, in which I believe I shall succeed."

With Clive on his side, the way was now clear for his re-employment, and at the end of 1768 he received an order, couched in highly complimentary terms, appointing him second on the Council at Madras, with the prospect of succeeding to the post of President when this should become vacant. He was delighted. The appointment brought to an end a long period of inactivity, hopelessness and growing pecuniary difficulties; these indeed had become so acute that he was obliged to borrow money to purchase his outfit for his return to India. But he now had good prospects before him, and he embarked on the *Duke of Grafton* in March 1769 in the very best of spirits.

In the eighteenth century a voyage to India was an ordeal. Something of its tedium, discomfort and danger has been revived in our own times, when, to reach that country, overcrowded transports have spent months at sea, traversing the Atlantic to America, doubling back to round the Cape, and sometimes disappearing altogether without trace. In Hastings' day the voyage normally took at least six months, and most of it was passed by the passengers in a state of considerable discomfort if not alarm. Hastings speaks feelingly of an "uneasy stomach and confused head, the inseparable companions of a sea life in a small vessel." And in a small vessel in bad weather life was not only unpleasant but unsafe.

Hastings' voyage in the *Duke of Grafton* was enlivened by the presence of a very attractive German lady, the Baroness Imhoff, who was going out to India with her husband and their child. The Baron, a native of Franconia, was badly off, but having some talent as a portrait painter he hoped to turn it to account among the rich 'Nabobs' of Bengal. During the voyage Hastings fell ill; the Baroness nursed him, and they fell in love.

Baron Imhoff seems to have entertained for his wife no strong feeling either of like or dislike. He needed money; and his skill as a painter was a doubtful asset. He was disposed, therefore, to be accommodating; and Hastings, as his first biographer [1] quaintly puts it, was "not firm enough to hold out against the strong temptation which the laws of Protestant Germany, in reference to the marriage contract, cast in his way." In other words, he and the Baron came to an amicable arrangement. This did not, however, take place immediately. At first the Baron obtained a post in the Company's service, and for over two years he and the Baroness lived together (with Hastings

[1] The Rev. G. R. Gleig, *Memoirs of Warren Hastings*, vol. I, pages 165–6.

in constant attendance) first at Madras and later at Calcutta. Then, in 1772, an order was received from the Company for the Baron's recall and a decision had to be taken. It was settled that the Baroness should remain behind at Calcutta and that the Baron should institute in Germany, at Hastings' expense, a suit for divorce on grounds of incompatibility of temper. It seems probable that Hastings, on his part, agreed to send the Baron back to Europe a richer man than he could ever have hoped to become by portrait painting.

The departure of the Baron left Hastings and the Baroness in a somewhat equivocal position; but it seems to have created no serious scandal. There was considerable delay in obtaining the divorce. The decree was not actually passed till 1775, and for some unexplained reason the news of it, enabling Hastings to marry the Baroness, did not reach Calcutta till 1777. During this long period of waiting Hastings displayed a patience and a constancy wholly admirable and wholly typical.

From a utilitarian point of view this second marriage was a remarkable success; in fact, few marriages can have been productive of such felicific consequences for all concerned. Hastings' love for his second wife was deep and lasting—an enduring passion which dominated the rest of his life. He was happy with her and she with him. Imhoff, freed from an attachment

to which he was indifferent, mended his fortunes, recovered his family estate and married
again. His two sons by his first wife gained the
advantage of an excellent upbringing and education which Hastings paid for.

What manner of woman was the lady who for
nearly fifty years commanded Warren Hastings'
unswerving devotion? She undoubtedly possessed good looks, and these lasted far into
middle life and even old age; and she had
sufficient address to win the respect of Calcutta society as well as the approval of George
III and Queen Charlotte. Men were unanimous
in admiring her. Even Philip Francis admitted
that she was "really an accomplished woman"
and "deserved every mark of respect." Women,
as might be expected, were not so uniformly
appreciative. Some considered that she gave
herself airs, tried to take too much of the
limelight and was needlessly extravagant
in dress and coiffure. She certainly liked to
create an effect and was fond of fine clothes and
fine jewellery. Whether she was always quite
discreet and sufficiently careful of her husband's
reputation may perhaps be doubted. His known
devotion to her made her a favourite channel
for requests and petitions, and she probably
accepted a good deal too freely what the peti-
tioners had to offer. One small point of interest
about her is that she never acquired a complete
mastery of English. "Wonderfully well as she

speaks the English language," Hastings wrote in 1803, "she does not always annex to words which are not in common use the precise meaning that belongs to them." This formula has the appearance of a meiosis. One may guess, however, that she exploited her imperfect knowledge of English as an added feminine attraction.

Mrs. Hastings was thirty at the time of her second marriage, and she lived to the great age of ninety. To Hastings' intense disappointment she bore him no children.

Hastings spent two years at Madras—perhaps the most peaceful, uneventful years of all his official career. He liked the Governor, Mr. Dupré, and was happy to find the greatest harmony prevailing among the members of Council —a marked contrast to his previous and subsequent experiences. "I never did business," he wrote, "with men of such candour, or in general of better disposition."

As second in Council his own personal duties were concerned with the superintendence of the Company's 'investment,'[1] and to this he gave a great deal of attention. Owing to the negligence or corruption of the Company's servants, the goods sent home from Madras had very much fallen off both in quantity and quality. Hastings decided on a complete change in the method of procurement, substituting for the

[1] i.e. the goods purchased for export to Europe.

contract system direct purchase by native agents working under the immediate supervision of the export warehouse-keeper. He carried through his reforms in the teeth of the opposition of vested interests, and had the satisfaction of receiving from the Directors a handsome acknowledgment of his services.

In the general affairs of the Council, he played no very conspicuous part. "The uncommon abilities and unwearied application of Mr. Dupré left me little room," he said, "to exert myself beyond the limits of my own particular department." He contented himself therefore with "the humble merit" of supporting the measures which Mr. Dupré proposed. He acquired, however, a first-hand knowledge of the politics and personalities of Southern India which was to be useful to him later on.

As a result of the Seven Years' War, French influence had by this time been practically eliminated. In the Carnatic itself, Muhammad Ali, the English nominee, was established as Nawab, and at the Court of the Nizam of Hyderabad English rather than French influence was now predominant. The main danger to the Company in Southern India came no longer from French rivalry, but from its own exposed position as the real power behind Muhammad Ali. This plausible rascal, of venerable appearance and charming manners, who to pay his debts to the Company borrowed

from the Company's servants at a higher rate
of interest, was little more than a puppet
Nawab, as Mir Jafar had been in Bengal. The
Company, therefore, though still in form only
a trading organisation, was liable to be drawn
into war through the predatory designs of neighbouring Indian powers on Muhammad Ali's
territories. There were successive threats from
the Nizam, from the Marathas and finally from
Haidar Ali, a rough Muslim adventurer of
genius who had made himself master of Mysore.
The Company had been involved in a useless
and costly war with him shortly before Hastings
reached Madras. Though he was defeated in
several engagements, he ravaged a large portion
of the Carnatic and caused consternation by
suddenly appearing before the gates of Madras
itself. Peace was hurriedly concluded a few
weeks before Hastings' arrival; but the evidence
of the panic and the desolation which he had
caused made a deep impression on Hastings'
mind, which was to be revived nine years later.

Hastings stayed only two years at Madras. At
the close of 1771 he received news that the
Directors had chosen him to take charge of their
affairs in Bengal—"an honour equally unsoli-
cited and unexpected on my part"—and early
in February 1772 he sailed for Calcutta. He had
been happy at Madras and regretted leaving its
friendly atmosphere. But Bengal had retained
a hold on his affections, and he knew that the

promotion offered real scope for his abilities. "I doubt whether I shall really profit by the change," he wrote to a friend a few days before departure, "but either pride, or partial attachment to Bengal, makes me much pleased with it."

Chapter Six

The Situation in Bengal

ONLY three years earlier Clive had said that Hastings was so much the dupe of Vansittart's policies that he ought not to return to Bengal in any capacity. How was it that he had now been selected as Governor?

The explanation lies partly in the fact that since Hastings' departure from England in March 1769 there had been a change in the Company's Directorate, and a faction headed by a forceful Director named Lawrence Sulivan had regained control. Sulivan was an unscrupulous but able man, and a bitter opponent of Clive. He had long disliked Clive's policy of political aggrandisement and distrusted his glowing pictures of boundless wealth which somehow never reached the coffers of the Company. Sceptical of Clive, whom he regarded as responsible for the Company's financial embarrassments, he was naturally sympathetic to Hastings and Vansittart. With his return to power, the latter returned to favour, while Hastings' own position became particularly strong. For Clive, as we have already seen, was not unfriendly towards him.

Apart from this, the Company badly needed a man of real ability to take charge of its affairs in Bengal. "Conquests are easily made in this country," Vansittart had warned, "but not easily turned into money." This proved only too true; victories and conquests had produced only deficits; and although supposedly master of all the riches of Bengal, the Company had been forced to raise a loan in order to pay a dividend. Complaints of misgovernment and oppression were loud and frequent. Shareholders and the general public were alike indignant. It was clear that there must be a thorough reorganisation; but the Directors in London could not tell what was really wrong, still less what remedies were required. Conscious of their ignorance, they decided to send out three Commissioners with full power to carry out such reforms as they might find necessary after investigation on the spot. The men selected were Vansittart and two of Clive's supporters, Scrafton and Colonel Forde. They left England at the end of 1769, and were never heard of again. After a year had passed the Directors concluded that their vessel had been lost and that fresh plans must be made. They turned to Hastings. What more natural? His abilities, industry and integrity were now well known. He had had fourteen years' experience in Bengal. He had been the trusted lieutenant and loyal supporter of the dead Vansittart.

And he was acceptable both to Clive and Sulivan.

So Hastings was appointed, albeit only by a narrow margin of votes, to be Governor in Bengal; and it fell to him, without the aid of any extraordinary powers, to do the work for which the Commissioners had been sent out armed with special authority. The task was formidable. One of his predecessors in Bengal, Verelst, summed it up as follows: "To reclaim men from dissipation, to revive a general spirit of industry, to lead the minds of all from gaudy dreams of sudden-acquired wealth to a patient expectation of growing fortunes." It was this; and it was much more than this. Government in Bengal had completely broken down: it was for Hastings to re-establish it. The people were starving and oppressed: it was for him to revive and protect them. The Company was still a trading organisation: it was for him to adapt it to the functions of a sovereign power. But before describing how Hastings set about his immense task, it is necessary to give some account of what had happened in Bengal since he and Vansittart left it at the end of 1764.

The Directors in England had been profoundly disturbed by the dissensions in Vansittart's Council and by the obvious corruption of many of their servants. The outbreak of war with Mir Kasim and the massacre of Patna threw them into a panic. The only solution, they felt,

was to send Clive back again, and he arrived in
Bengal for his second term of office shortly after
the departure of Hastings and Vansittart. The
military danger was quite over, and Mir Kasim
a helpless fugitive. But a settlement had still to
be made with the suppliant Emperor, Shah
Alam, and with Shuja-ud-daula, the Nawab of
Oudh. Clive, with undoubted wisdom, declined
to extend the Company's political commitments.
By the treaty of Allahabad Shuja-ud-daula was
permitted to resume possession of most of his
territories on payment of an indemnity, and an
alliance was concluded between him and the
Company. This was sound statesmanship. Oudh,
with the backing of the Company's troops,
became a useful buffer state between the Company's territories in Bengal and the dangerous
Maratha powers.

Clive's settlement with the Emperor was more
questionable. Shah Alam was without credit and
without power. He was really little more than
an adventurer, possessing in his name and title
his sole assets. He was anxious that the Company should lend him troops for the recovery
of Delhi, and Clive's immediate predecessors,
influenced no doubt by "gaudy dreams of
sudden-acquired wealth" had given him some
encouragement. Clive rightly refused to be
drawn into such foolish adventures; but he quite
gratuitously handed over to him the two districts of Korah and Allahabad—the only terri-

tories which he ever possessed in more than name—and agreed to pay him an annual tribute of 26 lakhs of rupees in return for the formal grant to the Company of the 'Diwani' of Bengal, Bihar and Orissa. An extra burden was thus needlessly placed on these provinces in return for a worthless scrap of paper. The Company was already in effect the supreme power in them, and the grant of the 'Diwani' by a nominal Emperor in no way strengthened its position. Clive of course represented the grant as a triumph, and in London there was an ignorant rush to buy the Company's stock. The price soared, whereas it should really have fallen, for the tribute, being an additional drain on Bengal's resources, diminished *pro tanto* the wealth which the Company could draw from the province.

So much for Clive's external policy. His internal policy was less clear-cut. The Company, by accepting the Diwani, had formally assumed an official authority. But neither Clive nor the Directors were ready to accept the implications. What exactly was meant by the Diwani? Under the old Mogul régime the Diwan was the chief financial officer in a province, responsible for the collection of the revenues and the control of expenditure, and, because of the close connection between the revenues and rights in land, responsible also for the administration of Civil Justice. In Akbar's time the Diwan in a distant province like Bengal was expected not merely to assist the Nawab or Viceroy, but also to act as a check on him lest he should become too independent of the Central Government. The Nawab was primarily responsible for the Nizamat, i.e. the military, police and criminal administration; his Diwan, for finance and Civil Justice. But, with the decay of Mogul power, the Nawab of Bengal became for all practical purposes an independent ruler, controlling all branches of the administration. He no longer had to accept as Diwan an official nominated by the Emperor in Delhi, and the distinction between Nizamat and Diwani, though not entirely obliterated, became somewhat blurred.

The grant of the Diwani to the Company by Shah Alam was therefore in form a revival of long-vanished imperial authority. The Nawab of Bengal—though himself now a mere puppet in the hands of the Company—was formally relieved of certain administrative responsibilities, and these were made over to the Company as Diwan. This at any rate was the theory. But in practice the Company ignored its new responsibilities. As though no change had occurred, the Directors continued to issue instructions to the Company's servants in Bengal not to interfere directly or indirectly in the business of government. The office of Diwan involved, they thought, nothing more than seeing that certain sums of money were paid into the Nawab's treasury at Murshidabad, certain sums paid out for the Nawab's agreed administrative expenses, and the balance transferred to the Company's coffers in Calcutta; and they appointed their Resident at the Nawab's Court to perform this simple duty. As for the actual mode of collecting the revenues and the supervision of the host of agents and officials engaged therein and the conduct of the Civil Courts—in fact, the real administrative duties of Diwan —all these, they fancied, could be left as before to the Nawab.

Clive himself was also in favour of leaving all these duties to the Nawab. His reasons were frankly cynical. He recognised that the real power was now entirely vested in the Company. It possessed overwhelming military force and had undertaken to provide all the troops that were required both for external defence and internal order. There remained to the Nawab, in Clive's words, "nothing but the Name and Shadow of Authority." But "to appoint the Company's servants to the offices of Collectors or indeed to do any act by an exertion of the English Power, which can be equally done by the Nabob at our Instance, would be throwing off the Mask, would be declaring the Company Soubah of the Provinces. Foreign Nations would immediately take umbrage and complaints preferred to the British Court might have very embarrassing consequences."

So they might. But the consequences of Clive's Dual System, as this calculated pretence was known, were equally embarrassing, viz. the failure of receipts to cover expenses, the collapse of the administration and the oppression of the people. These consequences were inevitable, because under this system there nowhere resided any real sense of administrative responsibility. The Company, which possessed the effective power, left everything to the Nawab and his servants; and they, robbed of all real power and independence, had no motive to govern well, but were content to let things slide and obtain for themselves what money and pleasure they could. Like all puppet Governments, the Nawab's Government was utterly degenerate and corrupt; and the Company's servants, hovering on the outskirts and using their real but unacknowledged power for personal rather than public purposes, added to the corruption. The Dual System failed from the moment of its inception.

Appropriately enough the Nawab was now a mere youth of eighteen. Mir Jafar had died shortly before Clive's arrival, and his eldest son, Najm-ud-daula, after the usual distribution of presents to the members of Council, had been permitted to suceed him. His Chief Minister, Muhammad Reza Khan, was selected for him by the Council—and, of course, paid the members handsomely for his selection.

Clive, during his first term in Bengal, had made a fortune by accepting presents. During his second term he endeavoured to repair the ill-effects of his own bad example. The Directors, with perhaps conscious irony, made him take out with him 'covenants' for their servants to sign, prohibiting them from accepting presents and engaging in inland trade. Having set himself to cleanse the Augean stable, Clive proceeded with characteristic courage and resolution. He vigorously enforced the rule about presents, and surprised his colleagues in Council by his indignant insistence that they should refund the 'immense sums' which they had received on Najm-ud-daula's appointment. Unpopularity he disregarded. Mutinies of disgruntled officers he firmly suppressed. But Clive was disqualified by his own past career for the task of leading men's minds from the "gaudy dreams of sudden-acquired wealth." Though he checked the open acceptance of presents, he could do little to correct the "Corruption, Licentiousness and want of Principle" which, he complained, seemed "to have possessed the minds of all the Civil Servants." Nor could he stop the inland trading. Though it was now expressly forbidden, and though in 1768 the Directors granted their servants special emoluments to compensate them for its loss, they were still engaging in it when Hastings took over. The immense havoc inflicted on the country by their virtual monopoly is widely attested.

Clive returned to England in 1767, prophesying for the Company dazzling returns from its Bengal possessions. His successors, Verelst and Cartier, reaped the inevitable deficits. Even without the burden of war the revenue receipts were insufficient to meet the cost of administration, there was no surplus to remit to the Company in England, and, in order to defray expenses, the Company's representatives in Bengal had to raise loans and to appropriate the bullion sent out to finance the China trade. A vicious system of Government, the derangement of economic life caused by the Company's stranglehold on trade, the determination of the shareholders at home and the Company's servants on the spot to wring immediate profits from the country—all these were combining to bring ruin and despair to the people of Bengal. The Company wanted profits without responsibility. Verelst, an honest man, explained to the Directors that this was impossible. "Experience must convince the most prejudiced that to hold vast possessions, and yet to act on the level of mere merchants, making immediate gain our first principle; to receive an immense revenue, without possessing an adequate protective power over the people who pay it; . . . are paradoxes not to be reconciled, highly injurious to our national character, . . .

and absolutely bordering on inhumanity." But the lesson took time to learn, and meanwhile the British taxpayer also demanded a share of the loot. In 1767 the Company was ordered to pay £400,000 annually to the Treasury and, being without funds both in India and England, it had to borrow.

Verelst and Cartier carried on Clive's Dual System as best they could. While a succession of youths, sons of Mir Jafar, occupied the position of Nawab, Muhammad Reza Khan remained the principal minister and the real head of the puppet Government. Verelst, however, had some ideas of his own. He had worked in the three districts of Burdwan, Midnapur and Chittagong, which had been ceded to the Company by Mir Kasim in 1760. Here for some years the English had had real responsibility for the administration; they had acquired some knowledge of the complexities of the revenue system and developed some interest in the welfare of the people. These districts were certainly happier than the rest of Bengal, where the English were still mere freebooters and the native administration cowed and corrupted. Verelst's own experience in these ceded districts led him to think that the introduction of an English executive would improve the administration in the Nawab's territories. A departure was therefore made from Clive's principles by the appointment of English 'supervisors' in all the principal Divisions of the country, with wide and imperfectly defined powers of controlling the Nawab's officials. This well-meant innovation did more harm than good. The Company's servants lacked the experience and the character for such difficult and responsible posts. The Supervisors, with their retinues of native dependants, were simply an addition— and, because the English were considered all-powerful, a formidable addition—to the number of officials battening on the people. There was a rush by the Company's servants to obtain these posts which, with their opportunities for unlimited graft and extortionate trade, afforded the surest means of getting rich quickly.

Some of the Supervisors "in the interval of making their fortunes . . . acquired experience and a real interest in the condition of their subjects." [1] Historically they were the forerunners of the British District Officer and hence mark the first beginnings of much that has been considered most admirable in British rule in India. But their initial effects were deplorable and, as we shall see, they were roundly condemned by Hastings.

Verelst's experiment increased the corruption of the administration and the misery of the people. During Cartier's régime (1770–72) a fearful drought and famine completed the ruin

1 Monckton Jones, *Hastings in Bengal,* page 66.

of both. Contemporary observers believed that one-third to one-half of the population perished, and modern writers accept a mortality of one-sixth to one-fifth as not improbable. Whole tracts of country were abandoned, and many of the cultivators who managed to survive took to vagabondage and dacoity.[1] The revenue of course fell, while expenditure remained unaltered. Debts instead of profits multiplied in Bengal, and the Company's financial distress became so great that early in 1772 it turned in desperation first to the Bank of England and then to the Government for a loan of one million pounds.

Such, then, were the depressing circumstances in which Hastings entered on his new office. He was himself fully aware that it was likely to be one of "trouble and difficulty"; and Clive, writing to him on his appointment, admits that it has come "at a critical time, when things are suspected to be almost at the worst and when a general apprehension prevails of the mismanagement of the Company's affairs." That he himself was in any remote degree responsible for the mismanagement had of course never entered his head. His whole letter, though full of admirable advice and obviously meant to be helpful, is superbly complacent and patronising. He points out to Hastings what he believes to be his weaknesses, viz. a diffidence in

[1] Armed robbery.

82

his own judgment and a defeatist tendency in the face of difficulty—surely an interesting criticism in the light of Hastings' subsequent career. But Hastings, he hints, has only to follow *his* example, and all will be well. "You are on the spot, and will learn my conduct from disinterested persons. I wish your Government to be attended as mine was, with success to the Company and with the consciousness of having performed every duty with firmness and fidelity." Hastings, when he received this letter, was aware that his old chief had made mistakes, and that his Dual System was a failure and would have to be scrapped. His reply, setting forth the main principles of his own intended policy, was courteous but guarded. "No man is better acquainted than Your Lordship with the political interests of the Company in Bengal nor with the difficulties and embarrassments of Government. I cannot therefore wish to profit by a surer guide than your counsel and your example. I shall adopt the principles of both and endeavour to carry them into execution, although in a different line from that which a different situation of affairs required Your Lordship to pursue. It will be my study to confirm without extending the power of the Company in this country, to cultivate the arts of Peace, to establish a regular Administration of Justice, to reduce the enormous expenses of the Company to fixed bounds, and to prune them as much as possible from remote wars and foreign connections.

"In most of these points I find myself supported by Your Lordship's judgment. They are rendered more particularly necessary at the time by the incredible injury which the country has sustained by the famine and mortality of 1770, and the general licentiousness which seems to have prevailed since we took the internal administration of the Provinces out of the hands of the former Government, and placed them without any fixed system in those of our agents."

Hastings clearly knew his own mind and felt that he knew his own business. He was about to undo much of Clive's work, and in this task he was not anxious to receive Clive's advice.

Chapter Seven

Hastings, Governor of Bengal

HASTINGS reached Calcutta in the third week of February 1772, but did not take over from Cartier till April 9th. He spent the interval, he says, in "reading, learning but not inwardly digesting." The orders issued from time to time by the Directors and still requiring attention were voluminous, going right back to the instructions drawn up in September 1769 for the three Commissioners who were lost at sea. These orders covered every conceivable subject, ranging from the general principles of government to the minutest details of the Company's trade; and, as will be presently mentioned, additional orders of vital importance reached Calcutta immediately after Hastings had assumed office.

His private correspondence shows that by the time he took charge, he had already formed clear ideas of his own on the main lines of policy to be pursued. His views on foreign policy will be discussed in the next chapter. As regards the internal government of Bengal, he had two principal objectives; (1) to assert the Company's authority and assume full responsi-

bility for the administration in all its branches;
(2) to withdraw all the 'Supervisors' and confine
European control to the centre and seat of the
administration.

Nine years earlier Hastings had been insisting
on Mir Kasim's rights as a sovereign prince and
dissuading his colleagues from usurping those
rights just because they had the power to do so.
But experience had shown that the Company,
however much it might disguise its power, was
not prepared to surrender it. Hastings, accepting this now as an unalterable fact, desired
that the Company's power should be regulated
and exercised responsibly. This was impossible
so long as it operated covertly through the sham,
corrupted, puppet régime of the Nawab at
Murshidabad. Orders which were received from
the Directors in April enabled him to assert
openly, as he wished, the Company's authority.
Even before their receipt he had decided in his
own mind that the capital should be shifted
from Murshidabad to Calcutta, because Calcutta
was the seat of British power. "As the British
power supports and rules the Country," he
wrote, "that part of it, wherever it be, from
whence that power issues is the natural seat of
government—to substitute any other in its stead
is to surrender the rights and authority of
government with it, and to lay the sure foundation of anarchy and universal rapine."

But, though determined to assert British

power and authority, the last thing Hastings wished to do was to introduce a British system of administration. Except within Calcutta itself he desired all European institutions and European influence to be excluded from Bengal. The actual collection of the revenues and the dispensing of justice—indeed, all branches of the administration—should be left, he considered, entirely to the natives of the country. He even proposed that no Europeans should be permitted to reside outside Calcutta except at the factories in connection with trade. His plan was simply to restore the decayed Mogul system of government, with the English Governor and Council replacing the Nawab, but with the other parts unchanged and entirely native; and he believed that, of the regulations which would be necessary to achieve his aim, there would be "not one perhaps which the original constitution of the Mogul Empire hath not before established and adopted and thereby rendered familiar to the people."

His main objection to the employment of Europeans in the administration was his certainty that they and their native dependants would grossly abuse their powers. "There is a fierceness," he said, "in the European manners, especially among the lower sort, which is incompatible with the gentle temper of the Bengalee, and gives the former such an ascendant as is scarce supportable even without the additional weight of authority." He was determined therefore to get rid of the 'Supervisors' and to concentrate European authority solely in the Governor and Council where, he thought, it might be exercised with moderation and least injury to the habits and feelings of the people. The Supervisors, he complained, had originally been appointed to inspect and gather information regarding the machinery of government and the state of the country. But they had become in practice Sovereigns of the Divisions in which they were stationed, and enjoyed "more trust, dignity and consequence than the Governor of Bengal." His letters burn with indignation whenever he mentions them. "Will you believe that the boys of the service are sovereigns of the country under the unmeaning titles of supervisors, collectors of the revenue, administrators of justice, and rulers, heavy rulers of the people?" Despite prohibitions to the contrary they had, he believed, engrossed the trade in every district, "more especially rice and the other necessaries of life"; and, as they were ignorant and largely in the hands of their native agents or Banyans, the Banyan was in fact "the lord of every supervisorship," and, through association with European power, far more oppressive than he ever could have been alone.

The Supervisors were the seed from which

sprang the Indian Civil Service; yet from the very start of his term as Governor one of Hastings' main objects was to remove them.

So much for Hastings' general views at the time when he assumed charge. He had hardly done so when despatches arrived from the Directors conveying their "determination to stand forth as Dewan and by the Agency of the Company's servants to take upon ourselves the entire Care and Management of the Revenues." This far-reaching change, which meant the beginning of the English administration of Bengal, they left to Hastings "to plan and execute." It is quite obvious that they themselves had little conception of what was involved. Their motive for it was purely mercenary. They had reached the conclusion that the dishonesty of Muhammad Reza Khan was responsible for the revenues failing to cover expenses and yield a profit to the Company; and they hoped that by the change the revenue receipts would be increased.

On the strength of these orders Hastings decided without hesitation to assume responsibility for the whole administration, i.e. not only for the Diwani (Revenue and Civil administration), but also for the Nizamat (criminal and police administration)—a distinction of which the Directors had no appreciation. Muhammad Reza Khan, the Nawab's chief minister, was the head of both branches, and the first step therefore was to get rid of him. Here the Directors had been helpful. Believing that he had swindled them and realising that his prosecution would furnish a good excuse for the change which they wished to effect, they had sent Hastings secret instructions to arrest him and keep him in confinement till he had cleared himself of the crimes with which he was charged. These consisted only of vague allegations, but the Directors recommended Hastings to seek further information against him from "his jealous and penetrating rival," Nandakumar. "You are too well apprised," they wrote, "of the subtlety and disposition of Nuncomar to yield him any trust or authority which may be turned to his own advantage, or prove detrimental to the Company's interest . . . yet should his information and assistance be serviceable to you in your investigation of the conduct of Muhammad Reza Khan, you will yield him such encouragement and reward as his trouble and the extent of his services may deserve."

These were somewhat unsavoury instructions; but Hastings did not quarrel with them. He acted promptly and arrested not only Muhammad Reza Khan but also his deputy, Chitab Rai, who presided over the affairs of Bihar. He did not expect that anything would come of their prosecution—in the end both men were acquitted—and he found the proceedings irksome and a great waste of his own time. Nevertheless, he was glad to have these once-powerful officers out of the way while the new system of government was being introduced; and he deliberately allowed the prosecution to drag on for nearly two years so that their influence might be completely broken. Nandakumar proved less useful in this business than had been hoped. Finding that he was not going to step into Muhammad Reza Khan's shoes, his zeal or his envy abated. He was disappointed and deeply aggrieved at the cynical attempt to exploit his baseness without giving him the reward which he expected. Before the trials were over Hastings seems to have received some premonition of the trouble which was to come from this quarter. He speaks of his fears on account of "the dark and deceitful character of Nundcomar, whose gratitude no kindness can bind, nor even his own Interest disengage him from the crooked Politics which have been the Study and Practice of his whole life." His apprehensions were well founded.

The Nawab's chief minister having been removed, the next step was to deal with the Nawab. He was a minor, Mubarak-ud-daula by name, and Hastings considered that every possible advantage should be taken of his minority to establish and confirm the Company's authority. All the new arrangements were governed by this aim. Hitherto Muhammad Reza Khan, in addition to his other duties, had also acted as the Nawab's guardian and had superintended his education and the management of his household. Hastings now deliberately selected a woman to be his guardian, viz. the Mani Begum, the senior of Mir Jafar's wives but not the mother of Mubarak-ud-daula. This was preferable to appointing any of the Nawab's male relatives, who might have tried to assert themselves, or the Nawab's own mother, who might have been tempted to intrigue on his behalf. With the Mani Begum as guardian Hastings was assured of what he called a "passive administration." Moreover, she was inimical to Muhammad Reza Khan and would therefore be useful in eradicating his influence.

To assist her in her duties Hastings appointed Nandakumar's son, Guru Das, as Diwan Nazim. This post amounted to little more than that of Master of the Household and was far from satisfying Nandakumar's ambitions. If Hastings hoped by this favour to his son to stimulate him to uncover Muhammad Reza Khan's malversations, he was disappointed. But here again his principal object seems simply to have been to ensure that the Nawab would be surrounded by influences hostile to Muhammad Reza Khan, who, having run the administration for seven years, had a large number of adherents at Court.

Hastings effected these appointments with considerable adroitness. There was strong opposition to that of Guru Das, owing to his father's bad reputation. But Hastings pushed it through. He also himself undertook the laborious and invidious task—long neglected by his predecessors—of reducing the Nawab's Civil List. Retrenching "the idle parade of elephants, menageries, etc. . . . cost little regret," but Hastings "suffered considerably in his feelings," so the Council wrote in their report to the Directors, "when he came to touch upon the Pension List. Some hundreds of persons of the ancient nobility of the country, excluded under our Government from almost all employment, civil or military, had ever since the revolution depended on the bounty of the Nawab and near 10 lacs were bestowed in this way. . . . Even with some of the highest rank he could not avoid discovering under all the pride of eastern manners, the manifest marks of penury and want. There was, however, no room left for hesitation." The pensions were cut down and the Nawab's total expenses, including much of the cost of the criminal administration, reduced from 32 lakhs of rupees per annum to less than 16.

The Nawab of Bengal now passes out of history. From this time onwards he ceases altogether to be a figure in the politics of the country. The way was clear for the reconstitution of the Government.

The Directors at home had no notion of the magnitude and complexity of the work which they had airily told Hastings to plan and execute. The Government which he had to re-shape was, he says, "a confused heap of un-digested materials as wild as the chaos itself." He had no experience to guide him and very little trained assistance of any kind. "We must work," he wrote, "as an arithmetician does with his Rule of False. We must adopt a plan upon conjecture, try, execute, add, and deduct from it, till it is brought into a perfect shape."

The most urgent tasks were to arrange for the settlement and collection of the revenues and to establish regular courts of justice. Even before he actually assumed charge, Hastings, with extraordinary diligence and quickness of grasp, had prepared draft regulations on these subjects, and these in due course became the basis of the new arrangements.

It is necessary at this point to say a few words in explanation of the revenue system of Bengal. The persons responsible for the payment of the revenue were the 'zemindars'—a quasi-heredi-tary class to which there is no exact English equivalent. A 'zemindar' was generally a com-bination of revenue-collector, landowner and feudal lord. First and foremost he was a revenue-collector, responsible for paying to the Government such sum on account of his 'zemindari' as might from time to time be agreed. He was nearly always also a landowner in the sense that within the area comprising his 'zemindari' he usually possessed an estate of his own, i.e. land, of greater or less extent, which he himself had the right to cultivate; but the whole 'zemindari' was not his 'estate' in the English sense that he was the landlord and the cultivators his tenants. The cultivators had rights of their own in the land; the zemindar's right consisted of the privilege of collecting from them the Government's share of the produce, viz. the revenue, and passing on such portion as might be agreed. In addition to this, however, the zemindar generally had the responsibility or privilege of maintaining peace and order within his zemindari and dispensing rough justice. In this respect he resembled a feudal lord.

At the time when Hastings became Governor it was customary to settle annually with the zemindars the amount which each should pay. Historically this amount had a remote connection with an assessment made by Akbar's finance minister, Todar Mal, in the sixteenth century, and supposedly represented one-fourth of the produce; but by Hastings' time it had become a more or less arbitrary sum dependent on bargaining between the Government and the zemindars. As for the sums which the zemindars themselves extorted from the cultivators, information was lacking, or at any rate was not readily obtainable by the English; still less was it known what revenue the land might reasonably be expected to yield.

Hastings from the very outset was anxious to arrive at a just assessment of the land's productive capacity, and on this basis to fix the revenue for a term of years so that both zemindars and cultivators would know exactly what they had to pay and would be able to undertake improvements without immediate fear of increased exactions. This remained his constant unvarying aim, though he was never able fully to realise it. But in 1772 the data for a proper assessment were not available. There was no alternative but to employ rough-and-ready methods. Hastings' Council therefore decided simply to let the revenues in farm for a term of five years for such sums as might be forthcoming, and a Committee of Circuit was appointed, with Hastings as President, to tour the province and settle the leases. In the grant of these leases the intention was to give preference to existing zemindars; but the Committee, greatly underestimating the effects of the famine, considered the offers made by many of the zemindars too low and had recourse to the dubious expedient of putting the leases to public auction. The results were unfortunate. All sorts of disreputable speculators, whose sole object was to fleece the cultivators and make a quick profit, came forward to bid, and obtained leases.[1] Moreover, the bids were run up much too high, sometimes out of sheer malice in order to embarrass a zemindar who was keen to retain his traditional post. In a year or two there were almost everywhere heavy arrears and considerable distress. Hastings knew that he was only groping his way and that mistakes would certainly be made. The mistake which he and his Committee made in over-estimating the revenue which they could safely take from the land was one destined to be repeated in almost every province of India as it came under British control. Even seventy-five years later, when the accumulated experience of several generations was available, the first settlements made after the annexation of the Punjab were far too heavy. Hastings therefore cannot be seriously blamed. His enemies, of course, seized on the failure of these first settlements in order to discredit him; but he was fully prepared to answer them. Their criticisms, howsoever valid, were ignorant; his own knowledge, through constant unremitting application, steadily grew; and, as we shall see, he pursued unweariedly his own sound aim of a fair settlement for a fixed term based on knowledge of the real value of the land.

In addition to settling the leases, the Committee of Circuit had to make arrangements for the

[1] It later came to light that Hastings' own native Secretary held farms to the value of over Rs.13,00,000.

general superintendence of the revenue collections and for the administration of justice. In accordance with Hastings' desire to make Calcutta the capital, the Khalsa, or Chief Revenue Office and Treasury, was shifted to Calcutta from Murshidabad; and the revenue in all its branches was brought under the immediate control of the Governor and Council, who, for revenue business, resolved themselves into a Revenue Board with separate council house, secretary and offices. Within a year Hastings was able to report: "The business of the new board of revenue, and of the office of the Calsa, go on as regularly as if both had been instituted from the first establishment of Calcutta."

For the supervision of the collections in the districts the 'Supervisors' were for the present allowed to remain; but their title was changed to 'Collector,' and the way was prepared for their eventual removal by the appointment of native officials, called 'diwans,' to assist them. Hastings would have liked to remove them at once, but he found "that there were amongst them so many sons, cousins, or élèves of Directors, and intimates of the members of Council, that it was better to let them remain than provoke an army of opponents against every act of administration, by depriving them of their emoluments. They continue, but their power is retrenched; and the way is paved for their gradual removal, and the Court of Directors

98

have sufficient arguments furnished them to order their recall immediately." In the following year this order came, probably as a result of Hastings' private representations; but even then it was not considered possible to adopt immediately in its entirety Hastings' own plan of central British control at Calcutta and purely native agency elsewhere. The whole revenue system was felt to be still too loose and confused to be superintended entirely from such a distance. Hence, though the Collectors were withdrawn from the districts and most of their work made over to the native 'diwans,' as a temporary expedient these 'diwans' were placed under the control of six Provincial Councils, each composed of five senior servants of the Company. Thus European agency in the districts was not completely abolished.

Nowhere does Hastings' dislike and distrust of European administration come out more strongly than in his comments on these Provincial Councils. He admitted them to be necessary as a temporary expedient, but he feared that they would be "oppressive to the inhabitants, prejudicial to the revenue, and ruinous to the trade of the country." He had always considered "the Collectors as tyrants"; he thought that under the Provincial Councils "each Division would be liable to become a separate tyranny of the most absolute kind," all the more oppressive in that the members, unlike the Collectors, would be senior servants of the Company and therefore more difficult for the Governor to restrain. He seems to have taken it for granted —and this is some measure of contemporary English standards—that they would monopolise trade, in spite of the covenants prohibiting inland trading, and that for their own private profit they would make unauthorised exactions from the zemindars—in short, that they would unhesitatingly abuse their power in the crudest manner. He hoped that by paying them each Rs.3,000 a month some check might be placed on "the licentious exercise of their influence"; but even these substantial salaries were considered by the Company's servants inadequate "indemnification for forbearance." Hastings was under no illusions regarding native agency, but native oppression was less truculent, more easily punished, more familiar to the people and in every way preferable to the corrupt tyranny of overbearing Englishmen.

His endeavours to limit the field of English administration were not entirely successful. The use of British officials outside Calcutta, once established, was difficult to discontinue, such was the pressure from Directors and other influential persons for posts for their protégés. But it was Hastings' successor, Lord Cornwallis, who gave a deliberate impulse to the process of anglicisation. Hastings himself resisted it.

The other main task of the Committee of Circuit was to establish Courts of Justice. In regard to this the Committee readily fell in with Hastings' plan, which was simply to revive "the laws and forms established of old in the country, with no other variations than such as was necessary to give them their due effect, and such as the people understood and were likely to be pleased with." Owing to the decay of the whole administration since the death of Allahvardi Khan the jurisdiction of the various native courts had become uncertain, most of them had lost their authority and the only live fount of justice was the dubious tyranny of the zemindars. Hastings confined the jurisdiction of zemindars to petty disputes, and established in each district a regular civil court, the Mofussil Diwani Adalat, and a regular criminal court, the Faujdari Adalat, based on Mogul models. The civil courts were presided over by the Collector, aided by native revenue officers and professors of Hindu law; later, when the Collectors were withdrawn, the native 'diwans' took their place. The criminal courts were governed entirely by Muhammadan law, which was expounded by the Kazi and the Mufti (Muhammadan legal officers) under the Collector's general supervision.

In addition to the district courts, Civil and Criminal Courts of Appeal were established at Calcutta. Here again Mogul models were followed. Inasmuch as civil justice fell within the scope of the Diwani, which had been granted to the Company, the Governor and two members of Council, aided by a number of Indian officers, presided over the Civil Court of Appeal. The corresponding Criminal Court was presided over by an Indian officer known as the Daroga Adalat and nominally appointed by the Nawab. He was assisted by Muhammadan law officers. Hastings and the Council only exercised a general and indirect supervision.

Hastings maintained that in these judicial arrangements "the only material changes which we have made in the ancient constitution of the country are in dividing the jurisdiction in civil and criminal cases by clearer lines . . . and in removing the supreme Courts of Justice to Calcutta. There are other trivial innovations . . . but the spirit of the Constitution we have preserved entire." He admitted, however, that the interference with the criminal courts was "an usurpation," since criminal administration was a function of the Nizamat, of which the Nawab was still nominally the head. But he felt that division of authority would lead to endless disputes between the Nawab's officials and officials of the Company, of which he had had some experience in Mir Kasim's time. He therefore boldly went ahead with the reconstitution of the criminal courts; but he took the precaution of obtaining the Nawab's consent to the appointment of all the officers of the Criminal Court of Appeal.

Hastings had hardly completed this work when reports reached India that judges were going to be sent out from England to frame laws and new forms of judicature for Bengal. This filled him with alarm. He asks indignantly, "Is it not a contradiction of the common notions of equity and policy that the English Gentlemen of Cumberland and Argyle-shire should regulate the policy of a nation which they know only by the lacs which it has sent to Great Britain? . . ." He was at pains to dispel the notion then prevalent in England that the people of India had no regular laws of their own. Muhammadan law was contained in a digest prepared by the order of Aurangzeb and universally acknowledged by Indian courts. Hindu law, though of vast antiquity, had not hitherto been systematically codified. So Hastings invited to Calcutta ten of the most learned pundits in the country and commis-sioned them to prepare a digest for the guidance and convenience of the civil courts. This digest he caused to be translated into Persian and English,[1] and transmitted sample portions of it to the Directors and to Lord Mansfield with a view to convincing them that "the people of this country do not require our aid to furnish

[1] No Englishman at this time knew Sanskrit, so a direct translation into English was not possible. The Persian trans-lation was retranslated into English.

them with a rule for their conduct, or a standard for their property." It was, in his view, their sacred right to retain their own system of law and justice. To deprive them of it would be a grievance, to compel them to accept another a wanton tyranny. "Even the most injudicious or most fanciful customs which ignorance or superstition may have introduced among them are perhaps preferable to any which could be substituted in their room. They are interwoven with their religion, and are therefore revered as of the highest authority. They are the conditions on which they hold their place in society, they think them equitable, and it is therefore no hardship to exact their obedience to them. I am persuaded they would consider the attempt to free them from the effects of such a power as a severe hardship." So long as Hastings governed Bengal these views prevailed; and the courts which he established were popular and on the whole successful.

Within the space of a single year all the work already described had been completed and Hastings was able to write: "By the translation of the Calsa to Calcutta, by the exercise of the Dewanny without an intermediate agent, by the present establishment and superintendency of the Nabob's household, and by the establishment of the new courts of justice under the control of our own Government, the authority of the Company is fixed in this country without

any possibility of a competition, and beyond
the power of any but themselves to shake it.
The Nabob is a mere name, and the seat of
Government most effectually and visibly transferred from Moorshedabad to Calcutta, which
I do not despair of seeing the first city in Asia,
if I live and am supported but a few years
longer."

There were, however, innumerable other
sides to Hastings' activity besides those already
described. The range and variety of his work,
the amount which he attended to and the
amount which he accomplished before, in 1774,
his hands were tied, is really astonishing. Owing
to the effects of the famine and the decay of the
native Government, there was widespread disorder in Bengal when he took over. Dacoity
was rampant, and queer bands of marauders,
in the guise of naked mendicants called
Sanyasis, overran many parts of the country.
The Bhutanese also descended from the
mountains into the neighbouring state of
Kuch-Behar and plundered the adjoining
Bengal districts. At the request of the Rajah of
Kuch-Behar, who placed himself under the Company's protection and agreed to pay tribute, the
Company's troops expelled the Bhutanese from
his territories. Military operations were also
undertaken against the Sanyasis. These banditti,
whose origin and real character are somewhat
obscure, were hard to hunt down owing to the

celerity with which they disappeared into the woods and to the veneration in which they were held by the people on account of their supposedly religious character. Hastings gave personal attention to the operations against them, which were ultimately successful.

For dacoity Hastings had no mercy. The evil had assumed enormous proportions, many of the zemindars were mixed up in it, and Hastings considered it necessary to prescribe draconian penalties. The Muhammadan law was in his opinion inadequate, as it only permitted sentence of death if robbery was accompanied by actual murder. He persuaded his colleagues that every convicted dacoit should be hanged in his own village, his family made State slaves and the village fined; and that this punishment, when it differed from the sentences passed by the courts, should "be superadded to them by an immediate act of Government."

Hastings recognised that the principal cause of these disorders was economic distress; and this in turn, to the extent that the famine was not responsible, was believed to be mainly due to the decay of trade consequent on the virtual monopoly of it by the Company and the Company's servants. This view was frankly expressed by Mr. Becher, who had been in the Company's employment in Bengal ever since 1743. "I well remember this Country when Trade was free," he wrote in

1769, "and the flourishing State it was then in; with concern I now see its present ruinous condition, which I am convinced is greatly owing to the Monopoly that has been made of late years in the Company's name of almost all the Manufactures in the Country." The Directors at home had by now grasped that the abuse by the Company and its servants of their trading privileges so as to engross the whole of the inland trade was not only ruinous to Bengal but detrimental to the Company's own immediate interests. For, now that the Bengal revenues belonged to the Company, the Directors did not wish to see the customs revenue disappear through their own servants monopolising trade and claiming exemption from customs dues on the strength of the Company's privileges. In other words, now that the Company was in Mir Kasim's shoes it would not tolerate that which he had found intolerable. The Directors, learning that their servants were disregarding the ban on inland trading, followed it up in 1771 by orders prohibiting altogether their use of the Company's 'dustuks.'

Strengthened by these orders Hastings proceeded to a complete reform of the Customs. A careful survey was made of the channels of trade and of the returns from all the various customs houses. After this had been studied, new regulations were issued (March 1773) by which all customs houses except five central ones were swept away, duties were reduced to $2\frac{1}{2}$ per cent., the 'dustuk' totally abolished and restrictions placed on Europeans settling in the districts. As a result of these regulations native merchants could once more resume their activities without fear of invincible European competition, and goods, having once paid duty at $2\frac{1}{2}$ per cent., could travel without let or hindrance to any part of the province. Only for salt and opium were monopolies retained; and these were placed on a regular footing under the control of the Government.

With the introduction of these changes commerce with Oudh, which the Nawab of Oudh had completely prohibited, was once more reopened. The Nawab's prohibition was due to fear lest his own province might become exposed to the oppressions practised by the English traders in Bengal. It had had the effect of cutting off Bengal entirely from all the markets of northern India. With the abolition of the 'dustuk,' Hastings was able to reassure the Nawab and to make arrangements with him for "free and mutual interchange of trade" between his territories and Bengal.

Hastings also attempted to open up trade with China and Tibet by the despatch of an envoy, Mr. Bogle, to wait upon the Grand Llama at Lhasa. Bogle never reached his destination and his mission was abortive, but the minute instructions for collecting information, which Hastings,

amid all his other preoccupations, found time to
send him, are a remarkable illustration of his
diligence and unquenchable thirst for knowledge. When he learnt that Bogle was not likely
to get through to Lhasa, he instructed him
humorously not to return "without something
to show where you have been, though it be but
a contraband walnut, a pilfered slip of sweet
briar, or the seeds of a butte or turnip taken
in payment for the potatoes you have given
them gratis."

Of all the measures which Hastings undertook
at this time none were of greater interest to the
Directors than those calculated to improve the
Company's finances. His drastic reduction of the
Nawab's allowance has already been mentioned; and in the next chapter the financial
advantages accruing from his foreign policy will
be noticed. The Directors on their part had
ordered him (1) to make a minute examination
of all civil and military expenditure, and (2)
to conduct enquiries into the past conduct of a
number of the Company's servants from whom,
they believed, considerable sums were due.

The first of these tasks Hastings carried
through with such success that economies were
effected amounting to about 50 lakhs of rupees.
His skilful financial management, which included a successful reform of the currency and
the establishment of a Bank, and the general
confidence which his administration inspired,

so much improved the Company's credit that in
June 1773 he was able to raise a loan in Calcutta
at 5 per cent. instead of at the previous rate of
8 per cent.

The enquiries into past delinquencies, some
of them involving his own colleagues in Council, were exceedingly distasteful to him. "These
retrospections and examinations," he wrote, "are
death to my views, as I have not an hour to
spare from the business of the day, even if they
did not interfere with it. . . . No good will be
got by them; they breed dissensions, and they
retard the course of real business." The Directors, with incredible folly, pressed him to
proceed with them ("arming," as he said, "my
hand against every man, and every man's of
course against me"), and yet left him, without
any special powers, entirely at the mercy of his
Council. Very wisely he kept putting them off,
and finally, at the end of 1773, he informed the
Directors quite plainly that he had no time for
"endless researches which can produce no real
good, and may expose your affairs to all the
ruinous consequences of personal malevolence
both here and at home."

The blame for past delinquencies was, he
thought, not so much imputable to the conduct
of individuals as to the lack of a system of
government commensurate with the extent of
the Company's new responsibilities. "Our constitution is nowhere to be traced but in ancient

charters which were framed for the jurisdiction of your trading settlements, the sales of your exports, and the provision of your annual investment. I need not observe how incompetent these must prove for the government of a great kingdom, and for the preservation of its riches from private violence and embezzlement." Hastings was writing of what he knew by personal experience. He had himself witnessed Vansittart's attempts to curb the rapacity of the Company's servants and his impotence in the face of a hostile majority in his Council. He knew that there could be no real reform until the Governor was endowed with ample coercive powers and the Company's servants paid regular salaries and debarred altogether from the entanglements of private trade. He himself had no special powers, such as Clive had enjoyed during his second administration and such as were given to the ill-fated Commissioners. If a majority in his Council opposed his policy, he had no alternative but to appeal to England and wait months or even years for the result. Aware of "the nakedness of his authority," he avoided a head-on collision with long-formed habits of licentiousness. He could only hope to carry through the reorganisation required to rescue the Company's affairs from ruin by securing the cordial co-operation of the members of his Council; and this was not compatible with inquisitions into their past conduct or a

sudden hard pruning of their means of enrich-
ment.

It says much for his tact and persuasiveness
that he was able to obtain his Council's consent
to the innumerable measures and the considerable retrenchments of his first two years of
office. Much that he did was highly contentious,
and he was not by any means entirely free from
opposition. General Barker, the Commander-in-
Chief, was impatient of control by the civil
power, and it needed firmness and discretion to
check his habits of independence and to enforce
proper discipline among subordinate military
officers. Another source of opposition and obstruction was Mr. Barwell, a Councillor of
ability but intolerable prolixity. Hastings'
patience was severely tried by his "altercations,
doubts, dissents, replies and rejoinders on points
of the most trivial nature," and he told the
Directors that he could not at one and the same
time "conduct their affairs and a literary war
with those who ought to help me bear the load
of their service." However, after a time Barwell
was won over and Hastings, writing towards the
end of 1773, was able to speak happily of "the
cordial disposition of the members of the Board
to co-operate with me in every measure for the
public good."

With such loyal support, he did not feel so
keenly the want of extraordinary powers. Nevertheless, he was convinced that changes were

necessary in order to give the Government greater vigour and consistency and to check intrigue among the Company's servants. He suggested that Governors should be appointed for a longer period than the three years then customary. "God forbid," he wrote to Lawrence Sulivan, "that the Government of this fine country should continue to be a mere chair for a triennial succession of indigent adventurers to sit and hatch private fortunes in." On this point his views were accepted. He also urged that the Governor should have the power of vetoing any civil appointment and of overriding his Council in urgent and extraordinary cases. He was certain that the powers which he recommended would be granted "at some period not far distant," as indeed they were to his successor. He himself was never to enjoy them.

During these first two years as Governor of Bengal Hastings was at his best. His temper had not been hardened and his character warped by years of bitter opposition and a deadly struggle for power. He was fresh; he was at his prime; he was confident and determined, yet not intolerant and overbearing. He had not yet developed the egotism and conviction of his own infallibility which marred his later years. His work at this time saved the Company from ruin. If there had not been a strong hand on the helm, its affairs in Bengal would have drifted into bankruptcy and confusion; if the foundations of government had not been firmly laid now, the shocks of the succeeding years could never have been withstood.

No one who studies the records of this period can fail to be impressed by his prodigious industry, and by the rapidity with which he made his influence felt in every branch of the administration. A stream of orders and regulations issued from Council, remodelling every department. Most of them were drafted by Hastings himself; all bear the clear impress of his mind. He was a master of the minutest details of administration; but he did not allow details to impede the flow of business. Every problem was handled with a promptness and decision rarely equalled by any subsequent Government in India. Business, he insisted, must not be held up. There was so much to do that it was "more eligible to resolve without debate, than to debate without resolving, or, which is much the same, to give so much time on the prudent accomplishment of one measure, as to leave many others suspended." The burden and strain upon him were immense. Writing to his friend Dupré in October 1772, he gives a vivid account of his multifarious duties: "Here I now am, with arrears of business of months and some of years to bring up; with the courts of justice and offices of revenue to set agoing; . . . with the trials of Mahommed Reza Cawn and Raja Shitabroy to bring on, without

materials, and without much hope of assistance,
. . . and with the current trifles of the day,
notes, letters, personal applications, every man's
business of more consequence than any other,
complainants from every quarter of the province
hallooing me by hundreds for justice as often
as I put my head out of the window, or venture
abroad, and, what is worse than all, a mind
discomposed, and a temper fermented almost to
vinegar by the weight of affairs to which the
former is unequal, and by everlasting teazing."

His mind was not, however, unequal to the
weight of affairs; on the contrary it was suited
by them. Like many men, Hastings worked best
under pressure; and the task of bringing order
out of chaos had a fascination for him. Neither
his health nor his spirits gave way; and he soon
had the satisfaction of knowing that he was not
labouring in vain. His work bore fruit and was
appreciated in England. The first despatches
from the Directors conveyed warm approval of
his conduct and assured him—with what un-
truth he fortunately did not know—"of their
firmest support in accomplishing the task he had
so successfully commenced." Encouraged by
their favourable reception of his first measures,
he proudly confesses to them his ambition to
serve them for some years to come as Governor
of Bengal. "Those who know my natural turn
of mind," he says, "will not ascribe this to sordid
views. A very few years' possession of the govern-

ment would undoubtedly enable me to retire
with a fortune amply fitted to the measure of
my desires, were I to consult only my own ease;
but in my present situation I feel my mind
expand to something greater. I have catched
the desire of applause in public life . The
important transactions in which I have been
engaged, and my wish to see them take complete
effect, the public approbation which you have
been pleased to stamp on them, and the estimation which that cannot fail to give me in the
general opinion of mankind, lead me to aim at
deserving more; and I wish to dedicate all my
time, health and labour to a service which has
been so flattering in its commencement.

"Such are my views and such my sentiments.
I expose them without reserve, because I am
conscious you will find nothing unworthy in
them, whatever opinion you may form of their
expediency."

Chapter Eight

The Rohilla War

CLIVE bequeathed to his successors in Bengal a defensive alliance with Oudh and an obligation to pay tribute to the Emperor. The alliance Hastings strengthened; the obligation he repudiated. This, in brief, was the sum and substance of his foreign policy during the years 1772–74.

The great ambition of the Emperor Shah Alam was to repossess himself of the imperial city of Delhi. Having failed to obtain the assistance of the Company in the achievement of this object, he looked elsewhere. Delhi was occupied by the Marathas in 1771. The Emperor promptly left the protection of the Company, joined the Marathas in Delhi and became virtually a prisoner in their hands. He continued, however, to demand tribute from the Company. Hastings, from the first moment of his arrival in Bengal, resolved not to pay it to him. It was ridiculous, in his opinion, that the revenue of the province should be drained away "to supply the pageantry of a mock King, an idol of our own creation"; and much more so when he had become "the tool of the only

117

enemies we have in India." His Council supported him, and in 1773 the Emperor's customary demand for tribute was met by a
peremptory refusal.

During the same year the Emperor was persuaded by the Marathas to cede to them the
districts of Korah and Allahabad, which had
been assigned to him by Clive for the support
of his dignity. It was only the presence of a
brigade of the Company's troops at Allahabad
which had enabled him to retain control of
these districts. Hastings saw no reason why they
should now be tamely surrendered to a power
avowedly hostile, and he gave orders to Sir
Robert Barker, the Commander-in-Chief, to
hold them against the Marathas.

There remained the question how they should
be disposed of. They were at a distance from the
Company's frontiers; to retain them permanently would be a ruinous expense. In view
of the Company's financial distress, Hastings
wanted to make them a source of profit instead
of loss by handing them back on payment to the
Vizier of Oudh, to whom they had originally
belonged.

He was in any case anxious to put the alliance
with the Vizier on a more satisfactory footing.
It had so far proved costly to the Company.
Year after year it had been necessary for a
brigade to move up to Oudh on an alarm of a
Maratha invasion, and the sum of Rs.30,000 a

month, which had been fixed as the amount payable by the Vizier for the use of these troops, did not cover the extra charges actually incurred. To the Vizier also the alliance had not been an unmixed blessing. Owing to the support which he had given to Mir Kasim, he was viewed by the English less as an ally than as a potential enemy, and every opportunity was taken to weaken his power rather than to strengthen him as the only barrier against the Marathas. His relations with the Company were exclusively in the hands of the officers commanding the Company's troops in Oudh, who kept harping on his "great power and treacherous designs." Hastings was confident that these were non-existent. He perceived that the military had an interest in keeping him in a state of impotence, for he would then always need the Company's troops and they, in consequence, would "have the rule both of him and of his country." Hastings was determined that he should not become a puppet in their hands. He knew that if this happened Oudh would be ruined by extortion and oppression, just as Bengal had been in the time of Mir Jafar and Mir Kasim. He wished to "make the Vizier depend on government and not on the military power," and he wished the alliance with him to be based on equality and mutual confidence.

To the military such an alliance was impossible. They looked on Shuja-ud-daula as a crooked, faithless, oriental prince with whom ordinary fair-dealing on terms of equality was out of place. Hastings had more faith in him. He believed that Shuja-ud-daula could be trusted. With sure instinct he determined to meet him and to establish with him personal relations. His Council approved, and gave him full powers to negotiate on all outstanding questions. He left Calcutta in June 1773 and met the Vizier at Benares in August.

Shuja-ud-daula was one of those princes of India who quickly conceived a great liking for Hastings and felt that they could trust him. Hastings and he conferred together for several days in complete privacy—much to the annoyance of Sir Robert Barker and reached an agreement which both of them felt to be highly advantageous. The Vizier agreed to pay 50 lakhs of rupees for the restoration of the districts of Korah and Allahabad and to raise the payment which he made for the use of the Company's troops in defence of his territories to Rs.2,10,000 a month for one brigade. Hastings on his side agreed to assist him with a brigade of troops in a much-cherished project, namely, the conquest of the country of the Rohillas, which lay on his north-western border. In return for this assistance the Vizier was ready to pay the Company 40 lakhs in addition to the expenses of the troops.

It was further decided that, with a view to

maintaining close and cordial relations, Hastings should appoint a special personal representative to reside at the Vizier's court. Nathaniel Middleton was selected for this post.

Hastings was highly pleased with the pecuniary advantages which he had gained for the Company. The Vizier for his part was delighted at the recovery of his former territories and at the prospect of rounding off his dominions by the annexation of the Rohilla country. But on further reflection he seems to have felt some doubt whether he could fulfil all at once so many pecuniary engagements. He therefore asked that he might suspend for the present the Rohilla project and renew it again later if he so wished. Hastings readily agreed, for he was himself in two minds about it. Though it promised strategic and pecuniary advantages at negligible risk, he knew that the Directors were opposed in principle to offensive operations beyond the boundaries of Oudh. He had consented to it in the first instance because the Vizier had pressed it strongly, and consent had enabled him to purchase the Vizier's compliance with his own requests. But when the Vizier himself cried off, he was not sorry. His own doubts and hesitations are revealed in a letter to Lawrence Sulivan. "I was glad to be freed from the Rohilla expedition because I was doubtful of the judgment which would have been passed on it at home, where I

see too much stress laid upon general maxims
and too little attention given to the circumstances which require an exception to be made
from them."

He was not, however, freed from it. The very
next year the Vizier raised the matter again, and
Hastings, morally bound by his previous consent, felt obliged to advise his Council that "a
direct refusal after what had passed would have
an unfriendly aspect, and might admit of the
construction of artifice and insincerity in our
dealings with him." Half-heartedly, therefore,
Hastings was dragged into the Rohilla war.

The facts regarding this war have been
obscured by Burke's rhetoric and Macaulay's
brilliant inaccuracies. In themselves they are
simple and hardly disputable. About forty years
before this time some bands of Afghan adventurers, called Rohillas, had seized a fertile
stretch of country along the foot of the Hima-
layas, to which they gave the name of Rohilkhand. The original Hindu inhabitants continued to cultivate the land and to form the bulk
of the population. The Rohillas became their
overlords, and settled down with their families
and dependants to enjoy in true conqueror's
style the fruits of other men's toil. Macaulay has
described them as "the finest population in
India," distinguished alike "by courage in war
and by skill in the arts of peace." This is
mere rhetoric. The Rohillas were freebooters

and soldiers of fortune, neither better nor worse than others of their kind.

Though brave and turbulent, the Rohillas themselves were no serious menace to the Vizier, much less to the Company in Bengal. But the Marathas, after some years of quiescence, had recently reappeared as an active force in northern India, and the Vizier's dominions would be exposed to serious danger if the Rohilla country fell into their hands: for it lay between the north-west boundary of Oudh and the line of the river Ganges; and if once the Marathas crossed the river and established themselves firmly in Rohilkhand, there was no natural barrier to check their advance into Oudh or even into Bengal.

The Marathas were at this time the most aggressive and formidable of all the native powers. They had first risen to fame under their great leader Sivaji in the early days of Aurangzeb; and as the strength of the Mogul empire declined, their name had become a terror throughout the length and breadth of India. Though little more than a loose confederation of predatory chieftains occupying the tangled hill country of Central India, their marauding bands ranged far and wide, extorting a tribute, called chauth, as the price of immunity from molestation. Their nominal head was the Peshwa, who resided at Poona and was the hereditary minister of Sivaji's descendant, the Rajah of Satara. But the Rajah had long since become a mere Rajah fainéant, and the Peshwa had also lost much of his former authority, with the result that various chieftains like Sindhia, Holkar and the Rajah of Berar had become practically independent.

In 1761 the Maratha forces were utterly defeated at Panipat by an Afghan invader named Ahmad Shah Abdali. This tremendous disaster shook the cohesion of their confederation and for the time being wrecked their hopes of reviving the Mogul empire under Hindu leadership. They recovered, however, with remarkable rapidity, and, as already mentioned, in 1771 they occupied Delhi and secured the person of the Emperor, Shah Alam, who deserted the Company and threw himself into their arms.

In the following year they invaded Rohilkhand and demanded chauth from both Oudh and Bengal. The approach of the monsoon and of a brigade of the Company's troops, which the Vizier had summoned to his aid, induced them to withdraw. But the Vizier rightly judged that they would return again. He therefore entered into an agreement with the Rohillas (which the British Commander, Sir Robert Barker, witnessed) to come to their assistance if the Marathas again threatened them. The Rohillas on their part promised to pay him 40 lakhs for his services.

As the Vizier had expected, in 1773 the Marathas again advanced against Rohilkhand; but on a threatening movement by the Vizier's army, which was accompanied by a strong detachment of the Company's troops, they hastily withdrew, and soon afterwards they were recalled to their home bases in Central India by internal dissensions at Poona.

The behaviour of the Rohillas during these operations was highly ambiguous. Despite their alliance with the Vizier, they entered into secret communication with the Marathas, and were only prevented from deserting to them by the timely arrival of the Vizier's army accompanied by Sir Robert Barker and the Company's troops. Their game was, as Barker put it, "to treat with both parties and adhere to neither." Furthermore, when, on the Marathas' withdrawal, the Vizier claimed his 40 lakhs, they failed to make payment.

The Vizier was probably not displeased at this failure. He had for some time wanted to annex their territory; he was now furnished with an excellent excuse for doing so. Though one may feel some sympathy for the Rohillas, who, with the Vizier on one side and the Marathas on the other, were very awkwardly situated, it is undeniable that they had proved faithless. Judged by any ordinary standards of political morality, the Vizier's proposal to annex their territory was in the circumstances neither wicked (as

Macaulay suggests) nor even unjust; and it was highly advantageous; for it would add both to his wealth and to his safety, and would neatly round off his dominions on the north-west by bringing them up to the line of the Ganges.

Hastings summed the matter up with his usual force and clarity: "I own that the convenience of possessing the Rohilla country was not sufficient reason for invading it. I never said it was; but if they had afforded a just provocation for invading their country, and we saw advantages in invading it, though neither cause was alone sufficient to produce that effect, yet both united would certainly justify it, and the most rigid speculators would approve so fair a conclusion." Neither he nor the members of his Council doubted for a moment that the Rohillas by their own faithless conduct had afforded ample moral justification for the attack on them. Barker, the one member who opposed it, did so, not on moral grounds, but because he thought that with the annexation of Rohilkhand the Vizier would become too powerful. If *per impossibile* Hastings and his Council had attempted to excuse themselves from assisting the Vizier on the sort of moral grounds on which Macaulay has condemned them, viz. that to attack the Rohillas was wicked and for the Company to do so for filthy lucre was doubly wicked, the Vizier would probably not have understood them, and would certainly have con-

126

cluded that they were entirely dishonest. For the Company's own actions in India had never yet suggested that it was governed by some higher morality different from that to which Indian rulers were accustomed.

Hastings' own hesitations in the matter arose from the Directors' known dislike of offensive wars. It could be represented that the reduction of the Rohillas was an essentially *defensive* operation, since the object of it was to strengthen Oudh, and hence Bengal, against a possible Maratha attack. But Hastings was aware that the Directors might not accept this argument. It is clear that he had to make a rather difficult decision. As an honest servant of the Company he could not lightly turn down the considerable advantages, political and financial, which the Vizier's proposal offered. On the other hand, in agreeing to lend the Vizier troops for offensive operations beyond his frontiers, he ran the risk of incurring the Directors' censure. He can hardly be blamed for the decision which he took.

So much for the origin of the Rohilla war. Of its actual course there is little to be said. In the spring of 1774 the Vizier sent a formal demand to Hafiz Rahmat, the principal Rohilla chief, for payment of the 40 lakhs due to him. No satisfactory reply being received, the Vizier's army, together with a brigade of the Company's troops under Colonel Champion, who had succeeded

Sir Robert Barker, invaded Rohilkhand, defeated and killed Hafiz Rahmat in a single decisive engagement, and in the space of a little more than a month gained possession of the whole country. Most of the Rohilla chiefs surrendered. One of them, Faizullah Khan, fled to the mountains and held out there for some time; but he too finally submitted and became the Vizier's vassal. The objects of the war were thus easily achieved.

Macaulay has represented Hastings as callously folding his arms and looking on while the Rohillas' "villages were burnt, their children butchered, and their women violated." This picture is almost entirely imaginary. No children were butchered and no women were violated. A few villages were burnt, but the country as a whole was quite untouched, and the people continued to go about their business with little or no interruption, "as if there had been a profound peace." Moreover, as soon as Hastings received reports of excesses—reports subsequently proved to be very much exaggerated— he immediately instructed his representative, Middleton, to remonstrate with the Vizier in the following vigorous terms. "Tell him that the English manners are abhorrent of every species of inhumanity and oppression, and enjoin the gentlest treatment of a vanquished enemy. Require and entreat his observance of this principle towards the family of Hafiz. Tell him . . .

that no part of his conduct will operate so powerfully in winning the affections of the English, as instances of benevolence and feeling for others. If these arguments don't prevail, you may inform him directly that you have my orders to insist upon a proper treatment of the family of Hafiz Rahmat, since in our alliance with him our national character is involved in every act which subjects his own to reproach."

Whether these remonstrances were themselves productive of any result is uncertain. It seems probable that they were superfluous; for the Vizier had no wish to see the country which he was about to annex extensively ravaged and plundered. The war was not marked by any special atrocity or inhumanity; rather the reverse. Had it not been for the malice of Francis, the alleged 'atrocities' would never have been heard of, and the Rohilla war, like other petty Indian wars of that time, would have been completely forgotten.

It must, however, be admitted that Hastings quite failed to see the objections which might be taken to loaning the Company's troops as mere mercenaries to an independent Indian ruler. There was a danger, and a real danger, that they would become involved in actions which would, to use his own words, "subject the national character to reproach." There were, no doubt, plenty of apparent precedents for his arrangement with the Vizier. The hiring out of

European troops to India rulers had been common. For instance, after the battle of Plassey the Company's troops had, in effect, been hired to Mir Jafar for the defence of Bengal. But Mir Jafar, though in theory an independent ruler, had in fact been a puppet in the hands of the English. Clive, whenever he considered English honour or interests required it, had insisted on Mir Jafar doing exactly what he was told. English honour was thus safe (or unsafe) in English hands. Hastings, on the other hand, while willing to hire the Company's troops to the Vizier, was unwilling to browbeat or dictate to him. Just as he had once stood up for the rights and dignity of Mir Kasim, so now he insisted that those of Shuja-ud-daula should be respected. He was an ally in name; Hastings wished him to be an ally in fact, and to find his connection with the Company a source of "satisfaction and credit" rather than of humiliation and servile dependence.

For this very reason Colonel Champion, who commanded the Company's troops, was rigorously confined to the execution of military duties. All diplomatic relations with the Vizier were entrusted entirely to Middleton, Hastings' own personal representative; and Champion was more than once somewhat peremptorily instructed, not merely to treat the Vizier with every possible respect, but to refrain from encroaching upon his authority and from meddling with his negotiations with the Rohilla chiefs. Champion's business was to fight; it was for the Vizier to decide what use should be made of victory, and it was for him to reap its fruits. When Champion and his troops demanded prize-money—much to the annoyance of the Vizier, who was paying handsomely for their services—Hastings supported the Vizier in the rejection of the claim, and told Champion that the "very idea of prize money" was "to be avoided like poison." But the clearest example of the respect which he demanded for the Vizier's authority is to be found in his reply to Champion's complaints of the Vizier's excesses. Champion, chafing at the restrictions placed upon his own power and eager to demonstrate their impropriety, readily accepted every rumour of the Vizier's cruelty and loudly lamented his own inability to restrain him owing to want of authority. Hastings rounded on him: "No authority which the Board could have given could be capable of preventing the effects you mention, since they could give you no control over the actions of the Vizier further than the weight and influence of your counsel and advice. . . . You have a right, and it is your duty, to remonstrate against any part of his conduct, which may either dishonour the service or prove prejudicial to the common interest; but I protest I do not know what you could do more, or what the whole Board personally present and invested with their full authority could do more. They could exercise no coercive power over the Vizier without committing a violence equal to any of these we should complain of."

This unwillingness to coerce the Vizier or to usurp his lawful authority is typical of Hastings and creditable to him. It is part of the secret of his influence and popularity with the rulers of India. They realised that his respect for their rights and dignity was not a mere façade but entirely genuine, and sprang from a fundamental instinct to treat them as equals. But this being his attitude towards the Vizier, was it wise or proper to hire out to him as mercenaries the Company's troops? Were not the precedents misleading?

Hastings would perhaps have argued that from his knowledge of the Vizier's character he was confident that nothing would be done to expose the Company to serious reproach. And in fact the Vizier was certainly guilty of no gross outrage. Champion's complaints against him were inspired by personal pique; they were based largely on unverified rumours, and were subsequently proved to be much exaggerated. But even if Hastings' confidence in the Vizier was justified, even if he was the best of rulers and the mildest of men, a doubt must surely still remain whether the arrangement which Hastings made with him for the use of the Company's troops as mere mercenaries was not in itself a trifle discreditable. At a subsequent enquiry into the conduct of the Rohilla war, Colonel Leslie was asked whether the army had considered the service in which they were engaged as honourable to the British name or the reverse. Leslie discreetly replied that he could not answer for the opinions of others. But the question gave expression to an intelligible and defensible point of view which Hastings, in his anxiety to relieve the Company's financial distress, unduly neglected.

He was soon made to suffer for it. Ordinarily he might have expected that Champion's ill-temper and the army's discontent over the prize-money would quickly pass away and be forgotten, and that the Directors, gratified by the manifest advantages accruing to the Company from the war, would pocket its proceeds without minute scrutiny of its propriety. But the close of the Rohilla war in the autumn of 1774 coincided with a radical change in the government of Bengal. Hastings' two and a half years of vigorous fruitful administration were at an end. From now onwards for upwards of six years he was to be engaged continuously in a bitter, sterile strife; and from the very outset the Rohilla war was selected by his opponents as a principal target for their attack.

Chapter Nine

The New Councillors

PARLIAMENT'S interest in the Company's affairs had by no means waned since the enquiry of 1767, when Hastings and others had given evidence at the bar of the House of Commons. The fortunes of the Nabobs, contrasting so strangely with the Company's own financial embarrassments, the disquieting stories of misgovernment and oppression in Bengal, the growing fear that a vast mine of unexplored wealth might be wrecked by a handful of greedy adventurers, kept the public in a fevered state of anger, envy, excitement and speculation.

There was a widespread feeling that the Crown should take over, or at any rate share, the Company's immense new responsibilities and potential profits. But the Company enjoyed a strong Parliamentary connection and possessed in its Indian patronage a plentiful means of corruption. Any attempt to deprive it outright of its privileges would arouse powerful opposition; and there were many who felt that the Crown, if once possessed of Indian patronage and the wealth of Bengal, might become dangerously independent of Parliament and threaten the liberties won in the preceding century. The general inclination therefore was towards a more cautious approach.

Matters were brought to a head in 1772, when the Company, having exhausted its resources and its credit, was forced to apply to the Government for a loan of £1,000,000. Such a loan, Lord North said, could only be granted with the consent of Parliament; but on certain terms that consent could be obtained. The upshot of the application was the passing of the Regulating Act of 1773. The Company was permitted to retain its Indian possessions, but its management of them was brought under the definite, if only partial, control of Crown and Parliament. The Act may be regarded as Parliament's first attempt to construct a regular Government for India.

The Company's pressing financial embarrassments were relieved by the grant of a loan of £1,500,000 and by release from the obligation, imposed in 1767, to pay £400,000 annually to the Treasury. In return for these concessions its dividend, which in 1767 had been limited to ten per cent., was now limited to six per cent. till the loan was repaid; and its constitution was altered so as to secure greater continuity of policy and to make the Directorate more amenable to ministerial influence.

In India a new Council, consisting of a Governor-General and four Councillors, was created for the government of Bengal, with vaguely defined powers of control over the foreign relations of the other two Presidencies. The first Governor-General and members of Council were named in the Act itself. They were to hold office for five years, and were to be removable only by the Crown on an address from the Company.

A Supreme Court of judicature, appointed by the Crown and composed of a Chief Justice and three Puisne judges, was established for the provinces of Bengal, Bihar and Orissa. Its powers and functions were ill-defined.

Provision was made for the Ministry's general control over Indian affairs by requiring that all despatches received by the Directors from India should be submitted to one of His Majesty's Secretaries of State within fourteen days of their arrival.

The Act has been universally condemned. It did, however, represent a genuine attempt to reach a fair compromise between conflicting interests. Its defects seem to have been due more to loose thinking and careless drafting than to corrupt or sinister influences. Many of the objects which it sought to attain were laudable; but it was so lacking in clear and precise definition that conflict between the various parts of the new Indian Government was almost inevitable. Thus the decision to bring the three Presidencies under a

single control—a course which had been
advocated by Hastings—was unquestionably
wise, but the authority given to the Governor-
General and Council of Bengal over the
Presidencies of Bombay and Madras was so
vague as to be practically nugatory. The establishment of a Supreme Court in Calcutta was
also in itself a sound measure. The old Mayor's
Court, which had been established by charter
in 1726 primarily to administer English justice
to the Company's own employees, was staffed by
amateurs and was ill-equipped to dispense
justice to Calcutta's now large and rapidly
growing population. But the new Court's
jurisdiction was defined so vaguely as to invite
disputes and provoke a conflict with the
Governor-General and Council.

The worst evils, however, were to flow from
the constitution of the Bengal Government
itself. To vest the Government in a Governor-
General and four Councillors and to give the
Crown the final voice in their selection was
reasonable; but to arm the Governor-General
with no overriding powers was unreasonable.
All that Hastings had written about the necessity of strengthening the Governor's authority
was disregarded. He was left as before, with no
superiority over the members of his Council
save a casting vote in the event of a tie. Such an
arrangement was likely in any circumstances to
lead to a struggle between the Governor-General

and his Council; but with the Council composed as it actually was, such a struggle was almost a certainty. Two servants of the Company—Hastings, who was appointed Governor-General, and his old colleague, Barwell—were harnessed with three new Councillors brought out from England and dependent entirely on the Ministry. These new Councillors—General Clavering, Colonel Monson and Philip Francis —knew nothing of Bengal, had no previous connection with the Company and viewed all its servants with prejudice and suspicion. The chances that they would co-operate loyally with Hastings were obviously small.

Lord North's appointment of Hastings as Governor-General seems to have been due partly to an appreciation of the need for continuity and expert knowledge, partly to a desire to conciliate the Directors who were very pleased with his administration, and partly to a genuine recognition of his merits. During the passing of the Act he spoke of him in high terms as a "person, who though flesh and blood, had resisted the greatest temptations—that though filling great offices in Bengal during the various Revolutions that had been felt in that country, never received a single Rupee at any one of them, and whose Abilities and intense application would be apparent to any gentleman who would consider what he had done during the first six months of his Administration." It is clear that merit, though it did not generally weigh heavily with Lord North, had some weight in this case.

The reasons for Barwell's appointment are not exactly known. Probably the Ministry thought it advisable to give another place to a servant of the Company, and selected Barwell somewhat at random. According to Hastings' friend Sykes, "A certain gentleman told Lord North he (Barwell) was next to you in abilities." Barwell had by now entirely succumbed to Hastings' charm of manner and superior abilities and was prepared to give him his cordial support. Hastings seems to have facilitated matters by winking at his irregular methods of acquiring a fortune.

The remaining three appointments were all political. General Clavering was a peppery old soldier of narrow views and moderate intelligence. He had served with some distinction in the West Indies, where he led the successful attack on Guadeloupe in 1759; but his real claims to Lord North's consideration were the parliamentary votes which he commanded and the warm support which he received from the King; indeed, it was largely in deference to George III's wishes that Lord North pushed through his appointment, despite the strong claims of a rival candidate, General Monckton. Clavering was given the position of second in Council, with the right of succession to the

Governor-Generalship should it become vacant. He was also appointed Commander-in-Chief.

Colonel Monson had seen service in Southern India during the Seven Years' War but had never been to Bengal. He too was a man of very ordinary ability, and commended himself to Lord North because of his parliamentary influence. He had no real qualifications for the post.

Philip Francis, the last of the trio, was certainly the most remarkable. Lord North's motives for appointing him are obscure. He had no parliamentary influence nor, so far as is known, any connections or patrons whose good-will it was important for North to purchase. His father had been chaplain to Henry Fox, and through the latter's patronage he had been employed, when still a lad, as a clerk in Whitehall. His abilities attracted the attention of Pitt, through whom he obtained various posts of private secretary. From 1763 to 1772 he worked in the Ministry of War; but he resigned his post after a quarrel with his chief, Lord Barrington, and at the time of his appointment to Bengal he was without employment, without prospects, without wealth and without influence. All the more astounding therefore was his selection at the early age of thirty-three to a lucrative post in India. It has been suggested that Lord North had discovered that he was the author of the letters of Junius and offered him this appointment in order to silence him. But even if he was really Junius, there is no evidence that anyone at that time knew or suspected it. A more probable explanation is the simple one that Lord North felt that he needed someone of keen intellect to compensate for the dull mediocrity of Clavering and Monson. Francis' dependence on ministerial favour would ensure his subservience, and his ability would supply what Clavering and Monson, with all their parliamentary influence, lacked. He was probably brought to North's notice by Lord Barrington, who apparently had become reconciled to his former subordinate and out of gratitude for his services and respect for his talents was eager to find him fresh employment.

Francis was undoubtedly a man of uncommon ability. Some of his minutes are admirable examples of clear statement and forceful argument. But he had a doctrinaire type of mind and an uncharitable disposition. Having once adopted certain views or conceived certain antipathies, he would never modify them in the light of experience or of fuller knowledge and understanding. Arrogant, unaccommodating and vindictive, he stuck to his opinions and his enmities with unquenchable zeal and rancour. Unfortunately he came out to India with strong prejudices against the Company's servants and with certain outmoded ideas about Indian affairs which he had picked up from Clive. On both grounds he was predisposed against Hastings; for not only was Hastings one of the oldest of the Company's servants, but it was Hastings who had swept away Clive's Dual System. IIe had little difficulty therefore in convincing himself that Hastings, despite his fair name and fair seeming, was really a corrupt dissembler, secretly conniving at all manner of oppression and extortion. This view not only served his own ambitions—for if Hastings could be driven from office he would become the effective head of the Bengal Government—but also cloaked them in the respectable garb of patriotism and public spirit. His mission it was to cleanse the Augean stable, to uncover the iniquities which Hastings had perpetrated or concealed. And certainly there were still plenty of iniquities in Bengal which Hastings, for want of power to remove them or from a too kind regard for human weaknesses, had tolerated or excused. For Hastings never claimed to be a Reformer or lamented that other men were not as virtuous as he.

Francis, during the long voyage out from England, had ample opportunity of instilling into the minds of his two colleagues his own distrust of Hastings and his views of their duties both to the public and to themselves. Their first experiences on arrival in Bengal served to confirm their worst suspicions, to stimulate their zeal for reform and to unite them firmly in opposition to Hastings.

First information of the impending changes had reached Calcutta by the overland route in April 1774. Fuller details were received by sea later. Hastings was flattered yet puzzled by his appointment as Governor-General. It was clear that his conduct of affairs had met with approbation; but the choice of his colleagues and the want of any addition to his own authority filled him with misgiving. The dismal experience of the luckless Vansittart was always before his mind. If he was really trusted, why was he not granted powers commensurate with his responsibilities? Had he been appointed merely to afford continuity and was it the intention that real power should pass to others? The hypothesis seemed only too probable. The establishmen of the Supreme Court also caused him disquiet. He foresaw the likelihood of a conflict and disliked the idea of importing into Bengal all the paraphernalia of the English law. There was, however, one redeeming factor—his old school-friend, Elijah Impey, was to be the first Chief Justice. Nothing but this, he told Impey in a letter of welcome, could have reconciled him to the new Court. In the same letter he gave some hint of his anxieties regarding his own position, and said that he counted on Impey's friendship to afford him such assistance as might be possible "for the prevention and removal of

the embarrassments which I fear I am unavoid-
ably to meet with."

Despite these misgivings, Hastings resolved
to make the best of the situation and to do all
that lay in his power to secure the confidence
and good-will of the new Councillors. He sent
them each a courteous letter of welcome to greet
them when their ship touched at Madras, and
he made careful arrangements for their reception at Calcutta, according them all the honours
which had been paid to Clive and Vansittart
when they had arrived as Governors.

These civilities were insufficient to satisfy the
new Councillors. They arrived on October
19th, 1774. Francis described their reception as "mean and dishonourable." Why was
there no guard of honour? And why was there
a salute of only seventeen guns instead of
twenty-one? This was an inauspicious beginning. On the day following their arrival
there was a formal meeting of the Council,
at which were read the Commission establishing the new Constitution and a general letter
of instructions from the Court of Directors.
The Directors, amid many other orders
and recommendations, urged an enquiry into
past abuses. Hastings, it will be recalled, on first
becoming Governor, had likewise been saddled
with numerous inquisitions into past misconduct and had discreetly shelved them, knowing that they would breed dissensions in his

Council and distract attention from more pressing business. But the new Councillors immediately decided that enquiry into past abuses should take precedence over all else. They would have liked to begin then and there, and it was only with difficulty that Hastings prevailed upon them to wait a few days for the arrival of Barwell, who happened to be absent from Calcutta. In the meantime he promised to draw up a memorandum giving a general account of the measures and policies of the late Government.

At the next meeting this memorandum was duly presented, and the great battle began. The new Councillors at once seized on the Rohilla war for criticism. Though they had only been in India a week as against Hastings' twenty years, they condemned straightaway all his transactions with the Vizier at Benares and demanded to see the whole of the correspondence which had passed between him and Middleton, the Resident at the Vizier's Court. To this Hastings demurred. Much of his correspondence with Middleton had been private and confidential and was never intended to be laid before the Council. General principles, past usage and loyalty to Middleton all justified him in withholding it. When pressed by the Majority to produce it, he flatly refused; but he offered to show them every line of it which had any bearing on the subject under discussion.

This by no means satisfied them. On the contrary, they boiled over with rage, and proceeded at once to make use of their strength. Despite the protests of Hastings and Barwell, they proposed and carried a resolution for the immediate recall of Middleton from Lucknow, denounced the Rohilla war as unjust and impolitic, and ordered an enquiry into its conduct.

The abrupt recall of Middleton was a direct and deliberate insult to Hastings. Even if the Majority felt that the Rohilla war had been ill-advised, to signalise their disapproval in this manner was outrageous. Middleton was Hastings' personal representative at Lucknow; he had been appointed with the Vizier's express approval with a view to maintaining the close and cordial relations so happily established at Benares. His recall, as Hastings told Lord North, was "a declaration to all Indoostan that my authority was extinct, and that new men and new measures would henceforth prevail." The conduct of the Majority is only comprehensible if one remembers the assumptions with which they started. They had persuaded themselves that Hastings, like so many servants of the Company, was deeply infected by the corruption of the times, and they therefore suspected that all his transactions with the Vizier were really corrupt bargains from which he had derived huge personal profits. His refusal to produce his private correspondence with Middleton struck them at once as the strongest possible confirmation of these suspicions and appeared to justify the most vigorous action.

Hastings, on his part, conscious of his own rectitude and of his good reputation—to which Lord North had publicly testified—quite failed to read the minds of his opponents. He had not, of course, expected them to be particularly favourable to him; but he never imagined that they would assume *ab initio* that he was a corrupt scoundrel and regard a minute inquisition into his past conduct as their first and foremost duty. Surely it was not for this that he had been publicly honoured by selection as the first Governor-General? He was therefore totally unable to gauge the effect which his refusal to produce his correspondence with Middleton would have on their minds. Possibly, if he had realised how they would interpret this refusal, he would have taken a different line; for there was nothing incriminating in the correspondence. He subsequently had the whole of it copied and sent it to Lord North for perusal.

On learning of Middleton's recall the Vizier is reported to have burst into tears. He regarded Hastings as a friend and divined at once that he himself would be one of the first to suffer from the eclipse of Hastings' influence. He did not, however, survive to experience the full effects of the Majority's malevolence. In January

1775 he died, commending his son, Asaf-ud-daula, to Hastings' care and protection.

There was little that Hastings could do for him. The Majority had by now got the bit between their teeth. He could only protest against follies which he was powerless to prevent. They decided that the Vizier's death cancelled all treaties that the English had made with him and that his son, if he wanted English support, must enter into fresh engagements. Asaf-ud-daula was a weak, indolent youth who needed firm support and guidance rather than gratuitous additions to his burdens. But the Majority thought otherwise. They decided that he must pay for the Company's brigade of troops at the rate of Rs.2,60,000 instead of Rs.2,10,000 a month and that he must cede to the Company the large zemindari of Benares comprising several districts and ruled over by his vassal, Rajah Chait Singh. This was an act of wanton spoliation for which there is no parallel in any of Hastings' alleged oppressions of the peoples and princes of India. Francis, who was to be foremost in the indictment of Hastings, was himself directly responsible for it.

Having thus raised the cost of the Company's troops and at the same time diminished Asaf-ud-daula's means of paying for them, the Majority proceeded to let the wretched youth be robbed in another way. Shuja-ud-daula had left an immense treasure, reported to amount to more than £2,000,000, which was claimed by his widow and his mother—the famous Begums of Oudh—on the strength of a will that was never produced. Large sums were owing to the Company on account of the Rohilla war, the pay of the army was many months in arrears and the troops were mutinous. If Asaf-ud-daula had possessed any firmness of character, he would have insisted on the treasure being used for the discharge of these outstanding obligations. Under Muhammadan law the Begums had no right to it, and they were amply provided for otherwise. The Resident, Bristow—a creature of the Majority who had succeeded Middleton— instead of encouraging Asaf-ud-daula to take a firm line with his women-folk, as the interests of the Company and the stability of Oudh both alike required, undertook to negotiate with them on his behalf and, for reasons which have remained obscure, concluded for him a very bad bargain. In consideration of the relatively small sum of 56 lakhs of rupees (about £500,000) Asaf-ud-daula gave up all further claims on the Begums, and Bristow, on behalf of the Company, guaranteed the agreement.

Hastings and Barwell vainly opposed all these impolitic transactions. The Majority went their own way, heedless of protest and of the disorders which inevitably ensued. The Nawab's troops mutinied for want of pay. The mutiny was suppressed by a massacre. To maintain order the

Nawab hired troops from the Company, found the expense too great and fell deeply into debt. The mishandling of Oudh at this time opened the long chapter of its exploitation, misgovernment and misery which was to end eighty years later with annexation and the Mutiny.

Chapter Ten

Discomfiture of Nandakumar

THE Rohilla war, with which the Majority
had begun their attack on Hastings, proved
much less productive of material against him
than they had at first hoped. Despite all their
probing and questioning of military officers,
they elicited little or nothing adverse to
Hastings—though they learnt a good deal about
the Rohillas of which they had previously been
ignorant. But their conduct had proclaimed to
all Bengal that Hastings' former power had
gone and that attacks on his character could now
be made not only with impunity, but with
every hope of future profit. The word went
round that the new rulers of the provinces
believed Hastings to be corrupt and would welcome evidence of his corruption. These rulers
had not been long enough in India to appreciate
that, in these circumstances, the evidence would
be forthcoming quite irrespective of the facts.
Blinded by prejudice, they readily accepted
calumnies from the most tainted sources; these
in turn confirmed their prejudices and spurred
them to further search for proofs of Hastings'
guilt. Clavering and Monson were not bad men;

but they were prejudiced, ignorant and stupid men, and they were dominated by the malevolent Francis. Adopting the principle that there is no smoke without a fire, they listened with eagerness and the utmost gravity to accusations brought against Hastings by notorious scoundrels from obvious motives of malice.

Hastings, who kept his ear pretty close to the ground, well knew what was afoot. The tool which he had used against Muhammad Reza Khan would now be used against himself. On March 11th, 1775, at a meeting of the Council, Francis produced a letter which, he said, had been delivered to him by Rajah Nandakumar for presentation to the Council. He disclaimed knowledge of its contents, but on his motion it was opened and read, and was found to contain, amid many insinuations against Hastings, specific charges of bribery. It was alleged that he had accepted sums amounting to Rs.3,50,000 from Nandakumar and the Mani Begum for appointing the latter as guardian of the Nawab and for giving the post of diwan to Nandakumar's son. Francis had all along been aware of the contents of the letter, as he was later forced to admit. Monson, too, was privy to it and so, probably, was Clavering; nor did it come as any surprise to Hastings.

Two days later a second letter was received from Nandakumar, reaffirming his charges and requesting permission to appear before the

Council Board to establish them by incontestable written evidence which he claimed to possess. Monson proposed that he should be called before the Board. Hastings, burning with indignation and quite unlike his usual calm, affable self, replied: "I will not sit at this Board in the character of a criminal, nor do I acknowledge the members of the Board to be my judges. I am induced on this occasion to make the declaration that I look upon General Clavering, Colonel Monson and Mr. Francis as my accusers." The words with which he closed his minute betray the intense emotion under which he wrote. "The Chief of this administration, your superior, gentlemen, appointed by the Legislature itself, shall I sit at this Board to be arraigned in the presence of a wretch whom you all know to be one of the basest of mankind? . . . Shall I sit to hear men collected from the dregs of the people give evidence at his dictating against my character and conduct? I will not. You may, if you please, form yourselves into a Committee for the investigation of these matters, in any manner which you may think proper, but I will repeat that I will not meet Nundcoomar at the Board nor suffer Nundcoomar to be examined at the Board; nor have you a right to it, nor can it answer any other purpose than that of vilifying and insulting me to insist upon it."

But to vilify and insult Hastings was just what

the Majority wanted. Monson's motion was carried and the Secretary was ordered to summon Nandakumar. On this Hastings declared the Council dissolved and together with Barwell withdrew from the Council Chamber.

The Majority proceeded to their examination of Nandakumar. He produced a document purporting to be a letter from the Mani Begum and bearing her seal, in which she mentioned in some detail various sums of money which she had offered to Hastings and which he had accepted. After a very perfunctory questioning of Nandakumar the Majority decided that Hastings had in fact received from the Mani Begum the sums alleged and that he should be required to pay them over to the Company. A resolution was passed to this effect and the papers made over to the law officers to advise how recovery should be made.

Hastings had no doubt that the letter produced by Nandakumar was a forgery, and that he would be able to prove this. The necessity to do so never arose, as the Company's legal advisers in London pronounced that the information given by Nandakumar was obviously untrue, and the matter was never pursued. In actual fact Nandakumar's charges contained one element of truth, and this was that Hastings, on his visit to Murshidabad in 1772, had received a sum of Rs.1,50,000 from the Mani Begum as a sumptuary allowance at the rate of Rs.2,000 a day. There was, however, nothing underhand about this. The payment was regularly entered in the accounts of the Nawab's treasury, and, though the allowance appears to have been grossly excessive, it was sanctioned by usage and had been paid at this rate both to Clive and Verelst. Apart from this, there was no substance in Nandakumar's stories.

But the falseness or absurdity of the accusations brought against Hastings afforded him for the moment no protection. Diligently assisted by Nandakumar and a disreputable European adventurer named Fowke, the Majority raked through all the filth of Calcutta in search of mud to fling at him. "The trumpet has been sounded," Hastings wrote, "and the whole host of informers will soon crowd to Calcutta with their complaints and ready depositions. Nandakumar holds his darbar in complete state, sends for zemindars and their wakils, coaxing and threatening them for complaints, which no doubt he will get in abundance, besides what he forges himself. The system which they have laid down for conducting their affairs is, I am told, after this manner: the General (Clavering) rummages the consultations for disreputable matter, with the aid of old Fowke; Colonel Monson receives, and, I have been assured, descends even to solicit, accusations; Francis writes. . . . Was it for this that the Legislation of Great Britain formed the new system of Government for Bengal, and armed it with powers extending to every part of the British Empire in India?"

Hastings, besides being powerless in his own Council and compelled to see his own carefully chosen officers deprived of their posts, was now daily subjected to personal insults and indignities. "There is no form of peculation," the Majority were pleased to remark on one occasion, "from which the honourable Governor-General has thought it reasonable to abstain." For a while he became despondent, and on March 27th 1775 he wrote to Colonel Macleane and Mr. Graham, two friends who had recently returned to England, that he had resolved to resign, if the first advices from home indicated that the Rohilla war had not been approved and that there is "an evident disinclination towards me. In that case," he said, "I can have nothing to hope and shall consider myself at liberty to quit this hateful scene before my enemies gain their complete triumph over me." He left it to them to take such action on his behalf as they might think proper. At the same time he wrote to Lord North, begging him either to order his recall or to give him proper authority. "The meanest drudge," he wrote, "who owes his daily subsistence to daily labour, enjoys a condition of happiness compared to mine, while I am doomed to share the responsibility of measures which I disapprove, and to be the idle spectator of the ruin which I cannot avert."

He had little chance of support from Lord North. A mere servant of the Company, what was he to the politicians in England? How could he hope to rival in their regard a man such as Clavering, with his powerful parliamentary connections and the patronage of the King himself? Hastings' strength lay, not in England, but in Bengal, the very scene of his torment, where, so it appeared, he was at the mercy of his enemies and could look only for ignominy and insult. But appearances were deceptive. The Majority, though all-powerful in Council and supported by a host of time-servers, were still profoundly ignorant of Bengal, and, unknown to themselves, its climate, its people and Hastings' superior knowledge of both were weighing heavily in the scales against them. Clavering and Monson had come to Bengal late in life. Its unpleasant and unfamiliar climate irked them, strained their tempers and secretly undermined their constitutions. In their dealings with the natives, the whole trio were quite out of their depth. Incautiously trusting themselves to such men as Nandakumar, they suddenly found that they were being swept to a shameful catastrophe—and that Calcutta was delighted. The truth is that they had failed to realise the strength of Hastings' influence and the worthlessness of their own tools. Public opinion, outraged by the men and methods which they employed in their attack on the Governor-General, turned strongly and decisively against them. Moreover, while they were busy with the slanders and tittle-tattle of the riff-raff of Bengal, far more devoted and reliable agents were secretly working in Hastings' interests. He had been connected with Bengal for a quarter of a century, for several years he had held high office, and he was liked and respected by the people for his sense of justice and the mildness of his manners. Far too many persons were bound to him by ties of friendship, gratitude or interest to let him be pulled down without a struggle. All these rallied ardently to his support. The worthless tools of the Majority buckled in their hands.

The first sign of the turning of the tide came on April 19th, when a certain revenue-farmer named Kamal-ud-din, who had been prominent amongst Hastings' accusers, waited upon him with a complaint against Nandakumar and Fowke. He told a long, rambling and somewhat confused story, but the general purport of it was that Nandakumar and Fowke had compelled him by threats to sign a petition containing various allegations against Hastings and Barwell. After questioning him closely, Hastings referred him to the Chief Justice. The next day Sir Elijah Impey and the other Judges held a preliminary enquiry. They concluded that there was strong suspicion against Nandakumar and Fowke, and asked Hastings and Barwell whether they wished to prosecute. Though Kamal-ud-din was an unreliable person who might easily go back on his statements, they bound themselves over to do so; and the defendants were admitted to bail.

Why was it that Kamal-ud-din, who had been actively assisting the Majority, suddenly turned against them? The reasons are not known, but it is hardly possible that he was actuated by the spontaneous prickings of his own conscience. He was a man of no character whose conscience was not likely to operate without some external stimulus. In other words, he must have been 'got at.' Someone working in Hastings' interests must have approached him and won him over. It is not necessary to suppose that this was done with Hastings' knowledge—in India such services are generally performed without the active connivance of the Great—but it must have been a deliberate act, consciously designed to enable Hastings to turn the tables on his opponents.

This, the first move in Hastings' counter-offensive, ended some months later in the conviction of both Nandakumar and Fowke for conspiracy against Barwell only. But long before these proceedings had reached their close they were overshadowed by a far more sensational prosecution. On May 6th Nandakumar was arrested for forgery, committed for trial and sent to the common gaol.

"The rage of the Majority," writes Macaulay, "rose to the highest point"; and well it might. Their principal witness against Hastings had been struck down. Lodged in gaol he was, as Hastings put it, "in a fair way to be hanged"; for forgery was a crime for which the penalty was death. It was useless for the Majority to complain to the distant Directors, as they did, or to heap honours on Nandakumar's son—as also they did. The law took its inexorable course. Nandakumar was brought for trial before Impey sitting with the three other Judges and a European jury, was found guilty, sentenced to death and executed. "The voices of a thousand informers were silenced in an instant. From that time, whatever difficulties Hastings might have to encounter, he was never molested by accusations from natives of India."

What is the truth about this extraordinary business? Macaulay said that no one, except idiots and biographers, had ever doubted that Hastings was the real prosecutor. Though this judgment has been ridiculed by some modern writers, at the time it was certainly assumed that Nandakumar was hanged because he ventured to attack the Governor-General; and it is hard to dispute that this contemporary assumption was correct. This is not to say that Hastings himself was the prime mover in the business,

160

still less that he and Impey deliberately acted in collusion. What is asserted is that, if it had not been for his attack on Hastings, Nandakumar would probably never have been prosecuted, and would certainly not have been hanged.

What are the facts? The prosecution arose out of civil litigation which had started as far back as 1772. The executor of a banker named Balaki Das had sued Nandakumar for over one lakh of rupees alleged to be due from him to the estate of the deceased. A pleader named Mohan Pershad acted for the plaintiff. Nandakumar resisted the claim, and a lengthy investigation of all the past transactions between him and the deceased became necessary. When these were gone into the plaintiff alleged that a certain bond, purporting to be signed by Balaki Das and to be an acknowledgment by him of a debt due to Nandakumar, was a forgery. The Court, seeing that matters were likely to take a serious turn, recommended arbitration. After much delay Nandakumar consented to arbitration; but he then delayed naming an arbitrator, and the case was still pending when the new Supreme Court was established in Calcutta (October 1774).

Nandakumar's dilatory tactics had caused Mohan Pershad as early as March 1774 to consider bringing pressure to bear on him by threatening him with a criminal prosecution for forgery. But in order to prepare an indictment it was necessary to obtain the original bond alleged to have been forged; this had been filed along with other papers of Balaki Das in the Mayor's Court as a Court of Record; and when Mohan Pershad applied for it the Court refused to give it to him and would only grant a copy.

With the arrival of a new Court, Mohan Pershad seems to have decided that it was worth trying again, especially as Nandakumar was still delaying settlement of the civil dispute. Accordingly, in January 1775, the Supreme Court was moved for the delivery of the required papers and the necessary order was obtained. There was, however, delay in complying with it, and on March 24th the Court had to be moved again. This time a peremptory order was issued for the delivery of the papers within one month. This order was complied with and the prosecution was then launched with the result already stated.

From these facts writers have sought to argue that the prosecution of Nandakumar for forgery at a moment so opportune for Hastings was sheer coincidence. They omit to notice that the existence of this long-postponed but potential criminal prosecution must have been known, if not to Hastings himself, at any rate to his dependants and well-wishers. It is almost inconceivable that it was not known to Hastings himself, as he was certainly in the habit of granting

audiences to the pleader Mohan Pershad—
indeed, Nandakumar made this a matter of
grievance against him. However this may be,
Hastings' supporters, especially among the
native population, must have known from
Mohan Pershad all the essential facts. Once,
therefore, Nandakumar came out into the open
against Hastings, they promptly saw to it that
life and vigour were put into the criminal proceedings. Hitherto these had been treated in a
leisurely, languid fashion; for the plaintiff in the
civil suit had regarded them merely as a means
of putting pressure on Nandakumar to pay his
debts, and would never have dreamed of going
so far as to have him sentenced to death. If
Hastings' interests had not become involved, the
criminal proceedings would probably never
have got fairly under way; if they had, they
would certainly have come to nothing in the
end. Nandakumar, as soon as things looked
dangerous, would have settled the civil suit and
with the plaintiff's collusion squared the prosecution witnesses. But once the Governor-
General's supporters had given their backing to
the prosecution, no such mild and amicable
termination to it was possible.

Before deciding to back this prosecution,
Hastings' supporters must have weighed carefully the chances of success. As so often in India,
the temper of the judge was of more importance
than the strength of the evidence; for the case

against Nandakumar, though a good one, was by no means cast-iron. An unfriendly judge might easily procure an acquittal. It was known, however, that Impey, the Chief Justice, was an old friend of Hastings; he therefore was not likely to show improper favour to Nandakumar. Nor was the jury likely to be unduly favourable to him, for he had long had a very evil reputation, and his attack on the Governor-General had been widely resented by the English community. The outlook was therefore as promising as could be expected.

It has been suggested that Hastings and Impey were in collusion; but it would have been superfluous for Hastings even to approach Impey on the subject. The case against Nanda-kumar being a good one, all that Hastings needed was the assurance that Impey would not wantonly incline in Nandakumar's favour. Against this his old friendship with Impey was in itself a sufficient guarantee.

There is, surely, nothing particularly dis-creditable to Hastings in all this. He used against Nandakumar, or allowed others to use on his behalf, a handle which had been for-tuitously presented to him. No one but a fool or a saint would have done otherwise. Moreover the trial itself and the actual verdict were not in any way unfair. Though perhaps few judges in India to-day would care to condemn a man to death on the evidence which was accepted against Nandakumar, the general weight of the testimony definitely pointed to his guilt, and, whatever may be thought of Impey or the European jury, the integrity of Impey's colleagues has never been impugned. It was not the verdict of 'guilty' which was indefensible, but the sentence of death. Viewed in the light of this ultimate result, the whole affair can hardly be regarded as other than the "scandalous travesty of decency" which modern writers [1] have termed it. For to Nandakumar and his compatriots forgery was a venal offence. To quote Macaulay, it "was regarded by them in much the same light in which the selling of an unsound horse, for a sound price, is regarded by a Yorkshire jockey." No doubt English criminal law, which prescribed death as the penalty for forgery, had for years been applied in Calcutta by the old Mayor's Court; but there is no record of any native of the country having actually been hanged for this offence. On the contrary, a few years earlier a prominent Bengalee, sentenced to death for forgery, had subsequently been pardoned. Nandakumar may have been a very bad man and may have deserved death on other grounds, but his execution for forging a document in order to swindle the heirs of Balaki Das out of a few thousand pounds was in itself indefensible. Basically, the con-

[1] Thompson and Garratt, *Rise and Fulfilment of British Rule in India*, page 135.

temporary Indian view that he had been hanged for daring to attack the Governor-General was not incorrect.

The injustice of hanging Nandakumar for forgery can have been apparent to no one more than to Hastings himself; for he had frequently complained of the injustice of "making men liable to punishments with which they have been unacquainted and which their customs and manners have not taught them to associate with their idea of offence." He took no steps, however, to prevent the execution of the sentence. For him to have done so would perhaps have been a work of supererogation. He was certainly under no compelling moral obligation to obtain a reprieve for Nandakumar. This obligation, if it rested on anyone, rested on the Majority. They had admitted him deeply into their confidence, they had freely availed themselves of his dubious services, they had encouraged him to denounce Hastings; yet when he was in mortal peril they did not lift a finger to save him. His Counsel drafted petitions to the Judges praying for a respite to enable a reference to be made to England. One of these was delivered to Francis in the hope that the Council might endorse it with a recommendation. Had this been done, the Judges might have found difficulty in rejecting it. But the Majority refused to have anything to do with it, and further piteous appeals addressed to them by

Nandakumar himself they ignored or purposely left unopened till he was dead. Their conduct is scarcely comprehensible; but they seem to have been utterly dumbfounded by the sudden, dramatic turn of events. Perhaps they felt that they were up against a diabolical cunning with which it was useless to contend further. Perhaps they were secretly abashed at the public revelation of Nandakumar's worthlessness. Whatever their motives, they left him to die and, by this startling betrayal of their own agent, threw away all chances of gaining the confidence of the people of Bengal. Hastings, on the other hand, went up in popular estimation. He had taken legitimate revenge on a bad man who had gravely injured him. He had done no wrong, and he had been successful. He gained more in respect than he lost in love.

Chapter Eleven

Hastings Recovers Power

THE trial and execution of Nandakumar was a decisive turning-point in Hastings' struggle against the Majority. Though he had to wait another year before he regained control in the Council, the direct personal attacks on him had failed ignominiously and from now onwards ceased. The Majority were discouraged by the set-back; Hastings was correspondingly cheered. His enemies had not gained that complete triumph over him which at the end of March he had expected. Recovering from the despondent mood into which he had fallen at that time, he abandoned his intention of immediately resigning if the first advices from England were unfavourable, and informed his agents on May 18th: "I now retract the resolution communicated to you separately in my letters of the 27th of March. Whatever advice the first packet may bring, I am now resolved to see the issue of my appeal, believing it impossible that men whose actions are so frantic can be permitted to remain in charge of so important a trust."

In the meantime, however, they remained in

charge and continued to criticise all that
Hastings had done and to persecute all those
whom he had protected or promoted. A disastrous spirit of partisanship spread right through
the administration, and even the zemindars
began taking one side or the other. At the same
time the new system of government, which
Hastings had taken such pains to introduce, was
rudely shaken; for the Majority lost no opportunity of repealing his measures or rendering
them abortive.

The revenue administration was one of the
earliest objects of attack. The excessive rents
which the revenue farmers had engaged to pay
at the five-year settlement of 1772 had led to
numerous defaults and a considerable accumulation of arrears. The Majority bitterly blamed
Hastings for having overestimated the rents
which could be paid, yet at the same time
reproached him for failure to realise them in
full, and refused to allow the smallest remissions.
Hastings, who admitted that mistakes had been
made, showed remarkable patience and courtesy
in face of their ill-natured criticisms; but he
adroitly took advantage of their profound
ignorance of the whole subject by suggesting
that each Member of Council should set forth
his views as to the best way of settling and
collecting the revenue. To this suggestion the
Majority could only reply weakly, "At this
moment we should be very much embarrassed if

we were called upon to make a new settlement of the lands, and were entrusted with power to do it." They were not in fact able to put forward any concrete proposals till nearly a year later. Francis then produced a plan for a 'permanent' settlement, based, without acknowledgment, on the views and advice of two of the Company's servants, P. M. Dacres and John Shore. Nine months earlier, with characteristic zeal and promptness, Hastings had drawn up with Barwell's help a far sounder plan of his own, embodying the principle of long leases for two lives, and public auctions with preference allowed to bids by zemindars. The plan was not sanctioned by the Directors and so unfortunately never took effect; but it is interesting as an index, not only of the soundness of Hastings' views, but also of his amazing energy and spirit; for he produced it just at the time when the struggle with Nandakumar was at its height and there seemed every prospect of his being driven from office by the calumnies of his enemies. Most men in such circumstances would have been far too discouraged to devote time and thought to the dry subject of revenue administration.

Faction being, in Hastings' words, the only principle which guided the Majority, they proceeded to close down the Bank which he had established, to suspend the superintendence of his Courts of Justice, to remove officials whom he had appointed, and to revive, so far as they could, the Dual System of Government which he had brought to an end. In this last measure we can trace the influence of Clive operating through the medium of Francis. But Francis sought to reintroduce Clive's system simply because it conflicted with Hastings' policy, regardless of the fact that, whatever merits it may once have had, it was quite inapplicable in the changed circumstances of Bengal. To attempt to revive now the pretence of the puppet Nawab's power was an anachronism, serving no political purpose—for the French and the Dutch had long since declared that the English Company was the ruling power—and entailing considerable administrative disadvantages. It was easy enough, however, for the Majority to prove that Hastings' creation of new Criminal Courts and virtual assumption of responsibility for the whole criminal administration was an encroachment on the Nawab's powers as head of the Nizamat. So, to redress the wrong which Hastings was alleged to have committed, they restored to the Nawab all the rights of the Nizamat, viz. full police and criminal jurisdiction; and, believing that the Nawab's old minister, Muhammad Reza Khan, would be inimical to Hastings, they brought him out of his retirement and put him in charge. Nominally he was the Minister of the Nawab; but in fact he was the agent of the Majority who, under cover of his pretended independence, wielded power uncontrolled.

As the weeks passed, Hastings, despite his powerlessness and his vexation at seeing his measures frustrated or repealed, became increasingly determined to stand his ground. The Directors' first despatches on the Rohilla war and on other early matters of dispute between him and the Majority had not been too favourable to him; a later despatch, written at the close of 1775, contained such sweeping condemnation of many of his actions that he was left with little doubt that they were turning against him. "It is replete," he wrote, "with the grossest adulation to the Majority, and as gross abuse to me. . . . But I regard it not. If those who penned the letter hope by it to provoke me to give up the battle, they have erred most miserably. Though ruin or death should attend it, I will wait the event, and if I must fall, I will not be the instrument of my own defeat by anticipating it."

The Directors, fully apprised now of the deep divisions in the Council, concluded their despatch with an exhortation to unanimity. This produced at any rate a momentary effect; for its absurdity, Hastings says, "so struck the fancy of every member of the Board when it was read, that they all at once burst out into a loud and hearty laugh, the only symptom of unanimity

172

. . . that I have seen in that assembly these two years."

During all this while Hastings, though unable to pursue his own policies, remained in a sense the mainspring of the Government. He never missed a single meeting of Council; and he "led and laboriously promoted the current business," frequently combining "the loose and incongruous opinions of the other members into a form which they might all approve, though foreign from my own." He could have thrown everything into the most inextricable confusion, but his own natural instinct for administration was always urging him to keep the wheels of government moving. Unable to make his own opinions prevail, he patiently adopted those of the Majority "for the sake of despatch, from a conviction that even wrong movements are preferable to inaction, which is the death of public affairs." The Majority themselves recognised, and deplored, their dependence on him. None of them could supply his knowledge, diligence and regular habits of business. Clavering, whose ambition it was to replace him, seems to have had secret doubts of his own capacity to do so. The climate was telling on him and he sometimes talked to Francis of resigning.

Hastings meanwhile laboured on indefatigably. One of his principal objects at this time was to prevent a really serious breach between the Council and the Supreme Court.

He had from the outset foreseen the probability of friction owing to the Court's lack of determinate relations with the civil courts, which he had himself established, and owing to the uncertainty regarding the extent of its jurisdiction. The main source of trouble was the Court's claim to entertain actions against persons engaged in the collection of the revenue. Were zemindars liable to the Court's jurisdiction in respect of irregular or oppressive acts alleged to be committed by them in the course of their collections? Admittedly the Court possessed jurisdiction over all 'British subjects' or 'persons in the employ of British subjects,' but it was uncertain who fell within these categories. Hastings perceived that the only sure way of preventing doubt and conflict was to extend the Court's jurisdiction to all inhabitants of the three provinces without limitation, but at the same time to bring it into defined relations with the existing courts which he had set up. In consultation with Impey he drew up a Plan for the better Administration of Justice, in which he proposed, *inter alia,* that the Judges of the Supreme Court should be united with the Council to form a Superior Court in direct control of all the subordinate civil or diwani courts. Here again we have an example of his unflagging enthusiasm and of the soundness of his judgment. If his Plan or something like it had been adopted, the serious

174

conflict between Council and Supreme Court which occurred later would have been avoided. He sent the Plan home early in 1776, but it was not accepted.

The Majority criticised this Plan in a long and academic minute, but could offer no practical suggestions themselves. They were now fast losing health and losing heart. In March 1776 Francis, in a gloomy letter, reported both Monson and Clavering in a "woeful condition." Clavering was "covered with boils" and Monson "obliged to go to sea to save his life." Francis himself was finding the heat a great deal too much for him. Barwell also was far from well, only alive, according to Francis, because death did not think him worth taking. Hastings, he complained, is "much more tough than any of us, and will never die a natural death." The fact is that Hastings' moderate and abstemious habits were more suited to the climate of Bengal than the fuller mode of life of his opponents. "I eat no supper," he says, "go to bed at ten, abstain wholly from wine, and from every other liquid but tea and water." Contrast this with Francis. Though he lasted better than the others, he dissipated his energies in amorous adventures, and spent night after night gambling with Barwell. On one occasion he is said to have won £20,000 from him in a single evening. Barwell, one of the richest of all the 'Nabobs,' could well afford it.

By the summer of 1776 Monson was seriously ill, and after lingering for over two months died on September 25th. Hastings, reporting the event to Lord North, comments drily, "It has restored to me the constitutional authority of my station." With the help of Barwell and his own casting vote he was at last master in his own Council. But how long would he remain so? "The General," he wrote just after Monson's death, "is sick, being covered with boils, but he has no symptom of danger." There was no immediate hope, therefore, of another casualty; and a successor to Monson would arrive in about a year, who would almost certainly be a friend of Clavering's, deliberately sent out to reinforce his party. Hastings was not therefore unduly elated by his temporary recovery of power. But he was more than ever resolved not to quit. "Having gone through two years of persecution," he wrote to his friend Graham, "I am determined that no less authority than the King's express act shall remove me, or death."

He had little idea how keenly the King and his Ministers wished to remove him, and how nearly they had succeeded in their wishes. While in Bengal his enemies were sickening, in England he was himself on the brink of disaster. Reports of the violent quarrels in the Bengal Council had reached the home authorities in the course of the year 1775. They had perceived that there was little likelihood of a reconciliation, and that in the interests of good government one or the other party would have to be recalled. Which party was it to be? Hastings knew that the scales were weighted against him, but he could hardly believe that the verdict would go in favour of men "whose actions are so frantic." He pinned his faith to Lord North, from whom and from whose secretary, Robinson, he had received several encouraging letters. He seems to have imagined that Lord North, having carefully gone through all the papers, would be convinced of the folly and impropriety of the Majority's proceedings and would give him the support which on merits he deserved. This was a complete miscalculation. There was never any chance of the case being decided on merits. Lord North was bound to back his own nominees—this was really a foregone conclusion. There might be some annoyance with Clavering and his two associates for provoking a crisis by their intemperate conduct, but there could be no question of abandoning them in favour of Hastings. Neither justice nor Hastings' superior abilities could outweigh the royal favour and parliamentary influence which Clavering enjoyed. Furthermore, there were still ideas afloat of confining the Company entirely to commerce and taking over on behalf of the Crown its territorial acquisitions. For the execution of such a policy Clavering, a soldier and the servant of the King, was more appropriate than Hastings, the servant of the Company.

A choice being necessary, it was Hastings who would have to be removed. To reach this decision was easy; to give effect to it was less easy. Lord North's Regulating Act, so productive of deadlocks between competing authorities, was now to operate against himself. The Members of Council were only removable by the Crown on an address from the Company, and there was no reason why the Directors and Proprietors of the Company should voluntarily ask for Hastings' removal. He was their own servant, and he had served them well, whereas the Majority had hardly troubled to conceal their dislike and contempt for them. A motion for the removal of both Hastings and Barwell was negatived by the Court of Directors.

Foiled by the Company's unaccommodating attitude, Lord North had no alternative but to resort to bribery. His agents set to work to tamper with the Directors and with some of the principal Proprietors. The success of their efforts was reflected in the Directors' despatches to Bengal, which became increasingly hostile to Hastings. Colonel Macleane, his agent in England, bewailed the defection of friends. "I live in constant dread," he wrote, "of the operation of loaves and fishes."

By the spring of 1776 Lord North's preparations were complete. On May 9th the motion for the removal of Hastings and Barwell, which had previously been rejected, was again brought before the Court of Directors at short notice and was passed by eleven votes to ten. The intention was to rush the whole matter through without delay and to address the Crown for Hastings' removal the very next day. But Macleane and Hastings' other friends were on the alert. As soon as the result of the ballot in the Court of Directors was known, they got a letter signed, demanding that a meeting of the Proprietors be called to consider the question. The Directors felt obliged to comply. The Court of Proprietors met on May 16th. There was an adjournment and the question of Hastings' removal was put to the ballot on the 18th. The Court was full; both sides had whipped up their supporters, and the Government had brought all their influence into play. But the Proprietors realised that more was at stake than a mere personal issue. Hastings' cause was the cause of the Company. His removal at the instance of the Ministry and Clavering's succession to the post of Governor-General would have meant the end of the Company's power in India. The Proprietors, therefore, too numerous to be bribed, rallied to his support, and by a majority of 106, or about two to one, reversed the decision of the Court of Directors.

The Government were disgusted. Their distribution of loaves and fishes to the Directors had been completely wasted. According to

Macleane, the size of the majority "stunned them. Lord North cannot bear the least mention of the India House, directors or proprietors." North let it be known that, in his opinion, Indian affairs could now be settled only by Parliament. The Company's territorial acquisitions must be taken from them, he said, without waiting for the expiration of their charter, and for this purpose Parliament must meet before Christmas. Meanwhile, the Proprietors might do as they pleased; the more violent and absurd their actions the better.

This brave and menacing language at first had no terrors for Macleane. He had reason to suppose that some of the Ministers were not in favour of proceeding to such extremes against the Company. But as the summer wore on he became anxious. Parliament was summoned to meet in October, principally for Indian affairs. The chances of putting up a successful fight against the Ministry in the House of Commons seemed small; and even if Hastings was not actually removed by a fresh Act of Parliament, there was no hope of his being permitted to be master in his own Council. When, therefore, the Ministry, acting through the indispensable Mr. Robinson, made overtures for a compromise, Macleane thought the moment opportune for Hastings gracefully to withdraw. After some weeks of negotiation it was arranged that he should resign on the express understanding that all employees of the Company, whether English or Indian, who had been displaced for attachment to him should be restored to their positions, and that he himself should be well received on his return and a vote of thanks promoted, if moved for. There was also some suggestion of an Irish peerage, but nothing definite was settled in this regard, lest it might appear that Hastings had been bribed to resign by the promise of a title.

These terms having been agreed upon, Macleane wrote a letter to the Directors saying that Hastings, with a view to ending the unhappy divisions in the Council, had directed him to signify his desire to resign his office of Governor-General. The Directors were doubtful whether Macleane really had proper authority to take this action. He relied on Hastings' verbal instructions and on his letter of March 27th.[1] After a little demur they accepted his assurances, and on October 16th communicated Hastings' supposed wishes to the Secretary of State.

Some of Hastings' friends were displeased with Macleane. They considered that the surrender was unnecessary and that he had no authority to offer Hastings' resignation. "Then Mr. Hastings will disavow me," Macleane replied. "His resignation is in his own hands." There is no doubt that he acted from the best of motives.

[1] See page 156.

News of Monson's illness and death had not yet reached England. It seemed that Hastings had nothing to gain and much to lose by remaining in Bengal. At best there was the prospect of continuing frustration; at worst the Ministry would proceed to extremes and secure, through Parliament, both his removal and his disgrace. There was much to be said for retiring with honour while he could. For the Ministry were not really ill-disposed towards him. They just wanted him out of the way, and were bound to be grateful to him for conveniently tendering his resignation. "You have freed them from a confounded puzzle," one of his intimates wrote to him; "you have saved them from the disagreeable task of a parliamentary discussion, and you leave them quietly to blunder on in the affairs of Bengal during the remainder of the term fixed by the Act; therefore when you come home you will be caressed by them."

The Ministry's first caress was, however, reserved for Clavering. In November the *Gazette* contained an announcement of his appointment to the Order of the Bath. Hastings received no mark of royal favour. Macleane regarded this discrimination as a direct breach of the spirit of the recent compromise. He wrote off at once to Hastings telling him not to resign until he received "authentic accounts from England of some equivalent honour being bestowed on you." The advice was superfluous. General

182

Clavering, by his own violent and precipitate conduct, had effectually removed all possibility of Hastings' voluntarily tendering his resignation.

Private information of the engagement which Macleane had made reached Hastings on June 14th, 1777. He was not pleased with it but, he told Lord North, "I held myself bound by it, and was resolved to ratify it." Official despatches containing full details of the transaction were opened and read in Council on June 19th, after which the Council broke up without any comment or resolution being passed. The next day, being a Friday, was the day for the weekly meeting of the Revenue Board. Hastings issued the usual summons, and he and Barwell met at the Revenue Council Chamber at 11 a.m. Barwell showed him a summons which he had just received from Clavering, signed by him as Governor-General, calling a meeting of the General Council for the purpose of taking charge of the Government from Hastings. Almost at the same moment a letter was delivered to Hastings from Clavering requiring him to hand over the keys of the fort and the treasuries. It was now learnt that while Hastings and Barwell were waiting at the Revenue Board, Clavering and Francis were holding a rival meeting in the General Council Chamber, and that Clavering, having taken the oaths as Governor-General, was presiding in that capacity.

Hastings acted with his usual promptness and discretion. He sent orders to Colonel Morgan, the officer commanding the garrison of Fort William, that he should obey him and none other, and he requested the Judges of the Supreme Court to pronounce whether he or General Clavering was Governor-General. This reference to the highest judicial authority was an adroit move. Clavering and Francis could not well refuse to accept the Judges' verdict, yet they could have little hope that it would be favourable to themselves, as Clavering's precipitate assumption of the office of Governor-General before Hastings had actually resigned was manifestly improper. The Judges met that evening, and at four o'clock the next morning delivered their unanimous opinion that Hastings was still Governor-General, since he was not dead, he had not been removed from office and—as was indeed a fact—he had not yet resigned.

Having obtained this decision in his favour, Hastings endeavoured to retaliate on his opponents. He and Barwell passed a resolution in Council that Clavering, by taking the oath as Governor-General, had vacated his seat as Senior Councillor. It was now Clavering's turn to appeal to the Judges. With excellent sense and moderation they unanimously advised that the Council had no authority to pronounce Clavering's seat vacant, that the parties should refer their several claims to England and that meanwhile they should all be placed in the position in which they stood before the arrival of the recent despatches. The advice was accepted and embodied in a resolution which was passed with a quite unusual unanimity.

Thus ended what Hastings described as "a convulsion of four days, which might have shaken the very foundation of the national power and interests in India." Clavering's extravagant behaviour had defeated its own object; for Hastings considered that the unmannerly attempt to wrest the Government from him by force absolved him from all obligation to resign. He would not be ignominiously hustled from office by an intemperate and choleric soldier. If he resigned at all, his resignation must not only be, but also appear to be, entirely voluntary. He informed Lord North of his intention to stand his ground; and by the time the letter reached him Lord North was in such difficulties elsewhere as to be content to let him do so.

Hastings' almost inexhaustible patience now reaped its reward. In the summer of 1777 there reached Calcutta the long-awaited news of the divorce which would enable him to marry Baroness Imhoff. Francis, who says that he had always been on good terms with the lady, did not "despair of being asked to the wedding." Whether he actually received an invitation is not known. The wedding took place on August 8th, and was followed only three weeks later by a funeral, which likewise can hardly have been unwelcome to Hastings. On August 30th, Francis noted in his journal: "Sir John Clavering, after a delirium of many hours, expired at half-past two p.m., and was buried at eight in the most private manner."

Chapter Twelve

Hastings and Francis

HASTINGS made no false pretence of regret at the death of Clavering. It came in fact as an inexpressible relief to him. He had dreaded the thought of his rival succeeding to the position of Governor-General, for he knew that "he would have made no other use of power but to persecute every man who had ever shown anything like attachment to me, and to undo all that remained of my doings in this Country." He regarded his 'political contests' as now at an end. His own five-year term of office, unless extended, had only two more years to run. It seemed probable that on its expiry a fresh set of men would be sent out to take over the Government, and that meanwhile there would scarcely be time to reconstitute the old unbreakable Majority, even if the Ministry wished to do this. In the period that was left to him he was quite prepared to brush aside Francis' opposition and to make effective use of his authority.

A year earlier, on the death of Monson, when it seemed likely that his newly recovered ascendancy would be short-lived, he had not been disposed to assert himself so vigorously. He had told Lord North that he intended "to avoid alterations which in the course of a few months may possibly be subject to new changes, and introduce weakness and distraction into the State." So long as Clavering lived and the early reconstitution of a hostile Majority seemed probable, he adhered to this general rule. But he made, and declared to Lord North his intention of making, one important and necessary exception to it. This was the institution of the 'Amini Office,' the function of which was to collect materials for framing a new settlement of the revenues to replace the five-year settlement of 1772.

While he was still in a minority, Hastings had determined not to propose or concern himself with any plan for a new settlement, as it would be useless for him to do so. But with Monson out of the way he was in a position to give effect to his own ideas, and he felt that in so important a matter as the new settlement "it would be criminally mean to give up my opinion to the crude and confused ideas of General Clavering." The first essential, in his view, was to obtain accurate information as to "the real value of the lands . . . so that the burden of the public revenue should rest with an equal weight upon the whole body of the people." The collection of this information was the primary purpose of the Amini Office. Actual measurement and

188

survey of the lands to be assessed—which has since become the basis of British revenue administration in India—was considered "too tedious, expensive and uncertain." Instead of this the Amini Office undertook a careful and systematic scrutiny of past accounts in the belief that the actual collections made from the different estates over a period of years would afford a good indication of their relative value.

Hastings' second main purpose in instituting the Amini Office was to provide the Ryot or actual cultivator with effective protection against arbitrary exactions by the zemindars. "It is the Zemindar's interest," he wrote, "to exact the greatest rent he can from the Ryots; and it is as much against his interest to fix the deeds by which the Ryots hold their lands and pay their rents. . . . The foundation of such a work must be laid by Government itself; all that I would propose is to collect materials for it."

The Amini Office represented the first attempt made by the British in India to put the assessment and collection of the land revenue on a solid, scientific basis. It is on this account of some interest in itself, and it affords a conspicuous example of Hastings' wisdom, insight and energy as an administrator; for the Amini Office owed its institution and the successful execution of its work entirely to his inspiration.

Francis and Clavering, with typical but unavailing perversity, opposed its creation, and

endeavoured to thwart its operations. Clavering
even went so far as to threaten to call to account
any member of the various Provincial Councils
who submitted to its authority. This gave
Hastings an excellent excuse for removing
Clavering's creatures from these Councils and
putting in men of his own, "For I will not
leave," he wrote, "such wretches as Goring,
Rosewell and James Grant (names that I blush
to write) in the power to render my designs
abortive. . . . God be praised, there are few
such in the service."

Francis supported his arguments against the
Amini Office by quotations from Adam Smith
and Montesquieu; and complained that it
would disperse "a multitude of indigent and
rapacious black officers through the Country."
Hastings refused to be drawn into academic discussion and went steadily ahead with his plans.
Three picked officers of his own choice, Messrs.
Anderson, Bogle and Croftes, were put in
charge of the work. They began their enquiries
at the end of 1776, completed them in the spring
of 1778, and submitted a report. This document
is the first comprehensive expert revenue report
written by British officers in India. Full profit
could not be derived from it, as the Directors
vetoed Hastings' plan for a long-term settlement and gave orders for reversion to the
pernicious system of annual leases; but it reveals
in a striking manner how, under Hastings'

leadership, the Company's servants were being insensibly transformed from mere trading adventurers into responsible administrators.

The Directors, when they came to know of the creation of the Amini Office, denounced it as a piece of jobbery, and wondered by what motives Hastings could have been actuated "save the meanest and the most corrupt." Such was the extraordinary attitude which in these early days of empire the home authorities adopted towards their representative on the spot. "You hurt yourselves," Hastings told them, "and your own affairs, by treating with indignities the man whom you leave in charge of your interests, and of the national credit in India." But he was by this time becoming accustomed and even indifferent to their censures; and with the death of Clavering, feeling his own position in Bengal to be more secure, he did not scruple, when it suited him, to disregard their orders. Soon after Monson's death he had replaced Bristow at Lucknow by his old nominee, Middleton, and had recalled from Benares the Majority's protégé, Francis Fowke —a son of the Fowke who had helped Nandakumar. In 1778 he proceeded to more sweeping changes of personnel, including the dismissal (for the second time) of Muhammad Reza Khan. When the Directors sent orders countermanding all these changes, he bluntly refused to obey them. They had fully earned this cavalier treatment.

Francis, grievously disappointed at Hastings' recovery of power, continued relentlessly in opposition. He was joined by the new Councillor, Wheler, who had been sent out to take the place of Monson and reached Calcutta at the end of 1777. A weak, pliant man, of little character of independence, he was one of those Directors of the Company who had been bribed by the Ministry to vote for Hastings' recall, the bribe in his case being the promise of a seat in the Bengal Council. On arrival in Bengal, he professed neutrality, but, in fact, succumbed immediately to Francis' influence. Hastings writes of him with well-merited contempt. "He is now, and must be, a mere cypher and the echo of Francis, a vox et practerea nihil, a mere vote." But with Barwell's steady support and his own casting vote he was "not the least afraid of any consequences from this confederacy." "I shall propose," he writes, "the same measures as I should with a united council, and some yet stronger, nor will it be in their power to deprive them of their effect, for there is a wide difference between the opposition of General Clavering, supported by the King, destined to the chair, and invested with a badge of honour, and men who have no known pretensions but in being the partizans of a cause which was his while he lived to animate it."

Hastings had many battles still to fight in the Bengal Council, but he was never again to be humiliated or rendered powerless as he had been during the reign of the Majority. We can see now that Clavering died just in the nick of time. Within a year England was at war with France, and soon after stood alone against a combination of France, Spain and Holland. Amid all these dangers her newly won empire in India survived virtually unscathed; but this would not have been possible if Clavering's timely death had not enabled Hastings to act once more with boldness and authority.

The main interest of Hastings' story shifts now from the internal politics and administration of Bengal to the field of diplomacy and war. Hitherto he has been a peace-time administrator, endeavouring to educe a rude order out of a frightful chaos; he now becomes a bold, resourceful war minister, planning expeditions, sending out armies and contriving all the while to find the means to supply them and to keep them in the field.

During the first three years of this new phase Francis remained in Bengal and kept alive the old discords. In every field of business he automatically opposed whatever Hastings suggested. All attempts to reach some kind of understanding broke down. Francis was irreconcilable. In secret and in public he never ceased to thwart and hamper the Governor-General, "to encourage disobedience to my authority . . . to excite and foment popular odium against me; . . . to keep alive the expectation of impending changes; to teach foreign states to counteract me, and deter them from forming connections with me."

What was the motive of this persistent opposition? Underlying the rivalry of the two men was there some vital conflict of principle? Or was it little more than a private feud—a clash of personalities rather than of policies? Before passing to the next phase of Hastings' career, it will be well to pause and try to give some answer to these questions.

Francis says that he arrived in Bengal with a poor opinion of Barwell but with a strong predisposition in favour of Hastings. His conduct hardly bears this out. From the very outset he was critical and censorious. It seems more probable that he started with a prejudice against Hastings—communicated to him, perhaps, partly by Clive—and that this was transformed into positive dislike when, on meeting him, he saw him to be a really formidable rival, superior to him in ability and vastly superior in knowledge and experience. Francis himself easily outclassed Clavering, Monson and Barwell, and believed that he could dominate them. But Hastings was more than his equal and, so long as he remained Governor-General, an obstacle to his ambitions. In addition to this he was a servant of the Company, and merely on this account objectionable to Francis. There were thus strong initial grounds for antagonism. The acute differences on policy were more the effects of this antagonism than its cause. Some of them, especially in regard to foreign policy, were genuine and perhaps irreconcilable. But many were far less deep than they appeared and could have been adjusted if the stubborn personal hostility had not prevented mutual understanding. There were no profound and memorable issues dividing them to redeem and dignify their quarrel. To a large extent their general political principles coincided. A frank interchange of views should have shown them how much they had in common. But time and closer acquaintance, instead of softening, hardened their differences. Francis' doctrinaire type of mind and uncharitable disposition were ill-fitted for compromise. He remained obstinately the slave of general principles, whereas Hastings knew by instinct and experience that these must be modified in practice.

The fundamental premiss from which all Francis' views flowed was that government of Bengal by the Company's servants was vicious in principle because they were traders and because they were foreigners. As traders their sole motive was profit, not the interest of the governed; and as foreigners they were wholly unqualified for the task of government. "Under a European Government," he wrote, "Bengal *cannot flourish*." His solution was to confine the Company strictly to trade, to declare the King of England the Sovereign of Bengal, to entrust the actual task of government to a native Nawab and native officials, and to limit the political connection between Britain and Bengal to the provision of armed forces and the receipt of tribute. From this there followed naturally his desire to revive Clive's Dual System and the power of the Nawab, his dislike of Hastings' new Courts of Justice—for the complete eradication of all foreign influence was, in his view, the first necessity—and his strong predilection for a permanent settlement of the Revenue; for if the demand was fixed, elaborate enquiries, close supervision of the collections and attempts to protect the ryots from oppressive exactions would all become unnecessary; the whole matter could be safely left to the Nawab, who would hand over a fixed sum to the British Crown without any interference by British officials.

Such were Francis' views. He imagined that they were diametrically opposed to those of Hastings. He never realised how warmly Hastings sympathised with his premises; still less did he appreciate the painful experiences which had compelled Hastings to draw somewhat different practical conclusions. For Hastings was aware, no less than Francis, how unfitted a trading Company was to rule a great

empire. He deplored as "a radical and incurable defect of British dominion" the conflict
of interest between the Company and the people
of Bengal. Like Francis he was deeply distrust-
ful of government by foreigners, acutely conscious of the corruption of the Company's
servants and anxious to reduce their share in
the administration to the minimum. Like
Francis, too, he was at pains—no one more so—
to preserve indigenous customs and institutions
and to avoid obtruding foreign notions and
methods. But the brute fact remained that the
English were the real sovereigns of Bengal, and
Hastings had learnt by experience that
sovereignty must bring responsibility. Unless
the English were prepared to renounce that
sovereignty altogether—and with it the tribute
which Francis wished to take—either the Company or the Crown must stand forth openly as
the real and responsible Ruler. To attempt to
retain the real power and yet to disguise it and
shuffle off responsibility on to a Nawab and
native Government had been proved by
experience to be disastrous. A weak Nawab, Mir
Jafar, and a strong Nawab, Mir Kasim, had both
been tried, and both had been failures. The one
was unable to control the province and to collect
the tribute; the other controlled it so well as
to threaten, or seem to threaten, English power;
and under both the province had been merci-
lessly exploited by private individuals.

197

Hastings had seen it all and suffered from it during his early service in Bengal. He would never willingly allow that experiment to be tried again. He knew that the system which Francis wished to reintroduce would serve "like all ostensible and covert systems . . . as a screen to private rapine and embezzlement."

But though experience had taught him that Francis' solutions must be rejected, the objection in principle to alien rule which he shared with Francis made him wish, first, that the Government of Bengal should be as much Indian and as little British as possible, and secondly, that British *sovereignty* should be confined to Bengal and not extended to fresh territories. The very fact that Francis failed to appreciate how closely Hastings' views on these matters coincided with his own is a measure of their estrangement. Hastings' objections to the 'supervisors,' his unwillingness to use the Company's servants for administrative purposes, his desire to place the management of the revenues entirely in native hands, save for a controlling Board at Calcutta, have already been described. They were quite lost upon Francis. He also quite misunderstood Hastings' intentions in revenue matters. He fancied that Hastings' objections to his own pet scheme for a permanent settlement were due to a desire to squeeze the maximum revenue from the country and to have an excuse for constant interference. He failed to grasp that a responsible Government, as distinct from a mere recipient of tribute, was bound to try to protect the ryots from the oppressive exactions of the zemindars and ought not to deny itself for ever all share in future accretions of wealth. But the extraordinary degree to which he misconceived Hastings' ideas and intentions is nowhere more strikingly revealed than in his comments on Hastings' Courts of Justice. He complained that Hastings had "rashly forced the accumulated wisdom and experience of ages to yield to the crude ideas of a few foreigners." This, as we have seen, is exactly what Hastings had not done—indeed, had been at pains to avoid.

His misunderstanding of Hastings in matters of foreign policy, though hardly less great, was perhaps more excusable. Hastings sought no accession of territory, and was opposed to the extension of the Company's sovereignty beyond Bengal—a fact which Francis seems never to have grasped. But he was not opposed to the extension of its influence; indeed, he admitted to friends that it was his aim "to extend the influence of the British nation to every part of India not too remote from their possessions." He proposed to achieve this, not by conquest of fresh territories, but by a system of alliances based on "conditions of mutual and equal dependence" such as had been his alliance with Shuja-ud-daula, the Nawab of Oudh. To Francis this penchant for foreign entanglements seemed clear evidence that Hastings was an incurable expansionist, determined to enlarge the area of the Company's misgovernment; and when war with France began to threaten and the Company's possessions were endangered, his strategy of active defence provided further cause for misunderstanding as well as genuine disagreement. Hastings believed that the best defence was attack. Francis disagreed, and preferred a purely passive policy. This was an irreconcilable difference of opinion on basic strategy, and revealed itself again and again in regard to all the military and diplomatic measures of the next few years of war. It was accentuated, no doubt, by the previous enmity and by Francis' settled habit of opposition; but it was not entirely factious; and, as will be shown in the next chapter, the views put forward by Francis were not on all occasions perverse and foolish.

Chapter Thirteen

Hastings Preserves British Dominion in India

THE outbreak of war between Great Britain and her colonies in America afforded the French a grand opportunity to recover the losses which they had suffered in the Seven Years' War. In India, as Hastings perceived, their best hopes lay in allying themselves "with one of the powers of the country." It was with alarm, therefore, that he learnt in the summer of 1777 that a French agent, the Chevalier de St. Lubin, had arrived at Poona, and had been most favourably received by the ruling party amongst the Marathas. The French, he believed, had "seized on the only means by which they can ever become formidable to us in India," and he immediately began to consider plans to "avert the dreadful consequences" of their designs.

When we last had occasion to mention the Marathas, their forces were in Northern India, threatening Rohilkhand and Oudh, but were recalled from there in 1773 by internal dissensions at Poona.[1] For an understanding of the

[1] Chapter Eight, page 125.

situation when St. Lubin reached Poona in 1777 a brief account of events in the intervening period is necessary.

The dissensions among the Marathas had been occasioned by the assassination in 1773 of the Peshwa, Narayan Rao. He was succeeded by his uncle, Raghunath Rao (better known as Raghoba), who may have been secretly responsible for his death. Raghoba was unpopular, and when in the following year Narayan Rao's widow gave birth to a posthumous son, this infant was proclaimed Peshwa, and Raghoba, who was away from the capital at the time, soon found himself without support. He turned for assistance to the Company's representatives at Bombay.

Though Bombay had once been the foremost Presidency, it had by this time fallen much behind Calcutta and Madras; for in face of the powerful Maratha confederacy there had been little scope for political or territorial aggrandisement. The dissensions at Poona seemed, however, to afford just such an opportunity for profitable intrigue as had already been exploited with such success in Bengal and the Carnatic. The Bombay Council coveted the port of Bassein, the island of Salsette and certain other islets adjacent to Bombay. Raghoba was willing to cede these to them in return for armed support for his pretensions. Without waiting to consult the Governor-General of Bengal, to whom in such matters they had recently been made subordinate, the Bombay authorities in March 1775 concluded a treaty with Raghoba, and thus imprudently involved the Company in war with the whole Maratha Confederacy.

Hastings, on learning of these proceedings, condemned them as "unseasonable, impolitic, unjust and unauthorised." The Majority, for once, agreed with him. Peremptory orders were sent to the President and Council of Bombay to cancel the treaty and to withdraw their troops; and the Bengal Government deputed an agent of their own, Colonel Upton, to negotiate peace with the ruling party at Poona. Hastings, with his usual practical sense, would have allowed the Bombay authorities rather more discretion. He felt that as they had already embarked on war, it would be unwise to reverse policy abruptly and to give up any advantage that might have been obtained. But he was over-ruled, and the Bombay authorities, who had already occupied Salsette and won the battle of Aras (which nearly ended in disaster), were obliged, much against their will, to desist from further operations.

After prolonged and unsatisfactory negotiations Colonel Upton concluded with the Marathas the Treaty of Purandhar. It was agreed that the English should retain Salsette and be paid an indemnity for the expenses which they had incurred, but that they should dismiss Raghoba, annul all their engagements with him and never assist him again. The treaty was signed on behalf of the Marathas by two Ministers, Sukaram Bapu and Balaji Janardhan (better known as Nana Farnavis), who at this time held charge of the Government in the name of the infant Peshwa.

All those most immediately concerned were dissatisfied with this treaty, and its terms were never fully carried out. The members of the Bombay Council resented the interference of the Bengal Government and, having received some encouragement from the Directors in their support of Raghoba, continued to countenance him and to grant him asylum. The Maratha leaders on their part made no effort to pay the indemnity, and never ceased to load the Company with reproaches. Hastings felt sure that the peace could not last long.

Such was the uneasy state of the relations between the Company and the Maratha Confederacy at the time of St. Lubin's arrival at Poona. Hastings learnt with disquiet, but little surprise, that he had been received with great pomp and attention, and that Nana Farnavis, one of the signatories of the Treaty of Purandhar, seemed particularly well-disposed towards him. In view of the strong probability of war with France, Hastings decided that the eradication of this French influence, established in the heart of the Maratha state, must be a primary object of policy; and on January 26th 1778 he laid before his Council a long and elaborate minute on the subject.

There can be no doubt that Hastings' basic assumptions in regard to the French menace were absolutely correct. He maintained, as against Francis, that successful invasion of Bengal by sea was impossible, and gave convincing reasons for this opinion. On the other hand, if the French formed an alliance with the Maratha Confederacy, they might with quite a small expenditure of effort "soon acquire the command of all its powers and resources" and threaten Bengal by land. "I lay it down as a point incontrovertible," he wrote, "that if a detachment of much less than 1,000 Europeans, with arms for disciplining a body of native troops in the European manner, shall have once obtained a footing in the Mahratta country, as the allies of that Government, all the native powers of Indostan united will lie at their mercy, and even the Provinces of Bengal be exposed to their depredations."

Hastings had scarcely laid his minute before the Council when a letter containing important proposals was received from Bombay. By the Treaty of Purandhar the Company was precluded from protecting or assisting Raghoba; but the Bombay Council now reported that an influential party in Poona, including Sukaram, the leading Maratha minister and one of the two signatories of the treaty, had requested help in his restoration. They considered that the request could be acceded to with great advantage—as this party was hostile to the pro-French Nana Farnavis—and without any violation of the treaty—as Sukaram, the chief minister of the infant Peshwa, could be regarded as the head of the Maratha state. They therefore sought approval for renewing their support of Raghoba's pretensions.

An interesting debate now took place in the Bengal Council in which Francis showed himself at his best. Though he wrongly belittled the French menace, he rightly pointed out that there were insufficient means of judging the real motives and intentions of Sukaram, and that in any case the party at Poona in favour of Raghoba must be conscious of its own weakness or it would not have sought the Company's aid. He was wholly opposed to the Company embroiling itself in the Marathas' intestine disputes. He wished to concentrate all resources on the defence of the Company's existing possessions rather than to attempt to meet the danger half-way by hazardous foreign entanglements and offensive tactics.

Hastings, deeply impressed by the reality of the French menace, felt that the opportunity of driving out Nana Farnavis and replacing French by English influence at Poona should not be missed. He knew, moreover, that the

Bombay Council had long been wedded to Raghoba's cause and had been encouraged by the Directors to support him. He believed that they would not willingly abandon their designs for his restoration, and that it was better to fall in with them than to risk the two Presidencies working at cross purposes. With Barwell's support and his own casting vote he could make his views prevail. It was resolved therefore to approve the Bombay Council's project, to supply them with money to the amount of ten lakhs of rupees and to assemble a body of troops which, if necessary, could be sent right across India to reinforce them.

The decision, as it turned out, was unfortunate, for it confirmed the Bombay Council in a course of action requiring a degree of military and diplomatic skill which they did not possess. But Hastings could hardly have foreseen the incredible folly and incompetence which they subsequently displayed.

The Bombay plan had hardly been approved when the Bombay Council's enthusiasm for it began to cool. Obscure intrigues at Poona suggested that no Maratha leader was really anxious to restore Raghoba, and though a political revolution led to the temporary eclipse of Nana Farnavis, the new party in power continued to countenance the French agent St. Lubin. The Bombay Council began to hint that their original plan would have to be abandoned. Meanwhile,

Hastings had mustered a force of six battalions under Colonel Leslie to march across India to Bombay, and at the end of May it crossed the Jumna and moved forward very slowly into Bundelkhand. Francis, who was strongly opposed to the expedition, lost no opportunity of urging that it should be absolutely counter-manded; and when news of General Burgoyne's surrender at Saratoga reached Calcutta he suggested that this disaster in America was portentous of Leslie's fate. In view of "the unfortunate event in America," it was not, he argued, "a season for hazarding offensive operations of any kind. . . . We should stand on our defence, and not weaken or divide the force on which the safety of Bengal may depend." Hastings' conclusion was exactly the opposite. This was no moment, he thought, for acting merely on the defensive or abruptly counter-manding an operation "in which we have now decidedly engaged with the eyes of all India turned upon it. On the contrary, if it be really true that the British arms and influence have suffered so severe a check in the Western world, it is the more incumbent on those who are charged with the interest of Great Britain in the East to exert themselves for the retrieval of the national loss."

More bad news, this time that France had declared war, was received in Calcutta early in July. The energy and promptness with which

Hastings now acted can be judged from the following sample of the measures immediately taken:

(i) The French settlement of Chandernagore was captured (July 10th) and orders were sent to Madras to seize Pondicherry and Mahé.

(ii) The Madras Council was empowered to form an alliance with Haidar Ali, the ruler of Mysore.

(iii) Orders were given to raise nine new battalions of sepoys.

(iv) Two vessels of forty guns each were manned and armed to reinforce the squadron of the Royal Navy under Sir Edward Vernon.

(v) Three months' provision of military and victualling stores were laid up in Fort William.

(vi) Chait Singh, Rajah of Benares, a tributary of the Company, was called upon to contribute towards the war the cost of maintaining three battalions of sepoys, computed to amount to five lakhs annually.

(vii) Alexander Elliott (one of Hastings' picked officers) was sent to Nagpur to offer an alliance to the Rajah of Berar.

Francis at this juncture could only cry "Woe." He opposed several of these measures, yet affected to regard them all as "insufficient, our resources already exhausted, a French invasion certain and impending, and the country incapable of resistance." Hastings was calm and even confident. Bengal itself, he knew, was secure, and its prosperity had increased so much in the past six years that it could liberally assist the other two Presidencies. In 1772 he had succeeded to a Government loaded with debt. By 1776 all this had been paid off and there was a surplus of 1½ crores for providing the Company's 'investment.' At the end of 1777 he reported the Government to be "in a more prosperous state than it has known since its first existence."

For the time being, therefore, he was not worried about finance; there were adequate resources for waging war. Nor did he share Francis' fear of a sea-borne French invasion of Bengal: he knew this to be impossible. His chief anxiety was still the Marathas. The French influence at Poona had not been eradicated; the Bombay plan for restoring Raghoba was in suspense; Nana Farnavis, backed by the great Maratha Chiefs, Mahadaji Sindhia and Tukoji Holkar, was worming his way back into power, and Leslie, instead of boldly marching forward to reinforce Bombay, was loitering in the "detested land of Bundelkhand," bewailing his difficulties. Some further move was clearly necessary. The Maratha Rajah of Berar was known to be friendly—Hastings had for years been in close communication with his 'vakil' or agent in Calcutta—and his friendship, if firmly secured, would counterbalance the hostility of the other Maratha chiefs. Immediately, therefore, on learning of the French declaration of war, Hastings despatched Alexander Elliott, a trusted officer and personal friend, to Nagpur to negotiate an alliance. The Bombay authorities, still trafficking with the party at Poona opposed to Nana Farnavis, were informed of this new negotiation and instructed to concert their measures with Elliott. Hastings himself entertained great hopes of the mission.

Everything, however, now went wrong. Elliott died on the road to Nagpur—"an irreparable loss" to Hastings both on public and private grounds. The unenterprising Leslie continued to dawdle, and by October was still hardly clear of Bundelkhand, having taken five months to cover a hundred and twenty miles. Hastings was obliged to supersede him and selected Goddard, a soldier of great initiative, to take his place. Goddard pushed on rapidly "without experiencing or expecting any of the many impediments of which his predecessor had complained." But many months had been wasted to no purpose and much needless expense incurred. To crown all, the Bombay authorities, in response to fresh solicitations from Poona, embarked suddenly on a wild expedition of their own and brought about a catastrophe of the first magnitude. They knew that Goddard was on his way across India to reinforce them; they knew also that Hastings was starting separate negotiations with the Rajah of Berar; they had received ample

211

evidence of the strength of Nana Farnavis' influence at Poona and the lack of real enthusiasm for Raghoba. Yet in November 1778, without waiting for Goddard, they set their own small army in motion in support of Raghoba's pretensions.

The military commander, Colonel Egerton, was a stranger to India and in very poor health. Accompanied in Dutch fashion by two civilian advisers and encumbered by a prodigious baggage train of 19,000 bullocks, he advanced towards Poona with a force of 4,000 men at a snail's pace of barely two miles a day. On January 11th, when his force was at last only sixteen miles from Poona, there was a sudden panic. A Maratha army, said to be 50,000 strong, lay ahead of them barring their advance. Egerton was by now too ill to command and the real direction of affairs passed to the civilian advisers. They strongly urged immediate retreat and, though some of the military officers wished to press on, the advice to retreat was taken. Stores and guns were abandoned and an attempt made to slip away stealthily by night. But the Marathas detected the move, pursued and surrounded the small force and induced its leaders to sign a disgraceful surrender, known as the Convention of Wargaon. The Company was required to restore Salsette and other places obtained by the Treaty of Purandhar, to renounce the cause of Raghoba, to withdraw

Goddard's force to Bengal, to give hostages and to admit war guilt.

Hastings said that the Convention almost made him sink with shame when he read it. It was immediately repudiated both by him and by the Bombay Council. But mere repudiation of the Convention could not efface the disaster. This could only be done by war—and war against the whole Maratha Confederacy; for all the chiefs were now united behind the triumphant Nana Farnavis. Even the Rajah of Berar, hitherto friendly towards the Company, turned cold and outwardly hostile. Elsewhere in India, too, the country powers saw the chance of gratifying smouldering resentments, and soon, thanks partly to the imbecility of the Madras Government, Hastings was threatened with a combination of all the strongest native rulers.

Francis received the news of Wargaon with characteristic defeatism. Secretly he was pleased at the disaster. He had consistently opposed meddling in Maratha affairs and predicted that no good would come of it. Events had proved him right. The only sensible course now, in his view, was to make peace on such terms as could be obtained—a peace of abject submission.

Hastings also wanted peace, but not 'peace at any price' such as would proclaim the Company's weakness and give courage to all its enemies throughout India. Wargaon had shattered his plans, but had not weakened his firmness of spirit. And he had one immediate cause of satisfaction. Goddard, hearing reports of the Bombay army's danger, pressed forward rapidly to the coast and reached Surat on February 26th, having covered the last three hundred miles in twenty days. He was too late to prevent Wargaon; but he was in time to restore Bombay's broken morale and to prevent further disasters.

The safe arrival of this seasonable reinforcement was for Hastings himself a tremendous personal triumph. He had staked his reputation on this seemingly hazardous venture; he had persisted in it, despite Francis' determined opposition and gloomy vaticinations; if it had failed, he would have been recalled to England, a ruined man. But it had not failed. Goddard's force had completed its great march and reached the western coast just in time to succour Bombay. Its timely arrival deeply impressed all India with the prescience, boldness and resource of the Governor-General. "Its way," Hastings wrote, "was long, through regions unknown in England, and untraced in our maps; and I alone knew the grounds on which the facility of its success depended." His confidence had not in fact been mere fool-hardiness; for, unlike Francis, he knew for certain that it would be assisted on its way through Central India by the friendly Rajah of Berar.

Hastings now had in Western India a soldier of his own choosing whom he could trust. Goddard, on reaching Bombay, was given command of the local forces and a seat on the Bombay Council; but he remained directly responsible to the Governor-General and Council in Calcutta. In this way Hastings managed to obtain over the military and diplomatic operations of Bombay the control for which the Regulating Act had failed to make adequate provision.

Goddard was instructed by Hastings to enter into fresh negotiations with the Marathas on the basis of the Treaty of Purandhar, but with the additional stipulation that no French force or French establishment should be permitted within the Maratha dominions. After their recent success the Marathas would not even consider peace on such terms. They demanded the restoration of Salsette and the surrender of Raghoba as essential preliminaries. Francis would have acceded to their demands. Hastings would not hear of such weakness. Clive had once thought him a defeatist, too ready to lose hope in face of misfortune; but he had long since profited by Clive's advice and Clive's own example. There was now no man more steadfast in adversity than he, and no one who knew better than he the value of such steadfastness in India. "Acts that proclaim confidence and a determined spirit in the hour of adversity," he wrote, "are the surest means of retrieving it. Self-distrust will never fail to create a distrust in others, and make them become your enemies; for in no part of the world is the principle of supporting a rising interest and depressing a falling one more prevalent than in India."

Hastings' strategy in the war with the Marathas which now ensued was simple. While Goddard, operating on the western coast, engaged the main attention of the Maratha chiefs, Hastings drew off the most powerful of them, Mahadaji Sindhia, by organising fresh expeditions to invade his territories from across the Jumna. In order to give effect to this strategy he was compelled to have recourse to some questionable expedients, which will be described later. His judgment and tenacity were, however, amply vindicated by the results.

Goddard, finding negotiation fruitless, took the offensive early in 1780, captured Ahmadabad, over-ran Gujarat and won over the Maratha chief, Fateh Singh, Gaekwar of Baroda. Later in the year, aided by Sindhia's withdrawal to defend his own territories, he took Bassein. Pressed by Hastings to force a decision, he next advanced on Poona itself. But this nearly precipitated a second Wargaon, and he was obliged to retreat with considerable losses of men and baggage.

This partial reverse was offset by successes elsewhere. The Rana of Gohad, a refractory feudatory of Sindhia, had appealed to Hastings for protection. Hastings sent to his assistance a small force under Captain Popham, which had originally been intended as a reinforcement for Goddard. Popham was an enterprising officer. He drove the Marathas out of the Rana's country "with great slaughter and fairly cleared it." Then, by a daring night escalade, he seized Sindhia's famous fortress, Gwalior, which had been deemed to be impregnable. This brilliant feat astonished India. "Its effect," wrote Hastings with intense delight, "is not to be described. Other congratulations which I have received on the many important successes of our arms were but coldly offered, but scarcely a man mentions this without enthusiasm. . . . I look upon it as one of the best concerted and most gallant enterprises that has ever been performed in India."

Sindhia came hurrying back from Western India to defend his own territories which a second and larger force under Colonel Camac had by now penetrated. Sindhia outmanœuvred this force and believed that he would compel it to surrender. But Camac extricated himself from a precarious position by a sudden night attack on Sindhia's camp, in which thirteen guns were captured. This unexpected defeat in the heart of his own country, coming on top of the loss of Gwalior, disposed Sindhia to peace. He had been greatly impressed by the courage and resource of the English and had conceived a considerable admiration for Hastings, whom he knew to be the heart and soul of the whole English effort. The war was bringing no advantage to him personally, and was impeding him in his design to make himself the effective leader of the whole Maratha Confederacy. So, in October 1781, he agreed to a cessation of hostilities and undertook to negotiate a peace between the Company and the Maratha Government at Poona. The negotiations were protracted, but Sindhia played his part as mediator honourably, and in the following year peace was concluded by the Treaty of Salbai.

There was nothing spectacular about its terms. Broadly speaking the *status quo ante bellum* was restored. The Company retained Salsette, but gave up Bassein and other conquests made since the Treaty of Purandhar; Raghoba received a pension; the Company agreed to help him no more, and the Marathas undertook to induce Haidar Ali of Mysore, who was now at war with the Company, to make peace, and to enter the war against him if he refused. But though unspectacular, the Treaty of Salbai was rightly regarded by Hastings as a triumphant vindication of his policy. Others— not only Francis, but even the intrepid Goddard—appalled by the overwhelming dangers of the year 1780, when all the native powers of India seemed leagued against the Company, when Haidar Ali swept through the Carnatic right up to the walls of Madras and when several thousand French troops were landed to support him—others, appalled by these dangers, had cried out for peace with the Marathas on any terms. But Hastings had refused to show weakness. "Feeble measures and advances for peace," he had written, "will but add to the strength and presumption of our adversaries, discourage our friends and perhaps induce them to become parties against us. . . . If you would employ effectual means for obtaining peace, you must seek them in the terrors of a continued war. . . . If you would expect to obtain it by concession and entreaty . . . you will be disappointed." He had persevered, and his courage and resolution had been rewarded. He had achieved his primary object, which was to prevent the French establishing themselves in the Maratha dominions; he had retrieved the disaster of Wargaon, and he had concluded with the Marathas a peace such as he desired—an honourable peace on equal terms. It brought no great material gains to the Company in territory or revenue; but it enormously enhanced British prestige. Single-handed they had fought off the Marathas and brought them to terms, even when engaged simultaneously in war with Haidar Ali and the French. They had thus shown themselves to be the strongest and most resolute power in India. The Treaty of Salbai gave peace with the Marathas for twenty years and the immediate assurance that the remaining dangers would be safely surmounted.

How was it that Hastings, when already at grips with the Marathas, became involved also in a war with Haidar Ali of Mysore? He owed this, as well as other dangers which he skilfully averted, to the wanton folly of the Madras Government. The cause and course of this wholly unprofitable war in the Carnatic must now be briefly described.

The moral atmosphere in Madras at this time was, if possible, even worse than that in Calcutta in the years immediately following Plassey. The Company's servants were engrossed in amassing private fortunes, regardless of the interests of their employers or of the wretched inhabitants of the Carnatic. Muhammad Ali, the nominal ruler, was a mere puppet Nawab, dependent entirely on English support. He was constantly in debt to the Company on account of the troops which they lent him, and to pay this debt he borrowed from the Company's own servants, who eagerly advanced him money at exorbitant rates of interest, ranging from thirty-six to forty-eight per cent. The usurious claims of these creditors he met by making them assignments of his land revenues; hence the seizure of fresh territory for the Nawab so as to enhance his revenues and swell the fortunes of his creditors became the dominant political interest at Madras. The whole scandalous system was devised and organised by the notorious Paul Benfield, originally an engineer in the Company's service, and nearly all the Company's senior servants in Madras had a stake in it. One Governor, Lord Pigot, who with more courage than tact opposed the interests of the creditors, was imprisoned by order of a hostile majority in his Council and died in confinement. His successor, Sir Thomas Rumbold, showed more wisdom. Like everyone else in Madras he applied himself to the advancement of his own private fortune.

Rumbold spent two years in Madras, during which time he embroiled the Company both with Haidar Ali and with the Nizam of Hyderabad. The quarrel with the Nizam was needlessly provoked. It related to five coastal districts south of Orissa known as the Northern Sarkars. These districts had originally been ceded to the French in Bussy's time. With the eclipse of French influence at the end of the Seven Years' War they had passed to the Company to be held by it as the tributary of the Nizam; but in accordance with an agreement made with him in 1768, one of them, Guntur, remained in the possession of his brother, Basalat Jang, and was only to pass to the Company on Basalat Jang's death. In 1779, without any reference to the Nizam, the Madras Government persuaded Basalat Jang to hand over to them this district, which they immediately garrisoned with an English force. The Nizam was naturally affronted at this arrangement being made behind his back and, to make matters worse, Rumbold chose this moment to ask him to remit the tribute due from the Company for the remaining Sarkars. Deeply suspicious of the English, he took the lead in fomenting hostility against them.

Haidar Ali, the ruler of Mysore, had several old grudges against the Company. Rumbold's Government gave him fresh grounds of complaint. On the outbreak of war with France they fitted out an expedition to seize the French port of Mahé which lay within his territory. Learning of their intentions, he warned them not to attack it. They disregarded this warning and captured the place. Then, without even seeking his permission, they marched a body of troops through his territories in order to take possession of Guntur, the district ceded by Basalat Jang. Haidar Ali resolved to crush the English once and for all. They were already at war with the Marathas, and the Nizam was ill-disposed. Here was an opportunity for a grand combination against them. Blind to the growing dangers, Rumbold went home in March 1780. In July Haidar Ali, having arranged for the co-operation of the Nizam and of the Maratha Rajah of Berar, burst upon the Carnatic.

The Madras Government were quite unprepared to meet this invasion. Their forces were scattered and they had no defensive plans. A detachment of nearly 3,000 men under Colonel Baillie was intercepted, while trying to join the main army under Sir Hector Munro, and completely annihilated. Shaken by this disaster, Munro, the former victor of Buxar, threw his stores and guns into a lake and retreated in panic to Madras. The sepoys were demoralised, the treasury empty; Haidar Ali raged through the Carnatic with fire and sword; and information was received that French troops were *en route* to India to join him. It seemed that nothing could save Madras itself. The Madras Government turned for help to Hastings.

The news of the disasters reached him in Calcutta on September 23rd. "The crisis demanded," he said, "the most instant, powerful and even hazardous exertion of this Government." He took one day to frame his plans. On September 25th he laid them before his Council.

Barwell had by this time gone home, and the Council consisted of Hastings, Francis, Wheler and Sir Eyre Coote, who had arrived in March 1779 to take the place of Clavering. Coote, though a man of notoriously difficult temper, was a fine professional soldier with great experience of India. He had fought at Plassey, he was renowned in Southern India for his victory over Lally at Wandiwash in 1760, and he was immensely popular with the sepoys. He had no political connections like Clavering, and endeavoured to keep clear of the faction in the Bengal Council. Generally he supported Hastings, who, knowing of old his explosive nature, wisely humoured him in the matter of allowances and army patronage. During the present crisis he stood by Hastings firmly.

The first essential was to send all possible military assistance to Madras. Hastings proposed that a force of European infantry and artillery, the flower of the Bengal army, together with a supply of fifteen lakhs of rupees, should be despatched at once by sea, and that a further force of 5,000 sepoys should be assembled at Midnapur under Colonel Pearse to march south later through Orissa and the Northern Sarkars as a reinforcement. He also proposed that Sir Eyre Coote should be requested to proceed himself to Madras to take command in the Carnatic. Only a soldier of his high repute, he said, could restore the confidence of the sepoys and retrieve the past disgraces.

Francis and Wheler agreed to Coote proceeding to Madras but, on the ground that Bengal would be left defenceless, objected to the other proposals. They were carried with Coote's support and Hastings' own casting vote. The troops left Calcutta on October 13th and Madras was saved.

In addition to these military measures diplomatic action was required. The disgruntled Nizam was contemplating hostilities, and the

Rajah of Berar, pressed by others to invade Bengal, had massed 15,000 cavalry at Cuttack. Hastings soothed the Nizam into neutrality, and by a timely cash payment converted the Rajah of Berar into an ally.

The Nizam had been aggrieved by the occupation of Guntur. Hastings had promised him redress and had ordered the Madras Government to withdraw their troops from the district; but they refused to obey his orders, and suspended from service their representative at the Nizam's Court, with whom Hastings had been in communication, on the astonishing ground that he had betrayed the secrets of his trust to the Governor-General! Hastings promptly reappointed him as his own representative, and instructed him to give the Nizam fresh assurances that Guntur would be restored to Basalat Jang. He also took stern action against the Madras Government. On October 10th, just before Coote sailed, he proposed that Whitehill, the acting Governor, should be suspended. The Council agreed, and Coote was instructed to suspend him on arrival at Madras. The Nizam, impressed like other Indian rulers by Hastings' vigour and evident good faith, abandoned his hostile intentions and gave no further trouble.

With the Rajah of Berar, Hastings had for many years been in friendly communication. He received from him a secret message that his real disposition towards the English was pacific,

225

and that it was merely "from a dread of a resentment of his associates," i.e. the Nizam, Haidar Ali and the Poona Government, that he had sent his cavalry to threaten Bengal. The conduct of these troops, who, as Hastings remarked, lay "for two months within marauding distances of our borders . . . as quiet as a herd of cattle," confirmed the sincerity of his professions. By skilful diplomacy, sweetened by a douceur of sixteen lakhs, Hastings soon converted him from a potential enemy to a firm friend and ally. He was induced to withdraw the cavalry which threatened Bengal, to assist the force under Colonel Pearse in its march southwards to reinforce Coote—just as he had previously assisted Goddard in his march across Central India—and to provide 2,000 cavalry for the war against Haidar Ali. A regular agreement with him was signed in April 1781, and was the first positive sign that the hostile combination of all the native powers of India had been broken. "The mere Fame of [the] Alliance," Hastings wrote, ". . . will have a great effect. We shall no longer be considered as sinking under the united weight of every state in Hindostan. The Scale of Power evidently turned in our Favour." The correctness of this judgment was soon proved; for the alliance was followed a few months later by the negotiations with Sindhia which brought the Maratha war to a close.

While these diplomatic moves were in progress, Coote in the Carnatic was slowly making head against Haidar Ali. On arrival at Madras he had tactfully executed the order for the suspension of Whitehill, and the next senior member of Council, who took his place, readily agreed to Coote assuming sole charge of the whole conduct of the war. Hastings hoped that in this way he would secure through Coote the same measure of control at Madras as he had obtained through Goddard at Bombay. Coote quickly restored the confidence of the Madras army and, in July 1781, defeated Haidar Ali at Porto Novo. Soon after this, Haidar Ali was reinforced by 3,000 French troops under the renowned Bussy. Fortunately, Bussy was but a shadow of his former self, and Coote, who had been joined by the sepoys from Bengal under Colonel Pearse, continued to hold his own, and in June 1782 won another victory at Arni.

The danger to Madras had been averted. Coote, by his courage, energy and good influence over the sepoys, had saved the situation. But though he marched strenuously up and down the country, relieving beleaguered garrisons and defeating Haidar Ali in the field, he was unable to drive him from the Carnatic; and he was soon completely at loggerheads with the Madras authorities, whom he bitterly blamed for failing to supply him with draught cattle and grain. He had never been an easy man for civilians to work with, and his natural

227

irritability was increased at this time by ill-health and anxiety. Hastings endeavoured to assist and to placate him by sending him money and by organising supplies of rice from Bengal. But he could not from Calcutta produce harmony at Madras; nor could he induce Coote to change his strategy and strike direct at Haidar Ali's dominions on the western coast instead of marching and counter-marching in the Carnatic.

By the autumn of 1782 Coote's health had become so bad that he had to take a sea voyage to Calcutta to recuperate. He was loud in his complaints against Lord Macartney, the new Governor of Madras, and, before returning to continue the war, wanted to be armed with powers to overrule and, if necessary, suspend him. Hastings would have consented to this, but the rest of the Council did not agree; and Coote sailed for Madras without the powers which he had demanded. He did not live to resume his command—or his quarrels with Lord Macartney. During the voyage his ship was chased by some French frigates. The agitation which this caused him brought on a fatal stroke and he died almost immediately after reaching Madras. Haidar Ali had died a few months earlier. His son, Tipu Sultan, succeeded him.

With Coote's death effective control of the war in the Carnatic passed to Macartney. Hastings continued to supply money from Bengal, but he could not influence strategy, and

Macartney, who was a man of some experience and ability and possessed a good deal of influence in England, did not hesitate to disregard or disobey his orders. The fighting went on for another year without either side gaining any decided advantage. The English were hampered by quarrels between the civil and military authorities and by the presence of a French naval squadron under the brilliant Suffren. The conclusion of peace between France and England robbed Suffren of the fruits of his skill and should have enabled the English to get the better of Tipu. But Macartney was tired of the war and, disregarding instructions which he received from Hastings, opened negotiations with Tipu and concluded a treaty of peace with him in March 1784. Both sides restored all conquests and released all prisoners. A severe struggle of nearly four years had ended in a draw.

Hastings disapproved of the treaty, but on account of its form rather than its substance. Its form was wrong because it contained no mention of the Nawab of the Carnatic, who certainly should have been a party to it, since nominally it was as his ally that the Company had been defending his territories against Haidar Ali. The treaty, as Hastings rightly objected, was "a public and avowed exclusion of the Nabob . . . from the sovereignty of the Carnatic, and an usurpation of it in the name of the Company." Furthermore, the treaty made no reference to Mahadaji Sindhia and the Marathas, who, in accordance with the Treaty of Salbai, had been pressing Tipu to come to terms and should have been made parties to the agreement finally reached. However, Hastings considered peace to be "an object too valuable to be rejected if it can be retained with honour," and the treaty was ratified.

"If the Carnatic is saved," Hastings had written in October 1780, just after despatching Coote to Madras, "I shall have the conscious satisfaction to reflect that it is saved by my exertions." He had indeed saved the Carnatic; but he had done much more. He had brought the Company through six perilous years of war not only unscathed but with vastly increased influence and prestige. "I cannot refrain from imparting to you," he told his Council with pardonable pride, "the pleasing satisfaction which I myself feel in observing the great and evident change that has within these few years taken place with regard to our Government in the opinion and dispositions of the principal powers of Hindustan. We seem to have regained our proper weight in the political system, and the neighbouring States, who formerly shrunk from our advances, are eager to participate in our views, and to connect their interests with ours." This was no more than the truth. The doggedness of the English resistance had astonished the native powers. It had been seen that they could withstand both the Marathas and Haidar Ali even when combined and supported by French forces. From a war disastrous elsewhere, the English had emerged in India, and in India alone, with increased strength and enhanced reputation.

The result would certainly have been very different if during these years the Company's affairs, instead of being in Hastings' hands, had still been conducted by Clavering and Francis. They would have concentrated solely on the defence of Bengal, left Bombay and Madras to their fate, and allowed the French to establish a paramount influence at Mysore, Poona and Hyderabad. The hostile combination of native powers, which Hastings broke up as soon as it was formed, they, by their passive policy, would have suffered to grow in strength and boldness, till all India was united against them in the hope of "partaking of the spoils of a falling Nation." At best the English would have ended the war with diminished influence and with the French established once more as formidable competitors. At worst they would have lost all territorial sovereignty and descended once again to the "humble and undreaded character of trading adventurers."

That the outcome was different was due to Hastings being a man of genius who, in his own words, was not content just to plod along quietly in the beaten tracks, as an ordinary man would have done, but had the spirit and courage to leave them and to "explore the wilds of peril and reproach." He himself gives an admirable picture of what he might have done if he had just been an ordinary, safe, sound mediocrity. "I could have guarded myself," he told Sulivan, "most effectually against their (the Directors') censures by avoiding all responsibility and covering myself with their orders in whatever I did. I could have kept their troops and treasure at home, when the Presidency at Bombay was engaged in schemes to which it was confessedly unequal. I could have suffered the disgrace of the unhappy affair of Wargaum to remain an indelible stain on the British name. It was no concern of mine. I could have suffered the Carnatic to fall an easy prey to Hyder, when Francis opposed the measures which I suggested for its preservation, and I could have justified it on the principle of self-preservation; the prior care due to the first possessions of the Company; the want of authority from home; the season of the year which would render it an act of madness to send their troops to perish by sea; and by a fair estimate of ways and means, which would prove that we had not assets for such an enterprise. I could have acquiesced in the violation of faith, which the Government of Madras were guilty of towards Nizam Ali, and contented myself with protesting against it. . . . I could

232

have sat quietly down when our ordinary resources would yield no more supplies for the war, and ruin threatened. What business had I at Benares [1]?

"But if I had observed this discreet and safe conduct, let me ask not you, my friend, but my most rancorous enemies, what would have been the state of the Company, or whether it is likely that it would at this time have existence?"

By such "discreet and safe conduct" he would have effectually liquidated an empire—but he would have escaped the censure both of contemporaries and of posterity. The loss of Madras and Bombay would have been attributed to circumstances beyond his control, and there would have been no one to show how by daring and energy these circumstances might have been overcome. He would have enjoyed the immunity from criticism so often reserved for the inert and unenterprising. Knowing, as he did, how easily and honourably he might have played for safety and lost everything, he had good reason to be proud of his actual achievement. The valour of others, he told the House of Lords, acquired for the British their dominion in India; "I preserved it; I sent forth its armies with an effectual but economical hand, through unknown and hostile regions, to the support of your other possessions; to the retrieval of one

[1] See Chapter Fifteen.

from degradation and dishonour; and of the other from utter loss and subjection. I maintained the wars which were of your formation, or that of others, not of mine. I won one member (the Nizam) of the Great Indian Confederacy from it by an act of seasonable restitution; with another (the Rajah of Berar) I maintained a secret intercourse and converted him into a friend; a third (Mahadaji Sindhia) I drew off by diversion and negotiation, and employed him as the instrument of peace. When you cried out for peace, and your cries were heard by those who were the object of it, I resisted this, and every other species of counter-action, by rising in my demands, and accomplished a peace, and I hope everlasting, with one great State (the Marathas); and I at least afforded the efficient means by which a peace, if not so durable, more seasonable at least, was accomplished with another (Tipu Sultan).

"I gave you all, and you have rewarded me with confiscation, disgrace, and a life of impeachment."

Chapter Fourteen

Internal Dissensions

DURING the critical years 1779–81 Hastings was to some extent relieved of anxiety regarding the attitude of the home authorities towards him. His original five-year term of office expired in 1779. By this time Lord North was far too much concerned with all the hazards of the American war to think of attempting any major changes in India. He had a high opinion of Hastings' abilities and, now that Clavering was dead, was only too glad that he should carry on. So for three years in succession he quietly continued him in office, and until Francis got back to England in 1781, "big with resentment, disappointment, spleen and envy," no serious attempt was made to remove him.

Hastings was thus reasonably assured of support at home. But in Bengal itself, at the very worst moment of the war, there were added to his other anxieties two violent quarrels threatening the stability of the Government itself—one with his bitter enemy, Francis; the other with Impey, his oldest and warmest friend.

The quarrel with Impey and the Supreme

Court was particularly painful to Hastings. "I suffer beyond measure," he told his friend Sulivan, "by the present contest, and my spirits are at times so depressed as to affect my health." He had done all he could to avert it; but his 'new plan of Justice,' designed to prevent friction between the Court and the Government, had been disregarded by the home authorities and no alternative remedy had been adopted. Disputes and disagreements multiplied and at the end of 1779 these led to what Hastings described as 'open war' between the Court and the Council.

Impey himself was a sensible man. While rightly jealous of the independence of the Court, he realised the danger of weakening the authority of the Executive and therefore, so far as possible, avoided clashes with the Government. But two of his colleagues, Hyde and Lemaistre, were petulant, petty-minded men, all too conscious of the majesty of the law as exhibited in their own persons. The jurisdiction of the Supreme Court was admittedly ill-defined, and they lost no opportunity of asserting and stretching it without regard for prudence or the public interest. So far from seeking to accommodate their views to those of the Government, they went out of their way to demonstrate their own independence.

The incidents which finally led to an open and scandalous rupture arose out of a summons issued by Hyde against a rich zemindar, the

Rajah of Cossijura, in a suit for debt. It was doubtful whether the Rajah was subject to the Supreme Court's jurisdiction, for though, as a zemindar, he was responsible for the collection of the revenue, he could hardly be classed merely on this account as a British subject or the servant of a British subject. He applied to the Revenue Board for instructions whether to obey the summons. The Board, on the advice of the Advocate-General, told him that he should ignore it. He did so; whereupon the Court despatched a sheriff's officer and a large number of armed men to seize his house and all his effects. The Rajah, making the most of these highhanded proceedings, complained bitterly to Hastings "of the violation of his zenana and of his religion, the former having been forcibly entered . . . the door of his temple broken open and his idol taken and packed like a common utensil in a basket, and sealed up with the other lumber." The Board promptly sent a party of sepoys to arrest the sheriff's officer and all his men, and published a notice to all the zemindars that they were not subject to the jurisdiction of the Court and could not be compelled to appear before it. The Court replied by issuing warrants against the sepoys and summonses against the Governor-General and the members of his Council. The Governor-General and Council ignored the summonses, prevented the warrants from being executed, and ordered the salaries of the judges to be stopped.

This scandalous quarrel, the first and most serious of the many which have disturbed the relations of the Executive and Judiciary in British India, went on all through the spring and summer of 1780. Both sides were partly to blame. The judges had asserted a doubtful authority in a rash, intemperate manner, and had outraged native opinion by the violence of their proceedings against a great zemindar. On the other hand, Hastings and his Council were to blame for not informally remonstrating with the judges, and warning them of the consequences of their action before opposing them by force and compromising their dignity. This omission seems to have been partly due to Hastings' belief that he could quietly settle the matter by inducing the plaintiff, at whose instance the summons against the Rajah had been issued, to drop his suit. He promised Hastings that he would do this, but did not keep his promise, and the next thing Hastings knew was that the Rajah's house had been broken into by armed men. After that there could be no compromise till tempers had cooled.

It was Hastings who found means of bringing about a reconciliation. His expedient, according to Macaulay, was a very simple one, neither more nor less than to offer Impey a bribe. Actually, what Hastings offered Impey was not just a bribe, but an arrangement which gave to him, under another form, the unlimited jurisdiction which he and his colleagues wanted. As already explained, the judges of the Supreme Court stood in no defined relation to the civil courts, modelled on native patterns, which Hastings had established. These were controlled and supervised by the Sadar Diwani Adalat or Chief Civil Court, which consisted of members of the Council aided by native officials; Impey and his colleagues had no concern or connection with them. Hastings had perceived that the best way to prevent friction between the Court and the Council and to assure the judges full opportunty of checking any oppression—which they believed to be their foremost duty—was to associate them with the members of Council in the control of the subordinate civil courts. If they themselves were made members of the Sadar Diwani Adalat, they would *ipso facto* obtain that unlimited jurisdiction throughout the provinces which they desired, and there would be no room for competition between rival courts and rival judicial authorities. His new plan of justice, embodying these ideas, had been rejected; but he now recurred to the principle of it, and proposed that Impey should himself be requested to assume sole charge and superintendency of the Sadar Diwani Adalat for which, he said, the members of Council had insufficient time. This proposal, he argued, would strengthen and improve the subordinate courts which "will be enabled to act with confidence . . . when their proceedings are held under the sanction and immediate patronage of the first member of the Supreme Court"; it would "lessen the cares of the Board, and add to their leisure for occupations more urgent and better suited to the genius and principles of Government," and it would "prove an instrument of conciliation with the Court," which would be precluded from the necessity of assuming a questionable jurisdicton. Impey, as head of the Sadar Diwani Adalat, would enjoy jurisdiction over the whole population without distinction, which was just what the judges desired, and he would exercise it through courts based on Mogul models and employing native forms and usages rather than the strange legal rites of England.

Francis and Wheler opposed this eminently sensible proposal, but with Coote's support Hastings carried it. Impey was appointed Judge of the Sadar Diwani Adalat at a salary of £6,500 and the quarrel between Court and Council was happily ended. For the unfortunate Impey, however, this was by no means the end of the matter. Francis returned to England shortly afterwards and at once began attacks on him, insinuating that the whole arrangement was a corrupt bargain. As a result of his machinations Impey was recalled to England in 1782 to explain why he, a servant of the Crown, had "accepted an office granted by and tenable at the pleasure of the servants of the East India Company." Though he vindicated himself before the House of Commons with complete success, the malicious innuendoes of Francis have been repeated by Mill and Macaulay as though they were established facts. The truth is that Impey, who has been charged with taking a bribe, never enjoyed a penny of the salary attached to his new office. He duly entered upon his new duties, and with commendable diligence prepared a whole series of rules and regulations for the Sadar Diwani Adalat. But he did not like to accept the salary until he had ascertained from the Lord Chancellor that there would be no objection; and the net result was that he got nothing whatever except an order of recall. "I have undergone great fatigue," he not unreasonably complained, "compiled a laborious Code, restored confidence to the suitors, and justice and regularity to the Courts of Justice . . . without any reward, and for my recompense shall have lost my office, reputation and peace of mind for ever." How widely different is Macaulay's conclusion. "The bargain was struck; Bengal was saved; an appeal to force was averted, and the Chief Justice was rich, quiet and infamous."

By the time that Impey was recalled the

authorities in England had at last realised that the provisions of the Regulating Act regarding the powers of the Supreme Court needed amendment, and in 1781 an Act was passed definitely excluding that Court from interference with agents of the revenue administration and recognising the courts established by Hastings.

The quarrel between Hastings and Impey had been followed by a reconciliation. An apparent reconciliation between Hastings and Francis was followed by a more deadly revival of their old quarrel. This, too, took place during the summer of 1780, when the Maratha war was at its height. But it did not shake Hastings' habitual calm. Even in the unfamiliar and, as he termed it, "odious character of a duellist," he retained his usual self-possession.

The reconciliation between Francis and Hastings was effected at the beginning of 1780. The occasion for it was the departure of Barwell for England. He had long wanted to return home to enjoy his enormous fortune, and in 1779 he had formally announced his intention of leaving; but Hastings had prevailed upon him to stay, pointing out that it would be fatal to the success of the Maratha war if complete power devolved on Francis and Wheler, who, as the Marathas well knew, were ready to make peace on any terms. With the arrival of Coote, Barwell again began to press for release. But

Coote was a man of wayward temper and was frequently absent from Calcutta on tours of inspection. Hastings could not depend on him for steady support and was therefore still most unwilling to let Barwell go. Torn between loyalty to Hastings and a desire to enjoy his wealth in England, Barwell set himself to arrange a settlement which would enable him to leave Bengal with a clear conscience. Barwell was a good mixer. His own social relations with the Majority had always been close. He had played cards with Francis; he had made love to Clavering's daughter; and his lack of success at both had by no means diminished his popularity. Everyone knew that he wanted to go home, and desired that his wish should be gratified. There was therefore a general disposition to promote a reconciliation between Francis and Hastings which would make possible his release. Early in 1780, through the mediation of Sir John Day, the Advocate-General, a definite agreement was reached between them, and on the strength of this Hastings, believing that he would "suffer no loss of power or influence," freely consented to Barwell's departure.

The most important article of this agreement from Hastings' point of view was an undertaking by Francis not to "oppose any measures which the Governor-General shall recommend for the prosecution of the war in which we are supposed to be engaged with the Marathas, or for the general support of the present political system of this Government." To prevent misconceptions and future cavils, the agreement was reduced to writing by Hastings and shown to Francis, who assented to it; but it was not actually signed. "I regarded it," Hastings said, "as a deed of faith and honour, not of law;" and, reporting it to Sulivan, he expressed complete confidence that Francis would abide by it.

In a very few weeks he was undeceived; for as soon as he began to develop his plans for Camac's and Popham's expeditions against Sindhia's territories he met with obstruction. At first, instead of openly asserting his rights under the agreement, he endeavoured to meet Francis' objections. Several times he modified his proposals; then, as Francis' opposition to the expeditions was based largely on grounds of expense, he offered a personal contribution of two lakhs of rupees towards the cost, and paid this sum into the Treasury. The money was not really his own, but a peace-offering which Chait Singh, Rajah of Benares, had made to him in the hope of escaping further exactions. But even this questionable device did not achieve its object. A gentle reminder to Francis of his engagements was equally useless. He persistently blocked the expeditions on which Hastings had set his heart—expeditions which in the end decisively influenced the course of the war and disposed Sindhia to peace.

"I debated with myself a long time," Hastings said, "how I should act. I now saw plainly that Mr. Francis had deceived me, and that I had no alternative but to let him take the rule and laugh at my credulity, or to make it a matter too serious for derision, and to expose the fallacy which he had thus unworthily practised upon me. This I did in a very strong but deliberate and temperate charge, which I had prepared for the next Council-day, which was Monday, the 3rd July."

Owing to a last-minute and unsuccessful attempt by Sir John Day to prevent a total rupture, this minute was not actually laid before the Council till August 15th. Hastings sent a copy of it privately to Francis the day before, so that he might be prepared for what was coming. It was a formidable indictment. He referred at length to Francis' persistent and factious opposition, the sole purpose of which was "to embarrass and defeat every measure which I may undertake, or which may tend even to promote the public interests, if my credit is connected with them. . . . Almost every measure has for that reason had his opposition to it. When carried against his opposition, and too far engaged to be withdrawn, yet even then and in every stage of it his labours to overcome it have been unremitted, every disappointment and misfortune have been aggravated by him, and every fabricated tale of armies devoted to famine or massacre have found their fast and ready way to his office, where it was known they would meet the most welcome reception." He then went on to charge Francis with breach of faith. He had entered, he said, into an agreement with Francis and on the strength of it had been induced to part with his friend and steadfast supporter, Barwell, and to throw himself "on the mercy of Mr. Francis, and on the desperate hazard of his integrity." This agreement Francis had broken and shown himself "to be void of truth and honour." "This is a severe charge," he wrote, "but temperately and deliberately made from the firm persuasion that I owe this justice to the public and to myself, as the only redress to both, for artifices of which I have been a victim, and which threaten to involve their interests with disgrace and ruin."

As soon as the Council had risen, Francis, as Hastings had expected, drew him aside and read him a challenge. Hastings accepted it, and the early morning of August 17th was fixed for the meeting. Both parties were quite inexpert in these matters. Francis declared that he had never fired a pistol before, and Hastings had only done so once or twice. The danger which they ran was not therefore really so great as might appear. Nevertheless, it was a serious affair. Hastings' own quaint but careful and objective account of it best reveals the grim deliberation with which he acted throughout.

"The next morning Colonel Pearse by appointment called on me, but before the time, at about a quarter after 4. I laid down again on the couch for half an hour. Then dressed and went with him in his carriage. . . . Arrived at Belvedere exactly at the time proposed—at 5.30, found Mr. F. and Colonel Watson walking in the road. Some time was consumed in looking for a private place. Our seconds proposed that we should stand at a measured distance which both (taking a recent example in England) fixed at 14 paces, and Colonel Watson paced and marked 7. I stood to the southward. There was (as I recollect) no wind. Our Seconds (Colonel W. I think) proposed that no advantage should be taken, but each choose his own time to fire —I should have said that Colonel Pearse loaded my pistols on the ground with two cartridges which he had prepared. I had resolved to defer my fire that I might not be embarrassed with his. He snapped, but the pistol missed fire. The Second put a fresh priming to it and chapped the flints. We returned to our stations. I still proposed to receive the first fire, but Mr. F. twice aiming and withdrawing his pistol, I judged that I might seriously take my aim at him. I did so and when I thought I had fixed the true direction I fired. His pistol went off at the same time, and so near the same instant that I am not certain which was first, but believe mine was first, and that his followed in the instant. He staggered immediately, his face expressed a sensation of being struck, and his limbs shortly but gradually went under him, and he fell saying, but not loudly, 'I am dead.' I ran to him, shocked I own at the information, and I can safely say without any immediate sensation of joy for my own success. The Seconds also ran to his assistance. I saw his coat pierced on the right side, and feared the ball had passed through him; but he sat up without much difficulty several times and once attempted with our help to stand, but his limbs failed him, and he sank to the ground. Colonel W. then proposed that as we had met from a point of honour and not for personal rancour, we should join hands (or that Mr. F. should give me his). We did so; Mr. F. cheerfully, and I expressed my regret at the condition to which I saw him reduced. He found most ease lying on his back. A cot was brought from Major Tolleys', he having no palikeen, and he was conveyed upon it to Belvedere, where he remains. Colonel P. and I returned to my house in town. We went to seek Dr. Campbell and I desired Dr. Francis to follow. Both immediately went. They found the wound not dangerous, having entered the side before the seam of the waistcoat a little below the shoulder, and passing through both muscles and within the skin which covers the backbone, was lodged within a visible distance of the skin in the opposite side.

"As soon as I returned home I sent Mr. Markham to Sir E. (Elijah Impey) to inform him of what had passed, and that I should wait the event, which if fatal I should instantly surrender myself to him, that the law might take its course against me."

Francis quickly recovered from his wound and resumed his seat in Council on September 11th. In reply to the minute charging him with breach of faith he asserted that he had never been a party to an engagement in the terms alleged by Hastings. He contended that the agreement in regard to the Maratha war was that he should not oppose operations already in progress, i.e. Goddard's operations on the Malabar coast, and did not apply to fresh measures not already in contemplation. Hastings was able to show that a diversion, such as was effected by Popham's and Camac's expeditions, had actually been projected before the agreement was concluded; and in a further exchange of minutes he had very much the best of the argument. Possibly there was a genuine misunderstanding —Hastings was certainly foolish not to obtain Francis' signature to the engagement so that all doubt and dispute might be avoided—but it seems rather more likely that Francis deliberately tried to take advantage of Hastings' credulous reliance on his good faith. This would not have been inconsistent with his character.

The duel was the culmination and the close of Francis' contests with Hastings in India. Disappointed and defeated, he decided to go home and seek his revenge in England. He disliked Bengal; he had already acquired by his savings and success at cards a fair fortune, and there was little prospect of regaining the power and influence which he had once enjoyed in the days of the Majority's triumph. Soon after the duel he engaged a passage home, and in December 1780 he departed.

"My antagonists," Hastings wrote some years later, "sickened, died and fled. I maintained my ground unchanged, neither the health of my body nor the vigour of my mind for a moment deserted me." After a conflict of six years he had gained a decided victory, and many were the congratulations offered to him. "But what a victory!" he wrote, "an exhausted treasury, an accumulating debt, a system charged with expensive establishments, and precluded by the multitude of dependants and the curse of patronage, from reformation . . . a country oppressed by private rapacity, and deprived of its vital resources by the enormous quantities of current specie annually exported in the remittance of private fortunes . . . the support of Bombay, . . . the charge of preserving Fort

St. George, and recovering the Carnatic from the hands of a victorious enemy; the entire maintenance of both presidencies; and lastly a war either actual or depending in every quarter, and with every power in Hindustan: these and many more evils which I could enumerate are the appendages of that authority which is devolving to me, and the fruits of that spirit of discord which has been permitted— how unaccountably. It has prevailed in this Government without an instant of remission, since the 19th of October, 1774, to the present hour." He goes on sadly to reflect that if he had been removed from office in 1774 and replaced by an honest man of only moderate ability who had enjoyed the full support of the Directors and the Home Government, "all the ills which have befallen the country might have been prevented." The Bengal Government's prestige would have steadily risen; its treasury would have been filled to overflowing; the Marathas would never have embarked on war: "Hyder Ally had not thought of invading the Carnatic; every state would have courted the Company's alliance, and the influence of the British name would have been felt, acknowledged and respected in every region of Hindustan and Deccan." As it was, the untrammelled power which had now temporarily fallen to him had to be employed "to retrieve past misfortunes, to remove present dangers, and to re-establish the power of the Company and the safety of its possessions."

Hastings always maintained that what he accomplished was only "by fits and intervals of power." The year 1781 was certainly one of those intervals. Coote was absent in the Carnatic and, as soon as Francis had departed, the pliant Wheler became entirely submissive. Hastings, who had previously scorned him, now could hardly speak too highly of him, and at once employed those crude methods, in which he so rightly believed, to secure his permanent attachment. "I have made it a rule," he wrote, "to give him the first option in most vacant appointments, and have provided handsomely for all his friends."

The war was still at a critical stage; the financial outlook was black; though Hastings was temporarily the unchallenged master of Bengal, most of his time and energy was indeed occupied in "retrieving past misfortunes." Yet despite distractions he seized the opportunity afforded by this interval of power to push through a whole series of administrative reforms affecting the Customs, the Salt monopoly, and the Revenue Administration, which led to a great increase in receipts. One of the principles embodied in these reforms was the remuneration of officials engaged in collecting any form of revenue by paying them commissions on receipts. By this means Hastings hoped to provide really liberal salaries—at which the Directors still jibbed—and "to eradicate every temptation and pretext for perquisites, embezzlements, and corruption." In several instances the resulting salaries were, by any reasonable standard, far too high; but the tradition of making large fortunes in the Company's service died hard.

Hastings' changes in the Revenue Administration included the execution of his long-cherished plan for abolishing the Provincial Councils—relic of the hated 'supervisors'—and placing all control in the hands of a Committee in Calcutta composed of four of the Company's best officers. This attempt at centralisation was probably premature. The revenue administration in the districts was still far too weak to be supervised adequately from Calcutta. It also proved impossible to adhere to his original idea of employing only native officers in the districts and confining the Company's servants to Calcutta. "The infinitude of claimants for posts" could not be accommodated at the seat of government. All the ex-members of the Provincial Councils had to be provided for as well as many fresh candidates. The result was that some of the Company's servants were allowed to remain in the districts as 'Collectors' with restricted powers, while some, for whom no other work was available, were appointed judges of the district diwani (civil) courts. In addition to their civil jurisdiction they were given 'faujdari' or police powers, enabling them to apprehend robbers and other capital offenders and to hand them over to the nearest native criminal court for punishment. The appointment of these English judges, which coincided with Impey's assumption of the office of Judge of the Sadar Diwani Adalat, and the combination of judicial with police functions, certainly marked a change of policy and helped to pave the way for the district officer of a later day. Yet it was "the curse of patronage and the multitude of dependants" rather than positive belief in European agency which was really responsible for the change. Hastings' own preference continued to be for Indian agency, as he showed during this very year when he took over from Chait Singh the administration of the zemindari of Benares. Instead of putting in English officials, he continued a purely Indian administration, complaining that there were already too many 'English Collectors' in Bengal. To establish them in Benares would be, he said, "to subvert the rights of the (Chait Singh's) family, to injure the revenues, and to lessen the attachment of the ryots which it will be ever good policy to conciliate." The British official was still very far from being the 'Cherisher of the Poor,' beloved of the ryots, which he was destined to become, perhaps in fact, and certainly in the imagination of a later age.

Chapter Fifteen

The Benares Outbreak and the Begums of Oudh

AT the outbreak of war in 1778, the Bengal Government had ample funds. Two years later, when Haidar Ali over-ran the Carnatic, the necessity of supporting Madras as well as Bombay began to put a serious strain on its resources. There was no longer any surplus revenue with which to provide the Company's 'investment' and to finance the China trade—both of which the Directors expected Hastings to do despite the war—and it became exceedingly difficult to find money to keep the armies in the field. In the autumn of 1780 the treasury in Calcutta was opened for loans, but the amount which could be raised in this way was limited. If the war was to be effectively carried on, it was necessary to look elsewhere for extra funds.

One possible source of supply was the Company's ally, Asaf-ud-daula, the Nawab of Oudh; another was the Company's richest and most powerful subject, Chait Singh, Rajah of Benares. Asaf-ud-daula owed the Company large

sums on account of the troops lent to him; but
it had become clear that, unless special arrangements were made, the debt would continue to
grow instead of being repaid. Chait Singh,
whose wealth was considerable, had each year
since the outbreak of war been called upon to
pay the Company a special subsidy of 5 lakhs of
rupees; but he had made these payments only
after much procrastination and many unreal
pleas of poverty. He was believed to be disaffected and in secret correspondence with the
Marathas.

With Francis out of the way, Hastings felt
that the time had come for him to settle accounts
with both the Nawab and the Rajah. Wheler
readily fell in with his plans. It was agreed
between them that, while Wheler remained in
Calcutta in sole charge of the internal administration of Bengal, Hastings should proceed to
Benares and Lucknow with full power to deal
with Asaf-ud-daula's debt and Chait Singh's
disaffection. He left Calcutta in July 1781,
accompanied by his personal staff and a body-
guard of about 500. The conjunction of unfettered power and financial stringency was to
lead him into the most questionable acts of his
public career.

Rajah Chait Singh had originally been a subject of the Nawab of Oudh, but, as already mentioned,[1] the Majority, in the early days of their

1 See page 148.

power, took advantage of the death of Nawab Shuja-ud-daula to detach the Benares zemindari from Oudh and bring it within the Company's territories. This change had been in accordance with Chait Singh's own wishes, but had not been approved by Hastings, who considered that it was unjust to the Nawab of Oudh and would unduly weaken him. Consequently Chait Singh regarded himself as the Majority's protégé, and certainly favoured them in their conflict with Hastings. This fact probably accounts in some degree for the severity with which Hastings treated him.

Chait Singh's zemindari was very large; but he was not, as Burke tried to represent him, an independent prince, paying the Company a fixed annual tribute. He was definitely the Company's subject, and the sum of 22½ lakhs of rupees which he was required to pay to them annually was land revenue rather than tribute. He was, in fact, a zemindar and, though a very big zemindar with special privileges and unusual authority, he owed loyalty and allegiance to the Company as the sovereign and ruling power.

The Company in its agreement with him had bound itself not to make any demands on him so long as he paid the 22½ lakhs. But Mogul usage fully recognised a sovereign's right to call upon his wealthy subjects for extra assistance in an emergency. There was, therefore, in Hastings' opinion, no question but that the Company was justified in demanding a special war contribution from Chait Singh, whatever might be the terms of its formal engagements with him. Francis consented to the demand, though with some demur, and the Directors, to whom the facts were in due course reported, raised no objection. Chait Singh himself, however unwilling he might be to pay the war contribution, knew that the demand for it was sanctioned by custom and that the amount fixed was by no means excessive. He held his zemindari on distinctly easy terms; it could yield nearly double the $22\frac{1}{2}$ lakhs that he was required to pay as annual revenue, and he was reputed—and subsequently proved—to be exceedingly wealthy. If he had been a really loyal subject, as loyalty is understood in India, he would have freely placed himself and all his resources at the Company's disposal; he would have paid up with alacrity, real or affected, the extra 5 lakhs demanded of him, and would have endeavoured to prove his zeal and devotion by offering more. Such behaviour was for him, in accordance with Indian traditions which survive to this day, almost a duty; for the Company had hitherto treated him with remarkable lenity: its hour of need was the moment for him to show his gratitude. But Chait Singh was not really loyal. Though Hastings was the head of the Government, Chait Singh still clung to Francis as his patron, and hoped by exploiting the divisions in the Council to escape his obligations to the Company. He himself had no direct interest in the war to which he was being required to contribute; he knew that Francis was opposed to Hastings' vigorous war measures, and he believed the rumours, assiduously circulated by Francis himself, that Hastings would soon be recalled. Hence, both in 1778 and 1779, he paid his war contribution of 5 lakhs tardily, reluctantly, with many absurd protestations of poverty and with an evident disposition to evade it altogether. He did not in fact pay it in 1779 until two battalions of sepoys were quartered on him at his expense.

In India the astonishing devotion which real loyalty will evoke makes suspect even the slightest backwardness in offering assistance. Many English historians, ignorant of Indian conditions, have failed to appreciate the contrast between Chait Singh's actual behaviour and what might reasonably have been expected of him. His unwillingness to pay up an extra 5 lakhs seems to them natural and excusable; to Hastings, with his far greater understanding of India, it seemed a sure symptom of disaffection. Chait Singh himself, of course, fully realised that his conduct had been such as to incur Hastings' just displeasure; and in the spring of 1780, finding that Hastings still continued in office and that there had actually been a reconciliation between him and Francis, he judged it expedient to make amends. He therefore sent a confidential agent to Hastings to beg forgiveness for his past misconduct and to assure him of his complete submission to his orders in future. Hastings accepted his excuses, promised to overlook his past delinquencies, and pledged his word that the annual demand for an extra 5 lakhs was purely a war measure, and that the fixed and stipulated sum of $22\frac{1}{2}$ lakhs due from him would not be permanently increased by any arbitrary addition. Having given this pledge, he demanded an extra 5 lakhs for the current year which Chait Singh unreservedly promised to pay. The payment, as usual, was made unpunctually, much to Hastings' justifiable annoyance.

Hastings was, however, guilty at this time of an indiscretion. Chait Singh, hoping to soften his temper and diminish the probability of further exactions, offered him a personal present of 2 lakhs. At first Hastings refused the money, but later accepted it and, having paid it into the Company's treasury, offered it as though it were his own as a contribution towards the expenses of Camac's expedition which Francis was opposing. After accepting this peace-offering from Chait Singh, it was hardly fair to make further peremptory demands on him without some word of explanation or reassurance. Yet this is what he did. In the autumn of 1780, at Coote's suggestion, he called upon him to furnish 2,000 horsemen to help in the defence of Bengal against an expected incursion by the cavalry of the Rajah of Berar. The demand was probably excessive, and was reduced first to 1,500 and then to 1,000. Chait Singh returned evasive answers, finally offered 500 horsemen—and sent none.

Hastings determined to teach him a lesson. "I had resolved," he wrote, "to draw from his guilt the means of relief to the Company's distresses, and to exact a penalty which I was convinced he was able to bear. . . . In a word, I had determined to make him pay largely for his pardon, or to exact a severe vengeance for his past delinquency." Before leaving Calcutta he confided to Wheler that he intended to fine Chait Singh 40 or 50 lakhs and, if he refused to pay, either to remove him entirely from his zemindari or to take immediate possession of all his forts and obtain the sum from the treasure deposited in them. He had a few months earlier taken the precaution of replacing Francis' protégé, the younger Fowke, as Resident at Benares by Markham,[1] a mere youth of twenty-one, who had been his private secretary and was entirely subservient to him.

The news that Hastings was coming up-country caused Chait Singh considerable alarm; for Hastings, whose resentment he had

[1] Son of Dr. Markham, Archbishop of York, a staunch supporter of Hastings in England.

rashly incurred, was now omnipotent. Chait Singh met him in a very contrite mood at Buxar on the borders of his zemindari, laid his turban at his feet in token of his complete submission, admitted his past faults, begged forgiveness, and assured him that all his property was at his disposal. Hastings told him that he could no longer be content with promises and verbal protestations, which cost nothing and in the past had proved delusive, and declined further conversation.

Hastings reached Benares on August 14th, 1781. Chait Singh again sought an interview with him, but was told that he could not see the Governor-General until certain matters had been settled which would be communicated to him through the Resident. The next day the Resident handed him a letter from Hastings complaining of his dilatoriness in paying the subsidy of 5 lakhs and his failure to comply with the requisition for horsemen, and demanding an immediate explanation. Chait Singh, having been repulsed at Buxar and then denied a further interview, seems to have despaired of appeasing Hastings by grovelling and a show of repentance. He sent a reply which Hastings described as "not only unsatisfactory in substance, but offensive in style; and less a vindication of himself than a recrimination on me." A modern historian [1] has expressed the view that

[1] P. E. Roberts, *History of British India*, pages 203–4.

it was "perfectly respectful, and, considering the way he had been treated, extraordinarily moderate." By modern English standards it was perhaps respectful and moderate; but it was seriously lacking in the submissive humility which in India is expected of a subject when addressing his lord and master, more especially when he knows that his conduct has given offence. As Hastings pertinently remarked, Chait Singh's reply expressed "no concern for the causes of complaint contained in my letter, or desire to atone for them; nor the smallest intention to pursue a different line of conduct." Whatever may be thought of the justice of Hastings' demands, it is undeniable that Chait Singh had, through his agent, assured him in the summer of 1780 of full compliance with all future orders, but thereafter had complied tardily, or not at all. When called upon for an explanation, instead of acknowledging his faults and throwing himself entirely on Hastings' mercy, he argued, with somewhat offensive emphasis, that Hastings was to blame for not answering his letters—which themselves were mere pretexts for evasion and delay. In the context of eighteenth-century India—and even of modern India—his whole reply could well be regarded as evidence of a refractory and insolent spirit which required to be broken.

It was in this light that Hastings regarded it, inflamed perhaps by the incendiary whispers of

Chait Singh's personal enemies. "An answer couched," he said, "nearly in terms of defiance to requisitions of so serious a nature, I could not but consider as a strong indication of that spirit of independency which the Rajah has for some years past assumed." He decided therefore on a drastic step. He directed Markham, the Resident, to proceed to Chait Singh's house with two companies of sepoys and to place him under arrest. This at once produced in Chait Singh a change of tone, if not of heart. He submitted quietly to his arrest and wrote humbly to Hastings, assuring him of his obedience. Hastings, relenting somewhat at this display of a more submissive spirit, replied kindly, telling him not to be apprehensive but to set his mind at rest. The Rajah, now thoroughly repentant, again expressed his complete submission. "Your gracious letter has been received, and has made me acquainted with your commands. You order that . . . I must not suffer any apprehension to disturb me, but remain at ease in my mind. My Protector! Wherever you spread your shadow over my head, I am entirely free from concern and apprehension; and whatever you, who are my master, shall as such determine, will be right."

Everything was now set for a reconciliation, and, if all had gone well, Chait Singh would have agreed to make amends for his past misconduct by payment of a considerable fine, and

264

Hastings would have released him and rein-
stated him with honour. But at this point other
forces came into play. Hearing the news of the
Rajah's arrest, a tumultuous throng of his armed
retainers swarmed across the river from his forti-
fied palace at Ramnagar on the other side and
surrounded the house in which he was confined.
Through some unexplained oversight, the two
companies of sepoys who were guarding him
had not been supplied with ammunition. A
third company, which was despatched to take it
to them, could not make its way through the
dense crowd blockading the building. There was
an altercation, a scuffle and then a massacre; for
Chait Singh's followers, on some sudden but
obscure provocation, fell upon the defenceless
sepoys who were guarding him, and killed or
wounded them to a man. The third company,
which had the ammunition, gradually dispersed
the crowd and occupied the building; but during all this confusion Chait Singh, scared out of
his wits at the bloodshed for which he would
be held responsible, had let himself down by a
rope of turbans into a boat in the river and
escaped to the other side.

Hastings' own position was now one of considerable danger. If Chait Singh's followers,
instead of recrossing the river pell-mell, had
proceeded to Hastings' quarters, they could
easily have overwhelmed him and his small
suite. But the whole tumult had arisen without

premeditation. Chait Singh had no plans except for flight, and Hastings was left quite un-molested in Benares. With his usual imperturb-ability he made immediate arrangements for taking over the administration of the zemindari, sent a report of what had passed to Wheler in Calcutta, and called up reinforcements from Chunar, Dinapur and Mirzapur. But he was not yet out of danger, for on August 20th a rash young captain who attempted against orders to seize Ramnagar was repulsed with very heavy loss, and Hastings' force at Benares was so reduced that he was obliged to withdraw to Chunar. Here, too, for some days he remained more or less in a state of siege.

Fresh troops, however, began to gather from the nearest military stations. Directions were given for clearing the country and suppressing the rebellion, and the whole episode was soon brought to a not very satisfactory conclusion. The wretched Chait Singh had no chance of putting up a successful resistance and was quickly hunted into Sindhia's territories; but he managed to take with him a considerable portion of his hoarded treasure, and the remainder, amounting to about 23 lakhs, was divided up amongst the troops as prize money on the capture of the fortress of Bijaygarh. Hastings was intensely vexed at the irregular appropriation of so large a sum; but he had only himself to blame, as an unguarded sentence in a private letter to Popham, the commanding officer, was quite reasonably taken as conveying his sanction. Thus the main object for which he had visited Benares, namely, "to draw from Chait Singh's guilt the means of relief to the Company's distresses," remained signally unfulfilled. So far from replenishing the public exchequer, he had burdened it with the cost of a minor war, and he himself was obliged to confess, when he finally journeyed back to Calcutta, "I return to an empty treasury which I left empty."

Hastings' efforts to wring money from Chait Singh have been criticised by historians for their failure no less than for their doubtful morality. But Hastings was not primarily to blame for their failure. It was primarily due to sheer mischance. Hastings, no doubt, did not foresee, as he should have done, the excitement which Chait Singh's arrest would arouse among his own people. The rapid gathering of an armed multitude round the building in which he was confined came as a surprise. But the situation could certainly have been controlled if the two companies of sepoys on guard there had been properly armed. Chait Singh's excited adherents were a mere tumultuous mob under no regular leadership and swayed by the blind impulse of the moment. Finding the sepoys defenceless, they broke wildly into the courtyard of the building and slaughtered them. They would never have done this if the sepoys had been able to meet them with a steady fire. Either they would have fled at once in panic or they would have kept their distance, and the remaining troops which Hastings had with him at Benares would have come up and dispersed them. Hastings had altogether 500–600 men at his disposal, and these should have been quite sufficient to deal with any sudden emergency. The loss of over 200 of them in the space of a few minutes was an event which no one could have foreseen.

Moreover, Hastings' failure to achieve the avowed object of his expedition to Benares was not really quite so complete as might appear. He obtained no *immediate* relief for the Company's distresses, but financial gains began to accrue in quite a short time. Chait Singh was deposed, and the Company, released now from all agreements, was free to take a revenue more in accord with what the zemindari could really yield. The amount payable was enhanced from $22\frac{1}{2}$ to 40 lakhs and, though this was not at once realised in full, there was soon an annual gain. The Company also secured a more direct control over the zemindari. Chait Singh's nephew, who was still a minor, was permitted to succeed to the position of zemindar, but the special privileges which his uncle had enjoyed were withdrawn, and the administration passed for all practical purposes to the Company.

Hastings himself inaugurated the new arrangements. Benares being a centre of pilgrimage for the whole of India, he was particularly anxious that the administration of the city should do credit to the Company. He established a regular police force and new courts of justice, and appointed as Chief Magistrate of the city a Muhammadan, Ali Ibrahim Khan, who was well known to him for his good sense and integrity. Ali Ibrahim did excellently, and when Hastings visited Benares again in 1784 he had the unusual experience of hearing "the voice of adulation directed even in my own presence from myself, in the eagerness of bestowing a better-merited praise on another."

The government of the rest of the Benares zemindari, also placed by Hastings entirely in native hands, was less happy, and in 1784 he was obliged to remove the principal official and to extend the authority of Ali Ibrahim Khan.

Hastings claimed, and has been adjudged entitled to, credit for the manner in which he extricated himself from his difficulties at Benares. It is clear that throughout the crisis he kept his head admirably, and his complete presence of mind in a perilous situation added considerably to his own and to the Company's prestige. He sent no alarmist reports to Wheler in Calcutta and made no requests to him for men or money, though for a time he was destitute of both. He forbade the Nawab of Oudh to come to his assistance, lest the Company should suffer in credit or dignity by appearing to rely on extraneous aid. In the most desperate period of his distresses he managed to send directions for negotiations with Sindhia, who had just then applied for a cessation of hostilities, and to bring these negotiations to a successful conclusion. His own rescue, he says with pride, "I obtained more from the affection than the obedience of my officers," who "flew to my assistance" from the neighbouring stations. The occasion did indeed afford a remarkable demonstration of the respect and even affection with which he was regarded, not only by his own countrymen and subordinates, but also by some of the conspicuous Indian figures of the day. The Rajah of Berar, so far from taking advantage of his embarrassment, sent to enquire after his safety, and the Rajah's Vakil, Beneram Pundit, who happened to be at Benares at the time, not only accompanied him on his retreat to Chunar, but personally made him a most timely advance of a lakh of rupees. The Nawab of Oudh, disregarding Hastings' injunctions, hurried to join him at Chunar, and immediately offered him personally a gift of 10 lakhs. Hastings accepted it and applied it to the public service. These examples of assistance generously offered by friends and allies at a moment of distress illustrate not unpleasingly the Indian tradition, and give a good indication of how a wealthy subject like Rajah Chait Singh might have been expected to behave if he had been really loyal to the Company's Government.

Yet, though the Benares incident was not wanting in its compensations and there was much in it which reflected credit on Hastings, taken as a whole it must be accounted a blot on his record. His actual demands on Chait Singh for assistance were not in themselves harsh or unwarranted by the despotic system of government to which he was heir. He also had good cause to be annoyed at Chait Singh's repeated recalcitrance. But his general treatment of him, judged even by despotic standards, was both severe and unwise; and, judged by his own high standards of courtesy and consideration towards Indian notables, it was deplorable. His demand for 2,000 horsemen shortly after his acceptance of the douceur of 2 lakhs, his unrelenting demeanour at Buxar when Chait Singh laid his turban at his feet, his refusal of another interview on arrival at Benares, his insistence on the frigid formality of a written communication demanding an immediate answer to charges— all these things were bound to make him appear to Chait Singh as a hard, unyielding tyrant whom nothing would appease. Such behaviour was both uncharitable and impolitic. It roused in Chait Singh a spirit of resistance and compelled Hastings to adopt the dangerous course of placing him under arrest and humiliating him before his own people. There should have been no need to go to such lengths. A hint of possible forgiveness at Buxar, the courtesy of another interview at Benares, would have given away nothing and would have coaxed Chait Singh into a spontaneous offer to compound for past delinquencies by payment of a reasonable fine. But Hastings was not in a mood to be mild and reasonable. His admitted intention of imposing a fine of as much as 40 to 50 lakhs shows that anger and arrogance had thrown him off his balance. He felt that he had Chait Singh in his power; and, yielding to the temptations of power and forgetting his own principles of justice and moderation, he provoked what proved to be a dangerous crisis and, instead of 50 lakhs, got, for the moment, nothing at all. Historians have found some excuse for him in his extraordinary financial perplexities; but the truth is that the fatal temptations of despotic power rather than financial embarassments were the real cause and must be the partial excuse for his conduct. Those who have actually experienced the temptations of power in the hot climate of India will judge him less harshly than historians.

From Benares Hastings was to have proceeded to Lucknow to settle affairs with the Nawab of Oudh; but, his plans having been upset by Chait Singh's rebellion, he met the Nawab at Chunar.

Asaf-ud-daula was a weak, amiable, foolish, incompetent prince. He had no proper control over his subjects or his revenues, and was chronically in debt to the Company on account of the troops which he hired to defend and keep order in his dominions. Originally these had been limited to a single brigade, but during the rule of the Majority another corps was raised and disciplined for him by English officers, so that in effect he became responsible for the charges of rather more than two brigades. With efficient management he should have been able to meet these charges without difficulty. But Asaf-ud-daula was not efficient. He dissipated his revenue among favourites and allowed himself to be imposed upon by the Company's military officers stationed in Oudh, who shamelessly sponged on him for presents and perquisites, lent him money at exorbitant rates of interest, and wrung from him pensions and jagirs [1] in return. According to Hastings, "Every Englishman in Oudh was possessed of an independent and sovereign authority. They learned and taught others to claim the revenue of lacs as their right, though they could gamble away more than two lacs (I allude to a known fact) at a sitting."

Apart from his own follies, Asaf-ud-daula had been handicapped at the outset of his reign by

[1] The grant of the right to collect and retain the revenues of a tract of land.

two foolish acts of the Majority. They had deprived him of the rich Benares zemindari, and they had confirmed the arrangement made by Bristow, their agent at Lucknow, whereby his mother and grandmother (the Begums) were permitted to retain, under the Company's guarantee, large jagirs and most of Shuja-ud-daula's hoarded wealth. Asaf-ud-daula had never recovered from these handicaps, and by 1781 he himself felt that his dominions were in such disorder and his revenues so much diminished that he must turn to Hastings for help. He had great faith in Hastings because his father, Shuja-ud-daula, had trusted him and been his friend, and on his death-bed had told his family to rely on him for support.

Hastings' chief concern was that the Nawab should discharge his debt to the Company in the shortest possible time. To this end he persuaded him to separate his public from his private expenses; to fix the amount of the latter; to put the control of the former in the hands of Ministers, who would act in close co-operation with the British Resident, and to reduce his army. The Nawab on his part desired to be relieved of all the Company's troops except one brigade, and to be assisted in ridding himself of the superfluous English officers who were battening upon him. Compliance with his wishes meant incurring the ill-will of all those who would lose their jobs; it also meant throw-

ing the charges of the unwanted troops directly
on the empty Bengal treasury. But the requests
were reasonable and Hastings did not hesitate;
he at once gave orders for the troops, which the
Nawab no longer required, to be withdrawn,
and he told the Resident to give all British subjects in Oudh notice to leave the country within
three months.

There was one further point on which agreement was reached, namely, that the Nawab,
in order to increase his revenue and so be able
to pay off his debts, should resume a large
number of jagirs. Hastings was primarily
interested in the resumption of jagirs held by
worthless favourites; but the Nawab himself
pressed for resumption of those held by his
mother, the younger Begum, which the Company had guaranteed. Hastings had never
approved of this guarantee, and was only too
glad to find a pretext for withdrawing it. The
Begums conveniently provided one; for just at
this time reports began to reach him that they
or their adherents had been aiding and supporting Chait Singh in his rebellion. He agreed,
therefore, that the younger Begum's jagirs
should be resumed, provided that cash payments
were made to her in lieu thereof.

More than two months passed, but in spite of
constant pressure from Middleton, the Resident,
no effective steps were taken by the Nawab for
the resumption of any of the jagirs. The truth is

that he was unwilling to deprive his favourites of what he had bestowed on them; and many of them kept armed retainers and were prepared to resist. At the beginning of December, finding Hastings relentless in his demands for payment of the debt, he proposed to Middleton that he should be allowed to lay hands on a portion of Shuja-ud-daula's treasure, which the Begums had appropriated, and that the Company should not, in discharge of its guarantee, interfere on their behalf. "This, my dear Sir," Middleton wrote to Hastings, "is a flattering proposition, and as to the point of right . . . you may possibly be of opinion that the conduct of the Begums in the late disturbance at Benares, as set forth in the several testimonies laid before you, has forfeited any claim they might originally have had to the protection and mediation of the Company. . . . For my own part I am so well persuaded of the disaffection of the Begums . . . to our cause . . . that I could very easily reconcile it to my conscience to assist the Nabob instead of obstructing him, in wresting from them every benefit they enjoy beyond a decent maintenance." Hastings, now in desperate need of money, found his conscience equally conciliable, and agreed that the Nawab should be "strenuously encouraged and supported" in his proposal "to deprive the Begums of their ill-employed treasure." He instructed Middleton to be personally present so as to prevent any abuse of power, but he also told him that he must allow no "negotiations or forbearance, . . . until the Begums are at the entire mercy of the Nabob, their jagirs in the quiet possession of his Aumils,[1] and their wealth in such charge as may secure it against private embezzlement."

The Begums lived in a palatial fortress at Fyzabad which had formerly been a favourite residence of Shuja-ud-daula. Accompanied by Middleton and some of the Company's troops, the Nawab marched there, invested the place, and called upon the Begums to hand over Shuja-ud-daula's treasure. They obstinately refused to do so. This refusal was, of course, inspired by others. Having lived all their lives in the Zenana, they took their cue from their servants and dependants, prominent amongst whom were two crafty and immensely rich eunuchs. It was they who really derived benefit from the Begums' wealth, and it was they who prompted or encouraged resistance to the Nawab's demands. Finding the Begums obstinate, the Nawab arrested the two eunuchs, put them in irons and kept them without food. These measures soon produced results, and in a few days the eunuchs brought out "from the most secret recesses of their houses" 55 lakhs of rupees (over half a million sterling). Similar pressure, exerted at intervals during the year 1782, ultimately

[1] Revenue Collectors.

extorted from them about 50 lakhs more. Most of these sums were paid over to the Company in discharge of the Nawab's debt.

Such are the bare facts regarding Hastings' treatment of the Begums of Oudh. It can hardly be maintained that the ladies themselves suffered any severity. No violence or insults were offered to them personally, and they were dispossessed of only a portion of a huge fortune to which they had no moral or legal right—for Shuja-ud-daula's alleged will in their favour was never produced. It is true that, without pressure from Hastings, Asaf-ud-daula would not have taken anything from them at all; but there was nothing particularly heinous in encouraging him to appropriate part of what should have been his by right. Nor did the Begums themselves bear Hastings any resentment. Though it was his pressure which forced them to disgorge, he had caused them no real hardship—for even after the loss of half their treasure they still retained about one million sterling—and, as they knew, he had been the trusted friend of the revered Shuja-ud-daula. With them this counted above all else. Because of this friendship they placed implicit confidence in him, rightly believing him to be the well-wisher of the family and the helper and protector of their weak and foolish Asaf-ud-daula. At the time of his trial they sent him letters expressing their gratitude and sympathy.

Responsibility for the ill-treatment of the eunuchs rests formally with the Nawab, for it was by his order that they were kept in confinement, in irons and on short rations. But all this was done under pressure from Hastings, who had expressly instructed the Resident that there must be no negotiation or forbearance. Hence Hastings can hardly escape some measure of responsibility for the measures that were taken against them. These, by the Indian standards of the time, were merely normal routine; by the standards of modern Europe they were abnormally mild; by the standards of a civilised government they were open to objection. But the eunuchs are not really entitled to much sympathy. They had no moral claim to the enjoyment of the riches which they were secreting, and such sufferings as they went through were due to their own miserly instincts which precluded them from yielding up a single rupee except under duress. In England to-day the true miser is almost an extinct species; but in the cities of India misers are still commonly met with—men of fabulous wealth who clothe themselves in filthy raiment, bemoan their poverty, part with even a rupee as though it were the last drop of their blood, and secretly brood over vast hoards of coined money and precious metals. The eunuchs were men of this type. They clung to their riches with every artifice of concealment and deception, feigning tears, offering for sale their household utensils as though they had nothing else left, and calling God to witness that they were doomed to pass the rest of their days in penury. Twenty years later one of them was still alive and was granted an interview by Lord Wellesley. He was at that time fat and well and reputed to be worth half a million.

Perhaps the most serious charge which can be brought against Hastings in regard to these transactions is one of breach of faith. The Company had guaranteed the Begums the possession of their jagirs and their treasure. Hastings permitted this guarantee to be violated. He had, however, colourable excuse for what he did. For it is clear from contemporary reports that immediately after the outbreak at Benares the Begums or their agents actively espoused Chait Singh's cause, sent armed men from Fyzabad to help him, and attacked isolated detachments of sepoys. Doubtless Hastings made the most of these reports, but they were quite precise, and certainly not without foundation. It may well be true that the Begums' disaffection had been caused by the scandalous misbehaviour of English officers in Oudh—according to Hastings Lucknow was "a sink of iniquity" and "the school of rapacity"—but, whatever its cause, it gave Hastings the pretext which he wanted, and, considering his difficulties, he was quite justified in making use of it.

One other incident in Hastings' dealings with Oudh at this time has attracted criticism and is of interest for the light which it throws on his ideas of financial propriety. As already mentioned, when the Nawab of Oudh met him at Chunar he offered him a gift of 10 lakhs of rupees (£100,000). Hastings accepted it and credited the sum to the Company. It has been suggested by some writers that the Nawab meant the gift as a bribe, and hoped thereby to be spared the necessity of despoiling his mother and grandmother in order to discharge his debt to the Company. This interpretation of the Nawab's motives is uncharitable and over-simple. Asaf-ud-daula certainly wished to please and conciliate Hastings; but he also had a genuine regard and respect for him as the friend of his father. The gift of 10 lakhs, just when Hastings was in desperate need of money after his escape from Benares, sprang as much from an impulsive generosity, typical of Indian character, as from any carefully calculated expectation of a return. It is in any case hardly conceivable that Asaf-ud-daula hoped by this gift to induce Hastings to remit the whole of his huge debt to the Company. Probably the most that he hoped for was that Hastings would agree to reduce the number of the Company's troops chargeable to him, and would help him to exclude English adventurers from Oudh. This hope was realised.

To modern ways of thinking, Hastings'
acceptance of this personal gift from a ruler
who was heavily in debt to the Company may
seem open to objection and excusable only by
his exceptional difficulties and the debased
standards of the time. Yet it has its modern
parallel. During the two great wars of the present century, the Viceroy of India and Provincial Governors have not hesitated to accept
gifts presented to them personally as contributions to various War Funds which they
sponsored. In some instances the motives of the
donors were far more crudely mercenary than
those of Asaf-ud-daula, and their financial
embarrassments no less serious than his. But
their gifts were accepted. Thus traces still
survive of a corrupt system which Hastings in
his day simply took for granted.

More extraordinary and more repugnant to
modern standards was the request which he made
to the Directors to be allowed to keep the money
for himself. The request was turned down; but it
was quite in keeping with the practice of the
times. Exceptional services were commonly rewarded by grants of money, and Hastings' services to the Company during a period of over
thirty years had certainly been exceptional. Clive
had retained without compunction the enormous presents offered to him, holding that he
was entitled to them by his services; and even
Bristow, an officer of little merit, was voted on

Francis' motion a gratuity of a lakh of rupees as a reward for work of doubtful utility as Resident of Lucknow. With these and other examples before him, Hastings felt that he could justly claim from the Company some special mark of their approbation. The Directors thought otherwise, and not without reason; for as Governor-General he drew a salary of £25,000 per annum. They demanded, quite rightly, a full account of all the presents which he had received and turned to public use—these amounted altogether to about 30 lakhs of rupees —and they indicated, again quite rightly, their disapproval of such transactions. To have allowed him to retain for himself any portion of the money would have been a fatal precedent.

Hastings was a trifle aggrieved at being excluded from the advantages enjoyed by others, but his vanity was tickled. "My name," he had written a little earlier, with an obvious thrust at Clive, "has received no addition of title, my fortune of jagheers, nor my person any decorations of honours"; and he went on to observe with evident satisfaction that he had dispensed with such amenities as a domestic surgeon and a private chaplain. "Neither my constitution nor my religious principles have been a charge upon the Company. These and other distinctions have been the lot of others . . . nor upon my honour has my envy been excited by them."

Chapter Sixteen

Last Years in Bengal

WHILE Hastings was away up-country a new Councillor, John Macpherson, had arrived from England and taken his seat with Wheler. He was a handsome, good-humoured, plausible rascal who had originally come out to Madras as a ship's purser and then wormed his way into the confidence of Muhammad Ali, the Nawab of the Carnatic, and later into the service of the Company. Hastings had known him at Madras and been friendly with him. At that time he was acting as private secretary to Dupré, the Governor; but he continued to be closely associated with Muhammad Ali's affairs and with Paul Benfield, the chief manager of his notorious debts. Lord Pigot, who as Governor opposed this party of fortune-hunters, very properly dismissed him from service; but, being a genial, attractive fellow with plenty of money—which he had sucked from Muhammad Ali—and the support of the whole corrupt Benfield gang, he soon made influential friends in England.

Hastings' star was at this time in the ascendant. The Majority had been defeated,

and Lord North wanted him to continue in
Bengal as Governor-General during the stresses
of the American War. With typical astuteness
Macpherson decided to throw in his lot with
his old Madras acquaintance. He resumed
correspondence with him, painted glowing
pictures of all that he was doing for his interest
in England, and did, indeed, bring to his support the corrupt influence which Benfield had
purchased in Parliament and in the Court of
Directors—a very dubious advantage. Having
thus established himself as Hastings' friend, he
could plausibly represent himself to the
Directors and to Lord North as just the man to
replace Barwell when Barwell returned to
England. The policy was to strengthen
Hastings' hands. Who more fitted to do this than
his old friend Macpherson? To Sullivan and other
supporters of Hastings in the Court of Directors
this seemed an excellent idea; it also commended
itself to Lord North. So Macpherson was
nominated to succeed Barwell. A more unsuit-
able and disgraceful appointment it would be
hard to imagine. Macpherson was an adventurer. His interest and skill lay in jobbery, in
shady financial transactions and in the accumulation of presents and perquisites. He was, in
fact, admirably qualified to perpetuate the worst
traditions of the Company's service.

Hastings was at first satisfied and even
delighted with his new colleague. He admits

that "a ray of inspiration very early flitted across my imagination more than once, and showed me the naked character of Macpherson, . . . but I either treated the warning as an illusion, . . . or chose rather to be deceived than to yield to doubtful suspicion." Macpherson heartily applauded and defended all his transactions with Chait Singh and the Nawab of Oudh. Hastings was extremely gratified. "I experience in him every aid and support that I expected, and an ease with a benevolence of disposition exceeding—even far exceeding—my expectations, and even my knowledge of him."

Throughout 1782 this happy harmony continued. Towards the end of the year Francis' successor, John Stables—also supposed to be friendly to Hastings—arrived in Calcutta and took his seat in Council. A surly, taciturn man, he devoted himself at once to the congenial task of assisting his relations. Two of them were provided with lucrative posts within a month of his arrival. Macpherson also helped his own friends liberally to profitable jobs.

The unwonted harmony in the Bengal Council did not last very long. It was broken by events in England. Hastings had foreseen that Francis, as soon as he got home, would start a regular campaign of calumny against him. In the hope of counteracting it, he despatched to England in 1781 an agent, Major Scott, whom he kept constantly supplied with material with which to refute Francis' slanders. Scott was an indefatigable and zealous — over-zealous — worker; he was also a bit of a fool. Francis was no fool, and hatred made him as tireless as Scott. He was not effusively received either by the Directors or the Minstry, but Burke and other enemies of the Company, of whom there were many, greeted him with open arms. Assiduously he diffused his poison among them. In the spring of 1782 two Committees of the House of Commons sat to enquire into Indian affairs. Well supplied by Francis with malicious mis-representations, they drew up reports casting severe reflections on Hastings' character and conduct; and in May, on the motion of Dundas, a resolution was carried censuring him for "having in sundry instances acted in a manner repugnant to the honour and policy of the nation," and calling on the Directors to remove him from the post of Governor-General.

Lord North a few weeks before this had fallen from power. Several members of the new Government of the Marquis of Rockingham were friendly to Hastings, but none of them were willing to exert themselves on his behalf, and among the Government's adherents in the Commons were Fox and Burke, his avowed enemies. The Directors, as a result of recent elections, were also unfavourable to him and disposed to take action on the House of Commons' resolution. Once again the Court of Proprietors came to his rescue. By a large majority they resolved that no order for his recall should be passed without their consent.

He had been saved; but his position was once more precarious. Its essential weakness lay in his inability to count on the steady support of any political party. The Proprietors of the Company might stand staunchly by him; but when once the dangers of war were over, no Ministry, whether Whig, Tory or Coalition, cared much about Hastings, a Company's man, commanding no votes or political influence and represented by that tiresome, importunate busybody, Major Scott. Rockingham died and was succeeded by Lord Shelburne; Shelburne, by a coalition of Fox and North, and they in turn by the younger Pitt. All of them were interested in Indian patronage; some of them professed interest in the reform of Indian government; but none of them were interested in supporting Hastings; for he stood between them and management of Indian affairs through a man of their own party or their own choice. When Scott besieged them with requests to rescind the censure and adverse resolutions of the House of Commons, they fobbed him off with fair words and promises and did nothing; and all the while Francis kept spreading among them his slanderous gossip. The treatment of Chait

Singh and the spoliation of the Begums provided him with plenty of new material.

By the beginning of 1783 it was clear to Macpherson in Calcutta that slavish support of Hastings would no longer pay. Friends in England advised him "not to attach himself to a fallen interest." His earlier enthusiastic defence of Hastings' conduct at Benares already began to appear imprudent; for the Directors stigmatised the arrest of Chait Singh as "unwarrantable and highly impolitic" and hinted that they might order his restoration to the Benares zemindari.

Hastings protested vigorously. In a long letter to the Directors written in March 1783, he told them that by their "proclaimed indisposition" towards him, and their partiality for Chait Singh, "a man universally considered in this part of the world as justly attainted for his crimes, the murderer of your servants and soldiers, and the rebel of your authority," they had annihilated his influence and had virtually invited his associates in Council to withdraw their support from him. He was weary of receiving from them, instead of support and encouragement, "reproach, hard epithets and indignities." If they still had no confidence in him, the time had come for him to make way for someone else. "I am become a burthen to the service," he wrote, "and would instantly relieve it from the incumbrance, were I not apprehensive of creating worse consequences by my abrupt removal from it." He went on formally to notify them of his intention to resign and to request them to nominate his successor. He also warned them that if they ordered the restoration of Chait Singh, "I will instantly give up my station and the service."

The warning had effect. Chait Singh was not restored. But there was delay in selecting a successor to Hastings, and for nearly two years he lingered on in Bengal—two years of little positive achievement and marred by constant wrangles with his Council. His irritation at opposition from Stables and Macpherson made him feel something like regret for his former antagonists. Writing to Major Scott he quotes from King Lear:

> "These wicked creatures yet do look well favoured
> When others are more wicked; not being worse
> Stands in some rank of praise."

He continues, "I in my heart forgive General Clavering for all the injuries he did me. He was my avowed enemy. These are my dear friends, whom Mr. Sulivan pronounced incapable of being moved from me by any consideration on earth." But Stables and Macpherson, certain now that Hastings' long reign was drawing to an end, were not disposed to tie themselves to him too closely. The time had come for them to show a little independence and to dissociate themselves from measures which might be unpopular with the authorities in England. Hastings, perhaps not unnaturally, resented this. Since Francis' departure at the end of 1780 he had enjoyed unfettered power. For two years his word had been law; Wheler, and later for a while Macpherson, had merely echoed his sentiments; and now he had grown intolerant of opposition, was irritated by the slightest hint of disagreement, convinced that he was always right and unwilling to conciliate or defer to the opinion of others. He was not the man he had been ten years earlier when, with infinite tact, he had carried his Council with him in all his measures of retrenchment and reform. He had been too long in India. His health was failing; he was peevish and irritable, and, as he himself admitted, too often "thrown off the guard of my prudence; for, my dear Scott, I have not that collected firmness of mind which I once possessed, and which gave me such a superiority in my contests with Clavering and his associates. My last year's sickness has left a debility upon my constitution which I cannot remove, nor shall till I try a colder climate."

Poor Wheler hated these contentions. Intimidated on the one hand by Stables and Macpherson, yet bound to Hastings by admiration, loyalty and gratitude—for Hastings had "provided handsomely for all his friends"—he did his best to keep the peace and steer a middle course. On the whole he comes out of it not too badly.

The conduct of Lord Macartney in Madras was one of the causes of disagreement between Hastings and his colleagues. Macartney had greatly annoyed Hastings by incautiously proclaiming his desire for peace and by opening unauthorised negotiations with Tipu without reference to the Marathas and the Treaty of Salbai. But he gave, if possible, still greater offence by his cavalier treatment of the Nawab of the Carnatic. Not long after the outbreak of hostilities with Haidar Ali, the Nawab had agreed to hand over to the Company for the duration of the war the administration of the revenues of the Carnatic, provided that his sovereignty remained unimpaired and that all appointments of Collectors and other revenue officials were approved by him and made in his name. For a few months all went well; but when the Nawab objected to two of Macartney's nominations for the post of Collector, Macartney, disregarding the terms of the agreement, brusquely made the appointments himself. The Nawab appealed to the Bengal Government, who roundly condemned Macartney, declared that by his violation of the agreement he had ended it, and directed him to restore to the Nawab the administration of the revenues. Macartney refused to obey. Hastings, though he did not formally propose it, wished to order his suspension; but at this point his Council declined to follow him. Macartney had powerful friends in England and was considered a likely candidate for the post of Governor-General in succession to Hastings. Macpherson, Stables and Wheler all preferred simply to do nothing rather than to incur his ill-will and that of all his connections at home. Hastings appealed in vain to their honour and their pride. Macartney was allowed to get away with a flagrant piece of insubordination.

Nor, if the truth be told, was his conduct altogether unjustified. He may have been somewhat tactless in his handling of the Nawab, but his aims appear to have been laudable. One of his main objects in taking over the management of the revenues had been to defeat the corrupt Benfield gang, who battened on the Carnatic and drew away its resources in payment of their monstrous interest charges. Muhammad Ali was a pawn in their hands, and his resistance to Macartney was almost certainly prompted by their sinister influence.

Whether Hastings in Calcutta was aware of this and was influenced at all in his conduct by the support which Benfield had given him in England is uncertain. What is clear is that Macartney had offended against two of his basic principles—he had violated a solemn agreement and he had usurped the rights of a sovereign prince; for a sovereign prince Muhammad Ali still claimed to be, and Hastings vigorously defended his rights just as he had defended those of Mir Kasim twenty years earlier. Actually Muhammad Ali was, in Burke's words, "a shadow, a dream, an incubus of oppression." His pretended sovereignty concealed a fraudulent conspiracy between himself and his creditors, of which the wretched inhabitants of the Carnatic were the victims. It was just one of those covert systems serving "as a screen for private embezzlement and rapine" which Hastings abominated. Macartney was as fully justified in trying to sweep it away as Hastings, in 1772, had been justified in ending the sham régime of the Nawab of Bengal. But Hastings does not seem to have grasped this; and Macartney certainly had broken an agreement.

The miserable affairs of Oudh were the other chief subject of dispute between Hastings and his Council. At Chunar, the Nawab had agreed to a number of suggestions for the reform of his Government and his finances. Middleton, the Resident at Lucknow, was held responsible by Hastings for seeing that these reforms were actually put into effect. He proved unequal to the task. Perhaps he can hardly be blamed, for the task which he had been set was well-nigh impossible of achievement. But he does appear to have been slack. He failed to straighten out the accounts relating to the Nawab's debt to the Company, and he failed to evict all the English adventurers from Oudh. Hastings was dissatisfied with him, and in the autumn of 1782 replaced him by Francis' old protégé, Bristow, whom the Directors had long been endeavouring to re-establish at Lucknow. If Middleton had been too weak, Bristow proved too strong, and the Nawab was soon complaining that he had usurped an undue authority and behaved towards him with disrespect. This, of course, at once roused Hastings. Bristow had never been a favourite of his, and he was now charged with what, in Hastings' eyes, were unforgivable crimes, "the commission of insults and indignities to a Sovereign Prince" and "the usurpation of his authority." Bristow made matters worse by pleading that he had only acted in accordance with Hastings' instructions. "There is not a syllable of my instructions," Hastings minuted angrily—and untruthfully—"which will admit of a construction of a power to assume any authority whatever in the administration of the Nabob Vizier." He demanded Bristow's removal from Lucknow. His Council refused to agree, and a long wrangle ensued.

Bristow was an officer of poor judgment and almost certainly corrupt; but Hastings' attitude towards him was unreasonable. He insisted on certain reforms being carried out in Oudh, but then blamed him for going beyond "advice and persuasion." He himself, no doubt, with all his great prestige and authority, could have persuaded the Nawab to agree to anything. Bristow's position was more difficult. The weak, incompetent Asaf-ud-daula, who could not maintain himself without the Company's armed support, yet chafed at the bondage to which this subjected him, might make promises to Hastings; but when Hastings had gone, there were many to urge him to kick against English control, and it was hardly possible for Bristow to keep him to those promises by mere persuasion and advice. Hastings would have done well to recall his own difficulties with Mir Jafar a quarter of a century earlier.

The members of his Council not only felt that Hastings was being unjust to Bristow; they also knew that the Directors had definitely ordered that he should be posted to Lucknow, and they were unwilling to draw upon themselves the Directors' displeasure by recalling him merely in order to please Hastings. Hastings had, however, lost nothing of his old tenacity, and after some months of wrangling he got the Council to agree, not indeed to the recall of Bristow, which would have been to cast a slur on him, but to the more drastic step of withdrawing the Residency from Lucknow altogether on condition that the Nawab gave the security of reputable bankers for payment of his debt to the Company. This was, of course, exactly what the Nawab and his ministers wanted. It was also, as Hastings well knew, the prelude to a request that he should himself visit Lucknow and help the Nawab to put his affairs in order.

"I have indeed conquered," he wrote to Scott early in 1784, "but I feel little inclination to triumph in my victory; for my hands are fettered; and such is the wretched state of the Vizier's affairs, that nothing can be more discouraging than the prospect before me. If the Nabob Vizier shall desire me to come to his assistance, I shall offer it to the Board, and shall be better pleased if they refuse than if they assent to it. Yet I will do what I can to gain their assent." The expected invitation duly arrived. Stables strongly opposed its acceptance; but with Wheler's somewhat reluctant support Hastings carried a resolution authorising him to proceed to Lucknow.

It was an extraordinary mission to undertake at the close of his career. He himself could hardly say what his motive was for "precipitating myself into such a scene of difficulty." Nearly a year had elapsed since he had notified the Directors of his intention to resign. His own health was failing, and the doctors advised that another year in India might be fatal to Mrs. Hastings. It would have been natural for him to accompany her when she sailed for England early in 1784; this indeed seems to have been his original intention. The war was virtually over, and there was nothing vital to detain him. But he changed his mind and resolved to let her go alone, painful though the separation would be to him, and to stop on for another year or until his successor arrived. He himself gave as the chief reason for staying "the distraction which I saw gathering in Oudh" and which "left that country and its Government without a resource, but in my exertions to retrieve it." Macpherson, he was convinced, "would observe no bounds with the Nabob Vizier" once he himself was out of the way. (In this he was not far wrong.) He felt also some obligation towards the wretched Nawab of the Carnatic, who, having been treated by Macartney as a mere cypher, "seemed to catch at me, for he had not a straw left besides, as his last resource." But these reasons appear to be mere pretexts. He was, it would seem, reluctant to part with power, certainly unwilling to let it pass to the unworthy hands of Macpherson and Stables. Possibly he still hoped against hope that political changes in England might lead to his continuation in office for a few years more with the enhanced powers for which he had always longed. If so, he was deluding himself.

Mrs. Hastings sailed on January 10th. "I followed your ship with my eyes," he wrote to her, "till I could no longer see it, and I passed a most wretched day, with a heart swol'n with affliction and a head raging with pain." His letters to her during the next year of loneliness show how much she meant to him. He reminds her with what delight he would "frequently quit the scene of business and run up to your apartment for the sake of deriving a few moments of relief from the looks, the smiles, and the sweet voice of my beloved." The doubt whether he had been right to part from her continually recurs. But the pressure of business did not leave him much time for repining. As he told his friend Impey, "I have a resource in the continual succession of occupations, which prevent my feeling so severe a sense of my loss as I should otherwise do." A threatened famine due to a severe drought gave him work and anxiety enough at Calcutta, and in the month following Mrs. Hastings' departure he set out on his long journey to Lucknow.

During his last trip up-country Hastings complained of languor and lassitude and a constitution "unable to cope with the sun." Yet his energy was still inexhaustible. He laboured, albeit to little purpose, with the same undaunted zeal as of old. From Benares, where he stayed five days, he sent his Council a long account of the state of that zemindari. Apart from the city, it was in a woeful condition. "From the confines of Buxar to Benares," he told them, "I was followed and fatigued by the clamours of the discontented inhabitants." The distress result-

ing from the severe drought was partly responsible, but the cause lay principally, he feared,
"in a defective, if not a corrupt and oppressive
administration." This was the administration
which he had himself set up barely three years
earlier, after Chait Singh's rebellion; but the
failure of his own handiwork does not seem to
have worried him. He proceeded to appoint
fresh officials and to draw up a new plan of
administration, which his Council somewhat
hesitatingly sanctioned. It did not lead to much
improvement. Two years later, Cornwallis
found Benares "a scene of the grossest corruption
and mismanagement." The British Resident,
whom Hastings, knowing only too well the
propensities of his countrymen, had carefully
excluded from direct share in the administration,
had in practice engrossed the whole of it and
was making out of it 4 lakhs a year as well as
vast gains from "the complete monopoly of
commerce."

From Benares Hastings journeyed on to
Lucknow. Bristow had left without properly
adjusting the accounts. Hastings laboriously
went through them, induced the Nawab to
accept without cavil a number of disputed
items, and recovered from him about one-half
of the outstanding debt of 73 lakhs. Arrangements were made for retrenching his expenditure, both public and private, for settling the
revenues for five years and for reforming his

military establishments; and a reconciliation was effected between him and the Begums. "The Nabob solemnly promised," Hastings reported, "that he would not break a single thread of my arrangements, and these, if undisturbed, will discharge all his debts to the Company in the course of a year, and leave him a free and independent man. His uncle, his mother and his grandmother, the most respected of his family, are all in my interest, and look upon me as the guardian of their house."

The object of Hastings' mission had been attained; so, at least, he informed his Council. Yet in his heart of hearts he knew what little reliance could be placed on the promises of poor, opium-eating Asaf-ud-daula, "bred and familiarised to the habits of sloth and dissipation." In order to "remind him occasionally of his obligations and engagements" he left behind his secretary, Major Palmer, to act as his agent and personal representative—thus reintroducing under another name the Resident whom he had previously withdrawn. It was all to no purpose. Palmer was no better—and no less expensive a burden on Oudh—than Middleton and Bristow had been. A few years later the Nawab's debt to the Company again exceeded 70 lakhs, his country was again overrun by European adventurers, his Government was as chaotic as ever, and he himself the helpless sport of low buffoons and parasites. In Oudh, as in the Carnatic and

301

earlier in Bengal, a weak Indian ruler had sought the support of European might only to lay his country open to European avarice. Well might Hastings bewail "our encroaching spirit, and the uncontrolled or even protected licentiousness of individuals," which "have done more injury to our national reputation than our arms and the credit of our strength have raised it." Ever since the days of Mir Kasim he had striven according to his lights to check them; and the object of his last intervention in Oudh had been to clear up the Nawab's debts and thus to rescue him from English clutches and "leave him a free and independent man."

But he was struggling vainly against the deep currents of history. Was he prepared to withdraw all the Company's troops from Oudh and let it fall a prey first to anarchy and then to the Marathas, and thus become a menace to the Company's dominions in Bengal? He was not; nor was the Company; nor was the Government of England. What they had they meant to hold. It was idle therefore to withdraw the Residency from Lucknow and to declare the Nawab a free and independent man. Through reliance on the Company's troops to protect and to keep order in his country, he had sunk from an ally to a vassal; and, as the Company's vassal, he was inevitably exposed to the rapacity of the Company and the Company's servants.

Hastings stayed about five months in Lucknow. It is lamentable to observe how deeply he had now fallen under the influence of incessant adulation. When Nawabs, Begums, Rajahs and Ministers told him that he was their sole resource, that they depended entirely on his wisdom and understanding—he who knew everything!—he veritably believed them. When the son of the Emperor Shah Alam, hearing of his fame, escaped from virtual imprisonment in Delhi and appeared at Lucknow to beg for his help, he was so flattered that he seriously proposed lending him a detachment of the Company's troops to expel the Sikhs from his father's nominal territories. The Council rightly vetoed this hare-brained scheme.

On his way back to Calcutta Hastings learnt of the death of his colleague, Wheler. The Council was once more reduced to three—himself, Macpherson and Stables. If he stayed on, the two latter, who had long been leagued together, could render him entirely impotent. But he was now in any case resolved to leave. News of Pitt's East India Bill, which reached him towards the close of 1784, destroyed any last lingering hopes that he may have cherished of being continued in office on terms acceptable to him. "My situation," he wrote, "is become worse than it was."

Hastings had never looked for anything but hostility from the Coalition Government of Fox and North which had taken office in the spring of 1783. Fox was a determined enemy of the

WARREN HASTINGS

Company. The Bills on India which he introduced were designed to supersede its authority
altogether and transfer power and patronage to
Commissioners nominated by the Crown. Fox
was supported by Burke, and Burke was
prompted by Francis. Their attacks in Parliament on the Company's rule were also direct
attacks on Hastings. But Fox's Bill, though
passed by the Commons, was rejected by the
Lords. The King, who hated the Coalition, took
this opportunity to dismiss them from office.
Pitt was called upon to form a Government,
and, after a General Election in the spring of
1784, he became firmly established in power.

Hastings' friends had taken an active part in
securing the defeat of Fox's India Bill which
led to the downfall of the Coalition. They therefore expected the new ministry to give him
their cordial support. Pitt was reported to regard
him as "a very great and indeed a wonderful man." The Chancellor, Lord Thurlow, told
Scott that he did not know a man "who cuts so
great a figure upon the stage of the world as
Hastings"; and he assured him, "This is
Hastings' administration . . . he put an end to
the late ministry as completely as if he had
taken a pistol and shot them through the head
one after another." These and other flattering
observations—"Good God, what shall we do if
Hastings should throw up the Government?"—
the foolish Scott passed on to his principal. But

Hastings was not taken in by them. "If it is expected that I should remain," he wrote to his wife, "why am I not told so by authority, and trusted with the powers necessary to my station? . . . To me it is apparent, from every observation that I have made, that it is not the wish either of the present or any other administration that I should remain but as a cypher to keep the office open for the gift of their own patronage. I am not pleased to be made so pitiful an instrument."

His view was confirmed by the reported debate on Pitt's East India Bill which was introduced in 1784. This Bill was a skilful compromise. While leaving the Company its trading privileges and patronage, it gave the Crown full control over policy through a Governmental Board of Control. It was by no means to Hastings' taste, chiefly because it left the Governor-General at the mercy of his Council.[1] But it was not so much the Bill itself as Pitt's speech when introducing it which disappointed him; for though Pitt did not mention him by name, it was on him that Pitt's criticisms of the Company's government really reflected. "It may not have been prudent or convenient for him to have proposed my removal from office directly; but it is impossible," Hastings rightly concluded, "that . . . he should desire me to

---

[1] This defect had to be corrected by an amendment of the Act before Hastings' successor, Lord Cornwallis, would consent to take office.

remain, afford me his confidence or add to my powers."

There was now no conceivable motive for staying on, and on January 13th 1785 he formally announced to the two remaining members of his Council his intention to relinquish the service. On February 1st he attended the Council for the last time and made over charge to Macpherson. A week later he was on board the *Berrington* and the shores of India had faded for ever from his view.

He left the country, where he had laboured for thirty years, conscious of having rendered great services—"I have saved India, in spite of them all, from foreign conquest"—but with his hopes and ambitions unrealised; for the powers which he felt ought to belong to his station had never been entrusted to him. "Yet may I feel a regret," he sadly recorded as he voyaged home, "to see that hope which I have too fondly indulged, and which I have sustained during thirteen laboured years with a perseverance against a succession of difficulties which might have overcome the constancy of an abler mind, of being in some period of time, however remote, allowed to possess and exercise the full powers of my station, of which I had hitherto held little more than the name and responsibility; and to see with it the belief, which I had as fondly indulged, that I should become the instrument of raising the British name, and the substantial worth of its possessions in India, to a degree of prosperity proportioned to such a trust; both vanish in an instant, like the illusions of a dream; with the poor and only consolation left me of the conscious knowledge of what I could have effected, had my destiny ordained that I should attain the situation to which I aspired, and that I have left no allowable means untried, by which I might have attained it."

Chapter Seventeen

Impeachment and Retirement

HASTINGS was only fifty-two when he returned to England, but his career was over. Though he lived for another thirty-three years, he received no further employment of any kind. He had hoped for a peerage, a seat on Pitt's new Board of Control, perhaps even a share in the Government of England. There awaited him impeachment and nearly a quarter of a century of peaceful retirement at Daylesford.

His first reception on arrival in England was flattering. He had returned to his native country a celebrity, yet known to few; and there was much curiosity to meet him. For some months, wherever he went, he enjoyed the experience of *monstrari digito*, and was gratified to find himself evidently held in high esteem. The Directors, from whom he had so often received "hard epithets and indignities," unanimously thanked him for his services; the members of the Board of Control were "more than polite"; and the King and Queen went out of their way to be gracious both to him and to Mrs. Hastings. He seems to have made a generally favourable impression. Fanny Burney, who met him at this time, was "quite charmed" with him and noted in her diary, "From all that I can gather, and all I can observe, he appears to be one of the greatest men now living as a public character; while, as a private one, his gentleness, candour, soft manners, and openness of disposition, make him one of the most pleasing."

Just a week after Hastings had landed at Plymouth, Burke gave notice in the House of Commons that he "would at a future date make a motion respecting the conduct of a gentleman just returned from India." Several months elapsed without his making any further move. The threat had caused Hastings no undue disquiet. He was confident that on an impartial review his conduct in India could only evoke applause, and he had no reason to suppose that the House of Commons which had been returned at the election of 1784 would be unfairly prejudiced against him. The party of Fox and Burke, the open enemies both of the Company and of himself, had sustained a heavy defeat at the polls. Pitt and the Tories, now firmly installed in power, were, if not conspicuously friendly towards him, at any rate not hostile; and Thurlow, the Lord Chancellor (prompted possibly by the King), was a particularly warm and vocal admirer. Burke himself was conscious that the tide of popular opinion was flowing strongly in Hastings' favour. He felt that it would be difficult to bring any charges home to him, and that the most he could hope for would be to get a respectable minority to support them. Most of the Whig leaders advised against pursuing the attack, and Burke, deeply influenced though he was by his friend Francis, might possibly have been induced to abandon it, had not Hastings, by throwing out a challenge, deliberately brought matters to an issue. On the first day of the Parliamentary session of 1786, Major Scott (now a Member of Parliament at a cost to Hastings of £4,000) rose in his seat and provocatively enquired when Burke was going to bring forward the motion of which he had previously given notice. To this open defiance there could only be one answer. Both Fox and Burke immediately replied that the matter in which Scott was interested would not be neglected. On February 17th Burke moved for papers and the battle began.

Scott has been blamed for challenging the opposition leaders to proceed with the impeachment. The blame, if it rests with anyone, should rest with Hastings, for it is inconceivable that Scott acted without his instructions. It was typical of Hastings not just to resist an attack but to anticipate it. He was never a believer in passive defence; and he had very strong motives for forcing the issue. Though he had been well received in England, official recognition of his services had been withheld, and it was understood that Pitt was reluctant to recommend him for a peerage so long as the censure recorded by Parliament in 1782 remained unexpunged and the serious charges, at which Burke had hinted, were still impending. Hastings believed that the obstacles blocking his path to honours and employment could be quickly and safely removed by challenging Burke to do his worst. Conscious of the strength of his own case and knowing that the majority of the House of Commons were not unfriendly towards him, he was confident that his honour would be completely vindicated and the stigma of the previous censure erased.

The opening skirmishes in Parliament confirmed this confidence. Pitt and other Ministers opposed Burke's attempt to obtain papers before the charges had been formulated, and defended Hastings' conduct in regard to the Maratha war. It seemed clear that the Government intended to support him. Early in April Burke brought forward his charges, and Hastings petitioned to be heard in his own defence. The prayer was granted, and on May 1st he appeared at the bar of the House of Commons. He complained to his friends that he had only been granted five days for preparation. The time allowed was short, but it would have been long enough if he had realised what the occasion demanded. As Macaulay has remarked, he would have been well advised "to make an eloquent, forcible and affecting oration." Instead of this he prepared a written defence of such immense length that he had to be assisted in reading it by Markham, his erstwhile secretary, and by two clerks of the House of Commons. The reading began at four in the afternoon and went on till after ten, when it was still unfinished. Naturally, few members stayed to listen and it fell completely flat. Hastings, however, thought it had been a great success. "I was heard," he wrote, "with an attention unusual in that assembly and with the most desirable effect; for it instantly turned all minds to my own way, and the ground which I then gained I still retain complete possession of." He was at this time quite confident of victory. "My credit," he told a friend, "now stands higher by many degrees than it ever did."

The debate on the first charge, relating to the Rohilla war, took place early in June. It was on this charge that Burke had most hopes of success; for the war had been condemned by the Directors, it had been condemned by the House of Commons, and it had been condemned by Dundas, the friend and lieutenant of Pitt and the Government's chief spokesman on Indian affairs. But Dundas, so far from supporting the charge, spoke in Hastings' favour, and maintained that whatever mistakes he may have made in regard to Rohilkhand had been amply atoned for by his subsequent services. Pitt, though he did not speak, voted against the charge, and Hastings was absolved by a hundred and nineteen votes to sixty-seven.

The result clearly indicated that the general sense of the House was against impeachment. It was assumed that the opposition would proceed with one or two more charges and then let the matter drop. On June 13th Fox brought forward the charge regarding the treatment of Chait Singh. Hastings' friends were in high spirits. Supporters of the Ministry had received a notice to be present to vote against Fox's motion. That it would be defeated by a substantial majority seemed a foregone conclusion. Pitt had himself a few days earlier requested Hastings to furnish him with a note on the status of a zemindar. It was known therefore that he would be fully armed to meet the argument that Chait Singh was an independent prince and that demands on him for war contributions were wholly unwarranted.

Pitt rose early in the debate and, as expected, proceeded to knock the bottom out of Fox's case. He proved that Hastings had been justified in his demands on Chait Singh, and justified in his proposal to fine him for his recalcitrance. That the charge had failed was the obvious inference. But Pitt, instead of drawing this inference, suddenly gave a sensational turn to the argument. Hastings, he said, though entitled to impose a fine, had intended to impose one which was "utterly disproportionate and shamefully exorbitant." To exact a penalty of half a million pounds for a delay in the payment of fifty thousand was to "destroy all relations and connection between the degrees of guilt and punishment." In view of this guilty intention—which had never been carried into effect—Pitt declared that he would give his vote in favour of Fox's motion.

The whole House was astonished, Pitt's own supporters confused. They had been asked to be in their places to vote against the motion. Their own leader had now announced his intention of voting for it. A considerable number, neither understanding nor approving his sudden *volte face*, refused to follow his lead; but others stuck to him with blind party loyalty, and their votes, combined with those of the opposition, sufficed to turn the scale against Hastings. Fox's motion was carried by one hundred and nineteen votes to seventy-nine. Francis had got his revenge, for by this decision the House, for all practical purposes, was committed to an impeachment. A motion on the charge respecting the Begums of Oudh was carried later by a still larger majority; numerous other charges regarding the acceptance of presents and fraudulent dealings in contracts and commissions were agreed to; and finally, on May 21st 1787, Hastings was arrested and brought before the bar of the House of Lords. The vote on the Benares charge had been decisive.

Pitt's conduct puzzled his contemporaries and has been a puzzle ever since. He himself felt that it required some explanation, and he was at pains to assure his friend Wilberforce that he acted from no ulterior motive. He had found, he said, some of Hastings' acts so bad that he could not conscientiously continue to support him. Wilberforce had no doubt that he was telling the truth, and certainly, in turning against Hastings on the Benares issue, he had some justification; for Hastings' treatment of Chait Singh, though it afforded insufficient ground for an impeachment, had been harsh and imprudent. Pitt rightly hesitated to defend it in its entirety.

Nevertheless, though Pitt himself may have acted, or thought he acted, from quite disinterested and honourable motives, other [1] influences must really have been at work. Hastings' conduct had not been blameless; but it was obvious to contemporaries, as it is obvious now, that on a dispassionate view of the real facts he did not deserve impeachment. Pitt was in possession of the real facts. He was not a man to be deceived by Francis' slanderous distortions or Burke's picturesque eloquence. He knew Francis' malignant character and he knew that Burke was in Francis' hands. How was it, then, that Pitt came to a wrong decision

[1] The view of the matter expressed here is not generally accepted by modern writers.

—a decision which meant ruin to Hastings as a public character?

The only convincing answer is that he succumbed at the last minute to the sinister influence and self-interested advice of his friend Dundas. Originally he had intended to defend Hastings on the Benares charge. Hence the notice to his supporters to be present to vote against Fox's motion; hence his own careful marshalling of arguments with which to demolish Fox's case. It was only on the actual day of the debate that he was persuaded to abandon Hastings' cause. The very weakness of his argument betrays how sudden and recent had been his change of plan. The ground which he gave for condemning Hastings was bad in logic and in law. Lord Thurlow not unjustly declared that "if a girl had talked law in such terms she would have been without excuse." If Pitt's conclusion, that the evidence against Hastings was so damning that he could not be defended, had been the fruit of mature deliberation, he would have stated the case against him in a far more cogent and convincing form. But it was not the fruit of mature deliberation. It was a hurried last-minute conclusion. Dundas spent three hours with him on the morning of the debate and talked him into it.

Whatever arguments Dundas may have employed, the advice which he gave was certainly not disinterested. In the past he had been a conspicuous opponent of Hastings. He had condemned the Rohilla war; he had moved the resolution of censure passed against him in 1782. Feelings of hostility had not entirely passed away; and, besides this ill-will from the past, there was jealousy for the future. Dundas was the leading member of the Board of Control and had already marked out India as a special preserve for himself and his Scots kinsmen. He had no wish to share it with a rival, and Hastings was potentially a dangerous rival. He was now a favourite of the King; and he was extremely popular with the Company. If his name was cleared of all stain, it would be hard to exclude him from a peerage and a seat on the Board; and, if once on the Board, his superior knowledge of Indian affairs and his long connection with the Company would give him an advantage over Dundas both in the determination of policy and (what interested that clannish Scotsman no less) in influencing the Company in its bestowal of patronage. Dundas was shrewd and worldly. It was not regard for justice or the public welfare but the more ordinary motives of dislike and self-interest which made him spend three hours with Pitt representing Hastings' conduct in the most unfavourable light and coaxing the young Prime Minister from a right to a wrong decision.

There was one other factor which contemporaries believed had had some influence on the decision. Lord Thurlow, the imperious and exceedingly able Chancellor, was one of Hastings' most vigorous supporters. In conversation with Major Scott he had spoken with contemptuous impatience of Pitt's hesitation to recommend Hastings for a peerage, and had said that if Pitt was afraid to take the responsibility he would make the recommendation himself. Scott, being a foolish, indiscreet man, gave currency to this tale, which is believed to have reached Pitt's ears. It was well calculated to nettle him. He was barely twenty-seven and very jealous of his power and privileges. He was bound to resent most keenly Thurlow's threat to go over his head in recommending Hastings to the King for a peerage. He had never been a great enthusiast for Hastings, and knowledge of Thurlow's over-zealous patronage rankling at the bottom of his mind may well have made him more prone to yield to Dundas's persuasions.

However this may be, Fate took revenge on both of them. Nineteen years later, in the last session of Parliament which Pitt attended, resolutions were moved reflecting on the integrity of Dundas and, to Pitt's bitter mortification, were carried by the Speaker's casting vote. Dundas was impeached and, like Hastings, acquitted; but he never held office again.

That the impeachment of Hastings was a mistake and cruelly unjust is now generally admitted. It was a monstrous reward for great services.

318

But if we look beneath the surface to the deeper laws which govern human destiny, we can see that he really brought it on himself; it was the inevitable consequence of an attitude of mind which invariably meets with a heavy retribution. The impeachment was simply an example of Ate following Hubris. During his long reign as Governor-General Hastings had grown convinced of his own infallibility. Whatever he did was right; whoever opposed him was wrong. Reading his writings and correspondence over the whole period from 1772 to 1785, one can trace the steady growth of this arrogance until, when he left India, this, the deadliest of the deadly sins, had gained almost complete possession of him. His dangerous state of mind is clearly revealed in the review of the State of India which he wrote during his voyage home. It is rendered odious by its egotism and complacency. A single illustration will suffice. "I have never yet planned or authorised any military operation, or series of operations, which has not been attended with complete success, in the attainment of its professed objects; and . . . I have never, in any period of my life, engaged in a negotiation which I did not see terminate as I wished and expected: and let this conclusion be offered as an undeniable proof of the propriety and efficacy of the principles on which I have regulated my conduct in both."

It is hardly surprising that Dundas and Pitt,

who were given this stuff to read, were luke-
warm in their enthusiasm for Hastings; and it
is also hardly surprising that he himself, blinded
by arrogance, should have dared his enemies to
do their worst and, by deliberate defiance,
courted his own disaster. If he had shown a little
humility and admitted that here and there,
amidst his manifold perplexities, he had perhaps
been hurried into ill-considered actions, the
House of Commons would probably have turned
spontaneously in his favour, disgusted by the
rancour and malevolence of his accusers. But
Hastings would not admit any error. He was
even unwilling to plead his great services as a
set-off, for this would imply that his conduct
had not been entirely impeccable. In his view,
all his actions were above criticism. He had
done nothing wrong, and therefore there was
nothing which his services could be required
to counterbalance. This may have been a *mens
conscia recti*, but it was also a pride waiting
for a fall.

The trial opened in February 1788, in a blaze
of splendour and publicity. It was a spectacle
and an entertainment for the fashionable world,
and there was a rush to buy tickets for a seat
in Westminster Hall. Burke, Fox, Sheridan and
the other managers of the impeachment prepared for their audience elaborate oratorical
displays which sometimes extended over several
days. To modern taste they would be intolerable

on account, not only of their length, but also of their artificiality and absurd exaggeration; but they delighted eighteenth-century listeners.

It very soon became apparent that the trial would be protracted. At the end of the first year it was calculated that at the rate of progress so far achieved it would go on for over twenty years. Parliament only sat five or six months in the year and had other business to attend to besides the crimes of Warren Hastings. At the end of the second year, when the court had sat altogether fifty-four days and was about to adjourn until the next session of Parliament, Hastings offered to waive his defence and requested their Lordships to proceed at once to judgment on the evidence already before them. He would have pleaded guilty, he declared, if he had known that the proceedings would be so prolonged. But the prosecution had not yet completed their evidence, and it was decided that the trial must continue.

The novelty had by this time begun to wear off, and the prosecution went slowly forward with their case in an atmosphere of increasing boredom. There were incessant disputes about the admissibility of evidence, and in 1790 the meeting of a new Parliament gave rise to lengthy arguments on the question whether, on a dissolution, an impeachment necessarily abated. It was decided that it did not, and so the trial went on; but the prosecution agreed to drop a number of the charges and in May 1791 they at last declared their case closed, and Hastings opened his defence.

He had grown, it seems, indifferent to the course of the proceedings and wished only for their end; but the end was not yet in sight. Though the Peers were so utterly weary of the whole business that they could hardly be induced to attend in sufficient numbers to form a Court, Burke persisted in cross-examining the defence witnesses at intolerable length, and three years were to pass before the defence was closed. In 1793 Hastings once more implored their Lordships to pass immediate judgment, reminding them that he might soon "be numbered with those among my noble judges whom I have, with sorrow, seen drop off from year to year, and in aggravation of the loss by their deaths, I may lose the judgment of their survivors by my own." However, after some debate his request was rejected, and the trial was adjourned to the Session of 1794.

It had long since ceased to attract public attention. Not only had the French Revolution and the outbreak of war with France given people other things to think about, but its own final outcome was seen to be a foregone conclusion. Burke alone seems to have retained a desperate hope that somehow or other he might obtain a verdict of guilty. Even after Lord Cornwallis had appeared as a witness and given evidence strongly in Hastings' favour, he still persevered, endeavouring at the last moment to introduce fresh material to replace charges which had clearly broken down. But the Court would not permit it.

The verdict was finally given on April 23rd 1795. One hundred and sixty peers had been present at the opening of the trial, but only twenty-nine had attended the proceedings with sufficient regularity to feel themselves justified in voting. On all the charges on which a verdict was recorded, Hastings was acquitted by large majorities. The number of votes given against him was highest on the charges relating to Chait Singh and the Begums of Oudh, the voting in each case being twenty-three to six. On the conclusion of the voting, he was called in, informed by the Lord Chancellor that he had been acquitted, and discharged. His honour had been vindicated, but it had cost him £100,000—rather more than the fortune which he had brought back with him from India. Financially, he emerged from the trial a ruined man.

Did the impeachment serve any useful purpose? It is commonly thought that Burke's denunciations of Hastings, however unjust in themselves, did at least focus public attention on the abuses of the Company's rule, and that out of the impeachment a new order of things arose in India. This notion is mistaken. The iniquities of the Company's servants were not brought to public notice by the speeches at Hastings' trial—they had been notorious and the constant theme of parliamentary discussion throughout the preceding twenty years, and all the essential measures which brought about a reform were taken before and not after the impeachment. The most important of these were the passing of Pitt's India Act in 1784 and the appointment of Lord Cornwallis as Governor-General in 1785. The Act, by establishing the Board of Control, laid firmly on Parliament the ultimate responsibility for the good government of India. The appointment of Cornwallis ensured that the reformation of the Company's servants, already begun in Hastings' time, would be carried on with still greater determination and effect. For Cornwallis was a man of sterling honesty and complete independence, and he was armed with powers which Hastings never possessed. He did not have to conciliate members of his own Council by conniving at their malpractices or finding lucrative posts for their friends, and, unlike Hastings, he could ignore the endless claims to patronage of the Directors—"that mine of oppressive rapacity," as Hastings described them. Sure of himself and sure of the support of Pitt's Government, he brought about a perceptible improvement in the standards of the Company's servants. While Burke declaimed, Cornwallis acted.

Thus the impeachment synchronised with a real change for the better; but it was not its cause. It served no useful purpose at the time; but it has acquired a symbolic value in the eyes of posterity.

After his acquittal, Hastings settled down to over twenty years of peaceful private life at Daylesford. He had realised his early ambition of recovering his ancestral home, and with characteristic improvidence had squandered enormous sums on rebuilding the house and improving the gardens. Altogether, including the purchase price, he expended on it about £60,000. This he could ill afford and, by the time the trial was over, he was not only penniless but heavily in debt. A petition which he submitted for reimbursement of his legal expenses was ungenerously rejected by Pitt, and, when the Directors came to his rescue and voted him his expenses and an annuity of £5,000 per annum, the Board of Control, whose sanction was necessary under Pitt's India Act, refused to grant it. However, the Directors took up the cause of their injured servant with commendable vigour, and eventually a compromise was reached. Hastings was granted an annuity of £4,000 and a loan, free of interest, of £50,000. After Hastings had repaid £16,000 the balance was remitted.

At Daylesford Hastings entered with zest into the life of a country gentleman. He amused himself breeding cattle, trying—unsuccessfully—to grow Indian plants in England, entertaining his friends and scribbling verses. Keen though his disappointment was at being tossed aside without honour or hope of employment, he gradually reconciled himself to retirement.

"Be this enough for me:
To bear contented my accomplished lot
Impeach'd, revil'd, acquitted and forgot."

He felt that he had much to be thankful for, not least that he could end his days amid the scenes of his childhood. "Though, perhaps, few public men," he wrote, "have had more right than I to complain of the world's usage, I can never express sufficient gratitude to the kind Providence which permits me to pass the evening of a long and I trust not useless life amid scenes that are endeared to me by so many personal as well as traditional associations."

As the years wore on he had the satisfaction of feeling that he had outlived the prejudices that had once been excited against him. Of this he had visible proof in 1813 when, at the age of eighty-one, he was once more summoned to appear before the House of Commons. The renewal of the Company's charter was under consideration, and he was required to give evidence on revenue and judicial matters. As he withdrew "all the members, by one simultaneous impulse, rose with their heads uncovered, and stood in silence till I passed the door of their chamber."

He lived on for several more years after this pleasing incident, happy, contented and without serious impairment of his faculties. "What age is it permitted to me to look back upon," he wrote to a friend in 1815, "with my body and mental faculties, though impaired, not destroyed; and as my memory presents to me the record of times past, to be able to say, *quorum pars non parva fui*; and like a grain of sand in the way of the ball of a billiard table, have given its excentrick direction to the rolling events of the world, which they would not have obtained, if I had never had existence." It was, he recalled, just sixty-five years since he had first landed in Bengal.

Three years after this he was taken seriously ill. He complained of confused sensations "as of the sound of distant multitudes," and for a few weeks suffered considerable pain. The end came on August 22nd 1818 after he had offered prayers for the Company's service, for his country, and for India, for which, he said, "I feel a sentiment in my departing hours not alien from that which is due from every subject to his own."

He was buried at Daylesford.

327

Chapter Eighteen

Hastings' Character and Opinions

HASTINGS' first loyalty was to the Company. No man, he told the Directors, ever served them "with a zeal superior to my own, nor perhaps equal to it." Herein lies the explanation of his career. His zeal saved the Company from disaster, but caused him to suffer for its sins. For the Company's political enemies came to regard him as the arch-villain. He had been for thirteen years the Company's most conspicuous servant. Twice the Proprietors, by rallying to his support, had thwarted the wishes of Ministry and Parliament. Hence, all the envy and moral indignation which the Company aroused among those [1] who did not share its privileges became focussed on him. In their eyes he typified tyranny and plunder.

Some of his accusers, who did not know him personally, were surprised to learn from their friend, Fanny Burney, that she had found this man of blood and avarice "so mild, so gentle,

[1] It is worth remembering that during the worst period of the Company's misrule Burke joined in the mad rush to purchase its stock and was a stout defender of its privileges. It was only after he had lost money and ceased to have a financial interest in the Company that he showed his awareness of its iniquities.

so extremely pleasing in his manners"; and when they first set eyes on him at the opening of the trial, his slight, frail figure and pale, emaciated face seemed hardly compatible with their preconceived idea of a ruthless tyrant and oppressor.

Fifty years later Macaulay found himself equally at a loss to reconcile his preconceived notion of Hastings' character with the actual reputation which he had left behind him in Bengal.[1] As a good Whig, Macaulay had to believe that he had been guilty of great crimes; otherwise the impeachment, which the Whigs had sponsored, would stand condemned as a gross injustice. The charges of rapacity and corruption were demonstrably unfounded; but there were incidents in Hastings' career which, if taken by themselves, might reasonably suggest that he was hard, ruthless and unprincipled. Macaulay fastened on these incidents, wrote them up in gorgeous prose, and depicted him as a statesman indifferent to the laws of morality and to the rights and feelings of others. Yet it was difficult to harmonise this portrait of a hard, unscrupulous ruler —behaving towards Chait Singh "with cold and repulsive severity," and remaining unmoved by the eunuchs' tears which "melted even the stout hearts of English warriors"—with the astonishing

[1] Macaulay was in India from 1834–38 as Law Member of the Governor-General's Council. His essay on Warren Hastings was published in 1841.

popularity which Hastings enjoyed among all ranks and classes of society in Bengal. On Macaulay's own admission—and having himself spent some years in Bengal he knew at first hand something of Hastings' reputation—"in the great art of inspiring large masses of human beings with confidence and attachment no ruler ever surpassed Hastings. . . . He enjoyed . . . a popularity such as other governors have perhaps better merited, but such as no other governor has been able to attain." How had he attained it, if he was as unfeeling and deficient in respect for the rights of others as Macaulay represented? Macaulay could only weakly explain the paradox by saying that his gravest crimes were committed against neighbouring states and not against the people of Bengal. Yet the rulers of neighbouring states had also been loud in his praises.

The truth is that Macaulay, owing to his Whig bias and preoccupation with Hastings' crimes, formed a one-sided view of his character. He paid ample tribute to his intellectual abilities, to his courage and resource and to his 'noble equanimity'; but his finer and rarer qualities of sympathy and moderation, which ran like a golden thread right through his career—never wholly lost even when long years in a hot climate and the constant irritation of opposition and censure had subjected him amid all his difficulties to an intolerable strain—these

330

finer qualities Macaulay quite failed to appreciate.

There was in Hastings, no doubt, as in most able men, a certain element of masterfulness, and this was greatly developed by power and responsibility. His early diffidence, with which Clive found fault, became changed into a self-fidence which found expression at times in wilfulness and arrogance. Francis was not the only person to complain of his desire always to have his own way and his tendency to monopolise the work of Government. But that early diffidence, and the gentler qualities of character from which it sprang—revealed so plainly in the early portrait of him by Reynolds—must not be forgotten. Cowper, his contemporary at Westminster, could only think of him as a good-natured boy. Macaulay recorded the fact, but missed its significance. He did not see that the good nature, which at school had impressed the shy poet Cowper, remained throughout Hastings' life an essential feature of his character. It struck all who met him from boyhood to old age; it was the secret of his popularity; and it was itself an expression of that naturally happy temperament which enabled him through all the years of depression and persecution to preserve, in his own words, "the durable state of his mental tranquillity."

This good nature baffled Francis. Believing Hastings to be a corrupt scoundrel, he was forced to conclude that his friendliness and charm of manner were the artifices of a hypocrite. "He can put on a smile," he said, "and assume an air of innocence and candour enough to melt or seduce a generous mind, and to deceive any man unacquainted with his arts." Others took his smiles and pleasant manners for what they really were—the indications of a naturally friendly and benevolent disposition. A contemporary Indian writer, [1] who met him in 1781, described him as possessing "a vast fund of innate goodness"; while from the Pundits and Brahmans of Benares—the scene of his harshness to Chait Singh—we get the following account:

"Whenever that man of vast reason, the Governor-General, Mr. Hastings, returned to this place, and people of all ranks were assembled, at that time he gladdened the heart of everyone by his behaviour, which consisted of kind wishes and agreeable conversation, expressions of compassion for the distressed, acts of politeness, and a readiness to relieve and protect everyone alike without distinction."

Here we have a charming picture of a great ruler—smiling, affable, and sympathetic. It is very different from that depicted by Macaulay of the stern realist whose "heart was somewhat hard" and whose "principles were somewhat lax."

[1] Ghulam Husain Khan, the author of the Sair-ul-Mutakherin.

Just as Macaulay failed to appreciate the gentler side of Hastings' character, so too he overlooked the profounder aspects of his achievement as a statesman. The British dominion in Bengal was the product of greed and violence. Macaulay had no illusions as to its sordid origins and atrocious character. The Company's servants, "daring, intelligent, eager to be rich," represented "the strength of civilization without its mercy." Against their irresistible strength the people of Bengal were helpless. The only protection which they could hope to find was "in the moderation, the clemency, the enlarged policy of the conquerors." That protection, Macaulay believed, at a later period they found; but he attributed this to the eloquence of Burke and to the acceptance by Parliament of certain great principles of government; he gave no credit for it to Hastings. He did not perceive that it was Hastings' example rather than Burke's eloquence that transformed, ennobled and, to some extent, redeemed the naked greed and violence of the Company's early rule, and that without the change of heart in the Company's servants on the spot, which Hastings' influence and example inspired, British dominion would have disintegrated at the outset through its own sheer lack of principle.

That Hastings towered above the mass of his contemporaries in India, whose sole object was to make quick fortunes, that he was a statesman, not a mere freebooter—"far too enlightened a man to look on a great empire merely as a buccaneer would look on a galleon"—Macaulay recognised. But moderation? Clemency? Enlarged policy? Were these characteristic of Hastings' statemanship? According to Macaulay, he followed with undeviating steadiness the principle that Might is Right. "The rules of justice, the sentiments of humanity, the plighted faith of treaties"—Macaulay sweeps on with majestice assurance—"were in his view as nothing, when opposed to the immediate interests of the State." How does this confident judgment square with Hastings' actual record and with his own recorded opinions?

Looking back at Hastings' career in the light of history, we can see that the ultimate effects of his actions were almost exactly the reverse of what he himself intended. By rescuing from bankruptcy and chaos the Company's government in Bengal and then bringing it safely through the critical years of war, he made possible and indeed ultimately inevitable: (i) the extension of British dominion over the whole of India; (ii) the reduction of such Indian rulers as survived to the status of mere puppets; and (iii) the establishment in India of an essentially British administration. He himself desired none of these things. The first he saw to be a possibility, but disclaimed all wish for its realisation; the second and third he unceasingly deplored and resisted; yet after his thirteen years of rule in Bengal nothing could prevent them coming to pass. He built, perhaps, better than he knew, yet worse than he intended.

As we have seen, he ended his career in India with a sense of disappointment. Why was this? His own declared ambition to be the instrument of increasing the Company's prosperity and extending the influence of the British name had been realised. He himself at the close of his administration claimed that in no part of the Company's annals had the Bengal Government known "an equal state, either of wealth, strength or prosperity." The claim was true. Why, then, was he disappointed? In what respect did his achievement fall short of his hopes?

The answer is simply that the increase in the Company's prosperity and in the influence of the British name might, in his view, have been very much greater. He believed that if he had not been thwarted, but had been permitted to exercise uninterruptedly the full powers of his station, British influence would have been extended to every region of Hindustan and Deccan "through a virtual submission" to British authority of every native power.

These prescient dreams of what might be accomplished caused him to be vilified by his contemporaries and applauded by his successors.

Both alike misunderstood and misrepresented him. His successors, impressed by his prophetic insight, liked to believe that he had consciously willed and worked for the creation of the comprehensive Indian Empire which later came into existence. He had certainly foreseen its possibility. "I am morally certain," he had written in 1779, "that the resources of this country (Bengal), in the hands of a military people and in the disposition of a consistent and undivided form of Government, are both capable of vast internal improvement and of raising that power which possesses them to the dominion of all India;" but he had added immediately in parenthesis the following sentence, *"an event which I may not mention without adding that it is what I never wish to see."* Lord Curzon, an intense admirer of Hastings,[1] quotes the passage as evidence of his far-sightedness, but omits altogether the significant addendum. He wished to praise him, but the praise had necessarily to be consistent with the imperialist ideology of his own day. Inevitably, therefore, he concealed both from himself and from his readers that Hastings, the second founder of Britain's Indian Empire, had not really wished to found that Empire as he and they knew it.

Hastings' contemporaries, misled by Francis, attributed to him ambitious schemes of conquest, ruinous to the Company's pros-

---

[1] *British Government in India,* Vol. II, page 157.

perity and repugnant to national honour and policy. He had foreseen that he might suffer for his "attempts to raise the power of my country and to extend the influence of the King's name;" for he knew the strength of the prevalent belief that schemes of conquest were both unrighteous and unprofitable. Indeed, he himself shared it; annexation and territorial expansion were never part of his policy. Right back in his early days as a member of Vansittart's Council he had opposed the infringement of Mir Kasim's sovereign rights as Nawab of Bengal; and throughout his later career he was closely associated with Sulivan, the leader of the party in the Company's directorate who were sceptical of Clive and disliked territorial acquisitions. Though he frankly confessed his wish to extend the King's and the Company's influence, this objective he proposed to attain not by conquest and assertion of sovereignty, but by attracting all the native powers of India into alliance with the Company. Explaining the policy which he would have pursued if he had not been deprived of power by the hostile Majority in his Council, he wrote: "I should have sought no accession of territory. I should have rejected the offer of any which would have enlarged our line of defence, without a more than proportionate augmentation of defensive strength and revenue. I should have encouraged, but not solicited new alliances; and should have

337

rendered that of our Government an object of solicitation, by the example of those which already existed."

The example which he had in mind was the Company's alliance with the Nawab of Oudh. He had himself put this on an honourable footing "of mutual and equal dependence" by the treaty which he concluded with Shuja-ud-daula in 1773. This alliance was to have formed the model for others. He believed that the Company, by combining its military power with a studied justice and moderation towards its allies and by "a sacred and undeviating observance of every principle of public faith," could have soon made itself courted as an ally by all the native powers of India. The arrival of the new Councillors, who immediately tore up the treaty with Oudh and wrested from its ruler the zemindari of Benares, cut short all these plans; and ten years later Hastings had himself abandoned them. He had by then grown doubtful whether the expansion of British influence through a system of alliances was advisable; and it was certainly in his opinion no longer practicable. All the powers of Hindustan, he said, wanted the Company's support, but all dreaded the connection "which they had seen attended with such mortifying humiliations to those who have availed themselves of it." Mir Jafar and Mir Kasim in Bengal, Muhammad Ali in the Carnatic, Asaf-ud-daula in Oudh, were awful warnings. All had accepted the Company's support, only to become the Company's vassals.

Hastings consistently resisted this process. He justly claimed that in all his dealings with the native powers he had scrupulously respected their rights and adhered strictly to the terms of treaties. His contemporaries disbelieved this, and arraigned him for his "atrocious" treatment of the rulers and princes of India. Even modern writers [1] have ridiculed his proud claim, "the faith of treaties I have ever held inviolate." The harsh treatment of Chait Singh and the spoliation of the Begums obscured, and still obscure, the real facts, so that even to-day it is not generally realised how extraordinarily fair and forbearing he was in his behaviour towards Indian rulers.

Yet the facts are incontestable, and were not lost upon Indian rulers of the time. All those with whom he came in contact—the members of the royal house of Oudh, the Rajah of Berar, Mahadaji Sindhia, the Nizam of Hyderabad— had absolute faith in him; it was he, indeed, who first persuaded them that the British, who were certainly to be feared, might also be trusted. His reputation among them was based upon his record. As a young man he had defended the rights of Mir Kasim, though this meant incurring the odium of his fellow-

[1] Thompson and Garratt, *Rise and Fulfilment of British Rule in India,* page 161.

countrymen: on appointment as Governor of Bengal, he had insisted on respect for Shuja-ud-daula's sovereignty even at the risk of a serious breach with the military; later, to secure justice for the Nizam of Hyderabad, he boldly suspended the Governor of Madras; and he devoted his last years in India to supporting the independence of Asaf-ud-daula and Muhammad Ali, worthless and helpless though they were. A minor, but signal, instance of his justice and good faith is provided by his treatment of the Rana of Gohad. The Rana, when he joined the Bengal Government in the war against the Marathas, had been promised the fortress of Gwalior; but as soon as it had actually been captured by Popham, all sorts of excuses were found for not delivering it to him. The Rana naturally became resentful, and was at once accused by British officers of disaffection. (The sequence is all too familiar in our relations with India.) This drew from Hastings a typical protest. "What right," he asked, "have we to his attachment? . . . We withhold from him the rights which we ourselves had given him, and yet resent every symptom which he betrays, or which we choose to impute to him, of indisposition towards us." In the end the fortress was handed over to him,[1] but, if it had not been for Hastings, his rights would have been brushed aside.

[1] He lost it later to Sindhia.

"I am not so desperate a politician," Hastings wrote on one occasion with reference to the Nawab of Oudh, "as to usurp his authority, and to divest him of all his rights, because I can do it." He was strangely slow to appreciate the rarity of such moderation. He had witnessed again and again the tendency for power to be exploited, either nakedly and shamelessly, or under cover of some plausible pretext such as the need for security or the obligation to succour the weak. In reference to specious fears that the Rajah of Berar, if made an ally, might become dangerously strong, he himself had warned prophetically "the reverse is more to be apprehended, that we shall commence as allies and end as tyrants and despots." His apprehension was fulfilled to the letter. Yet he clung irrationally to the belief that the Company, despite its proved superiority of military power, could form alliances with neighbouring Indian rulers "on conditions of mutual and equal dependence." Only towards the end of his time as Governor-General does he seem to have realised that this was impossible, and that what he called the "fixed policy of our nation in India to enfeeble every power in connection with it" was not so much "fixed policy" as the natural operation of power, which his own deliberate moderation was unable to reverse. Then at last he began to doubt the wisdom of his design for a far-reaching system of alliances; for he saw

341

that every ally must be broken like Mir Kasim, or become a puppet like Mir Jafar.

In resisting the transformation of princes into puppets, Hastings was battling against natural tendencies that were far too strong for him. His resistance to the transformation of the Government of Bengal from a Mogul into a British system of administration was equally hopeless. This is obvious to-day, but was not so obvious at the time. We to-day do not perhaps sufficiently realise how natural it was for Hastings and his contemporaries in India to think that in succeeding to the Mogul dominions the Company (or the Crown) should step directly into Mogul shoes and just carry on the Mogul system of administration. That system was, of course, completely despotic, and the contrast between it and the liberal oligarchy of their own eighteenth-century England struck them forcibly; but it did not occur to them as practicable to change it; it had to be accepted as a fact. Francis felt that, just because it was despotic and wholly repugnant to English ideas of civil liberty, the English should content themselves with receiving tribute and should leave the work of administration entirely to a native Nawab. Hastings, having witnessed the complete collapse of the native administration owing to the Company's violent intrusion, knew that, to restore any semblance of order, positive action by the Company itself was necessary; but this, he thought, should consist merely in reviving, under the Company's direction, but through mainly native agency, the forms of government belonging to the ancient constitution. "It will no doubt be most happy for the inhabitants of Asia," he told the House of Commons, "when the despotic institutes of Jhengheez Khan or Tamerlaine shall give place to the liberal spirit of a British legislature; and I shall be amply satisfied in my present prosecution, if it shall tend to hasten the approach of an event so beneficial to the great interests of mankind." But the approach of this event, which even to-day, after 160 years, hangs doubtfully in the balance, seemed to him so remote as to be quite without practical significance. He envisaged, therefore, a despotic, Mogul, and almost wholly Indian administration.

There were, however, two factors which, before he died and even before he left India, began to operate powerfully to introduce an essentially British administration. One was the influence of opinion at home, summed up in Burke's dictum that "it was the duty of a British Governor to enforce British laws, to correct the opinions and practices of the people, not to conform his opinion to their practice." The other (which has been too much overlooked) lay in the ever-increasing claims of patronage. These, as Hastings complained, the Regulating Act had not only failed to limit but had actually extended. It was useless for him to

plan to abolish the 'Collectors' and to confine
English officials to a few headquarter jobs at
Calcutta, when all the while he was being pressed,
not only by the Directors but also by Ministers
of the Crown, to find openings in India for their
friends and relations and when his own continuance in office depended on compliance with
their demands. Hence, despite his own views
and wishes, the anglicisation of the administration went on steadily during his period of
office; and after his departure it led rapidly to
the exclusion of Indians from all the higher
posts.

Hastings was utterly opposed to this policy
of exclusion. His opposition sprang partly from
a distrust of the virtue and moderation of his
own countrymen, but partly also from a deep
respect for the rights, the feelings and the
virtues of the people of Bengal. "Among the
natives of India," he wrote in 1812 to the
Marquis of Hastings, who had been appointed
Governor-General, "there are men of as strong
intellect, as sound integrity, and as honourable
feelings as any of this Kingdom. I regret that
they are not sufficiently noticed, sufficiently employed nor respected so much as they deserve to
be. Be it your Lordship's care (forgive, my good
Lord, this imperative style) to lessen this distance: be their especial Patron, friend and
protector, and by your example make it the
fashion among our countrymen to treat them

with courtesy and as participators in the same equal rights of society with themselves in all cases not excepted by the institutions of legal authority."

Nothing perhaps more plainly reveals Hastings' real character—and the perversity of Macaulay's judgment—than his sympathy for the conquered people who, by a strange twist of fate, were suddenly placed at the mercy of a handful of English adventurers. Born into the world of eighteenth-century cynicism and corruption, taken from school when still a boy and set down in a counting-house in Calcutta, this orphan from a country parsonage, brought up on the classics and the doctrines of the Anglican Church, displayed a restraint, a humanity, and an insight such as few of his successors have equalled.

There was one advantage which he enjoyed, but which was denied to them. For six years he lived among the people of Bengal—at Calcutta, at Kazimbazar, and at the 'aurang'—not as a lord and master, but as a humble clerk in a trading company which was itself "subject to the most slavish dependence on the Government." During these years he acquired an understanding of them such as no other Governor-General has possessed; while his own natural courtesy and amiability evoked all the best elements in their character. The affection and esteem which he conceived for them at this time survived the startling revolution in the Company's fortunes and his own unlooked-for elevation to a position of great power. Unlike most of the Company's servants in Bengal, he kept his head when suddenly transformed from a trader to a ruler. He saw that the mad rush for loot and the shameless trampling on the rights of the people of the country were not only wrong in themselves, but must also prove disastrous to the Company. "It is on the virtue, not the ability of their servants," he pregnantly remarked, "that the Company must rely for the permanence of their dominions."

When he left Bengal the Company's servants were still corrupt, and the whole administration still deeply tainted with jobbery. Though he endeavoured, especially in his early days, to pick able and honest men for important posts, he himself admits that virtue and ability were not the sole criteria. Throughout his time as a ruler of Bengal he had to conciliate the Directors at home and his colleagues in Council, and the stronger the opposition to him grew, the more necessary was it for him to satisfy his own supporters by providing them or their relations with lucrative posts. We must judge Hastings not by the complacent nineteenth-century standards of Macaulay (who during four years in India saved from his pay a comfortable fortune), but by the corrupt standards of the eighteenth century, which, it must be remembered, were almost as low in Westminster and Whitehall as in Calcutta and Madras. He did not claim to be a reformer; nor was he armed with the authority and coercive power by which alone a thorough-going reformation could have been effected. "It is not possible," he wrote, "that a body of men should refrain from illicit advantages, when the means are easy, not expressly forbidden, no penalty or disgrace annexed to them, and, falling within the reach of all, receive the sanction of general practice." Yet, what could be effected by the influence of example, Hastings achieved. Though his own pecuniary transactions were not all beyond criticism, his general integrity over a long period of years and in the face of great temptation was universally acknowledged and respected by the Company's servants in Bengal; and, if he did nothing else, at any rate by his example he infused into them habits of industry, an interest in administration rather than in mere money-making, and a sense of responsibility for the welfare of the people over whom they ruled.

Greed was not, however, in those days the only besetting sin of the Company's servants. They succumbed also to an arrogance which power and the submissiveness of the people of Bengal readily encouraged. It is to the credit of Hastings and some of his contemporaries that they recognised this as a fault and endeavoured to check it. In the instructions which his friend, Becher, drew up for the guidance of the Supervisors, humility is specially mentioned as one of the "national principles which should ever characterise the name of an Englishman." Humility was surely a remarkable virtue for a conquering race to lay stress on. Yet the fact is that even in the eighteenth century there were elements in England whose outlook was deeply Christian in origin, and for whom exhortations to specifically Christian virtues had a serious meaning. The importance which Hastings himself attached to these virtues is shown by his farewell message to the Company's servants in which he specially commends them for "the gentleness and moderation with which they have generally, and almost individually, demeaned themselves towards the native inhabitants." There can be no doubt that he sought by his own example to influence their conduct for the better.

He also endeavoured to give his countrymen in England a truer understanding of their Indian subjects. In contrast to Francis, who contemptuously condemned "the ignorant and unimproved native of Bengal," he tried to bring home to them that India possessed an ancient civilisation not inferior to that of the West. Thus it was that he sent to Lord Mansfield an English translation of the code of Hindu law, which he had caused to be compiled, "as a proof that the inhabitants of this land are not in the savage state in which they have been unfairly represented." He liked to cite instances of their chivalry and generosity and opposed the theory that they required moral enlightenment from England. With the consolidation of British dominion in India this theory gained in strength, and moved him in his old age to pay an eloquent tribute to Hindu virtues. "Our Indian subjects have been represented as sunk in the grossest brutality," he wrote to the Marquis of Hastings, "and defiled with every abomination that can debase humanity; and it is therefore said that as we possess the power, so it is our duty to reform them, nay to 'coerce' them into goodness by introducing our faith amongst them. If the debasement of their moral character is the only plea for the positive intervention of our Government to bring about their reformation, indeed, my Lord, it will be better to leave them as they are, especially that race of them, the Hindoos, against which these aspersions are particularly fulminated. These I dare to pronounce, and your Lordship will have ample means of knowing with what truth, are as exempt from the worst propensities of human nature as any people upon the face of the earth, ourselves not excepted. They are gentle, benevolent, more susceptible of gratitude for kindness shewn them than prompt to vengeance for wrongs sustained, abhorrent of bloodshed, faithful and affectionate in service and submission to legal authority. They are superstitious; but they do not think ill of us for not behaving as they do. Coarse as the modes of their worship are, the precepts of their religion are admirably fitted to promote the peace and good order of society; and even from their theology arguments, which no other can afford, may be drawn to support the most refined mysteries of our own. The persecuting and intolerable spirit of Mohammedanism has spared them through a course of three centuries, and bound them into union with its own professors: the least therefore that can be expected from the most liberal and enlightened of all nations, that which providence has appointed the guardian of their civil rights, is to protect their persons from wrong, and to leave their religious creed to the Being who has so long endured it, and who will in his own time reform it."

This striking passage is all the more remarkable when we reflect that Hastings' bitter enemy, Nandakumar, was a Hindu.

Hastings' interest in the civilisation, thought and languages of India dated from his early days at Kasimbazar. His attempt, on his return to England in 1765, to encourage the study of Persian at Oxford was unsuccessful, but he seems to have impressed Dr. Johnson both with his zeal and his capacity for oriental studies. "I shall hope," Johnson wrote to him some years later, "that he who once intended to increase the learning of his country by the introduction of the Persian language, will examine nicely the traditions and histories of the East; that he will survey the wonders of its ancient edifices, and trace the vestiges of its ruined cities; and that, at his return, we shall know the acts and opinions of a race of men, from whom very little has been hitherto derived."

Amid the cares of office Hastings could not carry out this ambitious programme in its entirety; but his own keen interest in everything touching the life and thought of the peoples of India was infectious and, with him as patron and preceptor, an increasing number of the Company's servants began to take to oriental studies. Several of them, notably Halhed, became proficient Persian scholars. It was Halhed who, with (Sir) Charles Wilkins' collaboration, translated the digest of Hindu law from Persian into English. Later, Wilkins turned his attention to Sanskrit, and a further impetus was given to these studies when in 1783 the great orientalist, Sir William Jones, came out to Calcutta as a Judge of the High Court with the professed object of devoting himself to scholarship no less than to judicial duties. Hastings cordially welcomed him and not long afterwards the four enthusiasts, Hastings, Jones, Wilkins and Halhed, founded the Asiatic

Society of Bengal for the furtherance of these studies.

Hastings, though he himself never learnt Sanskrit, was deeply interested in Hindu philosophy and enjoyed going off "Pundit-hunting" to Benares, as his contemporaries described it. Macaulay ascribes to his influence the willingness of the Brahmans to lay open to English scholars the secrets of their literature, one of the earliest fruits of which was Wilkins' translation of the Bhagavad Gita. Hastings contributed an introduction which admirably illustrates his broad humanity and affords, perhaps, some justification for the claim of eighteenth-century Englishmen to belong to "the most liberal and enlightened of all nations." After praising the moral doctrines and philosophy expounded in the Gita, with which he himself felt closely in harmony, he passes to the following more general reflections:

"Every accumulation of knowledge, and especially such as is obtained by social communication with people over whom we exercise a dominion founded on the right of conquest, is useful to the State; it is the gain of humanity: in the specific instance which I have stated, it attracts and conciliates distant affections; it lessens the weight of the chain by which the natives are held in subjection; and it imprints on the hearts of our own countrymen the sense and obligation of benevolence. Even in England, this effect of it is greatly wanting. It is not very long since the inhabitants of India were considered by many as creatures scarce elevated above the degree of savage life; nor, I fear, is that prejudice yet wholly eradicated, though surely abated. Every instance which brings their real character home to observation will impress us with a more generous feeling for their natural rights, and teach us to estimate them by the measure of our own. But such instances can only be obtained in their writings: and these will survive when the British dominion in India shall have long ceased to exist, and when the sources which it once yielded of wealth and power are lost to remembrance."

The transitoriness of British dominion in India, with which this passage concludes, was a theme to which Hastings constantly recurred. An empire so distant from the parent state, so much larger than it and more populous, was, in his view, unnatural and unstable. On many occasions it had "vibrated to the edge of perdition"; and though it had survived and might stand for some years to come, it held only "a reprieve from ruin." Yet, though precarious, it could not be abandoned. It was useless to enquire whether the Company or the nation had derived any substantial benefit from it, since it was impossible for them "to retrace the perilous and wonderful paths by which they have attained their present elevation, and redescend to the humble and undreaded character of trading adventurers."

To-day the wheel has come full circle. It is as impossible now for the British to remain in India as rulers as it was in Hastings' time for them to remain as mere traders. Consciously and willingly the British nation is obeying the logic of history and is resigning the political power which a British trading company acquired, half unconsciously and half unwillingly, nearly two centuries ago. It is as useless now, as Hastings felt it was then, to enquire whether the nation will benefit from the change; for the change is inescapable. "The most liberal and enlightened of all nations" is the slave of its own liberalism. It cannot reassert the dominance which it has pledged itself to surrender. Hastings perhaps would not regret it. "If our people," he had written in the days of Mir Kasim, "instead of erecting themselves into lords and oppressors of the country, confine themselves to an honest and fair trade, they will be everywhere courted and respected." His prediction may still turn out to be true.

Note on Books

THE following authorities will be found useful for further reading:

A. MERVYN DAVIES, *Warren Hastings: Ruler of British India.*

SIR ALFRED LYALL, *Warren Hastings* (English Men of Action).

THE REV. G. R. GLEIG, *Memoirs of Warren Hastings.*

SIR JOHN STRACHEY, *Hastings and the Rohilla War.*

SIR JAMES F. STEPHEN, *The Story of Nuncomar and Impey.*

H. BEVERIDGE, *Trial of Maharaja Nanda Kumar.*

MISS M. E. MONCKTON JONES, *Warren Hastings in Bengal, 1772–1774.*

SOPHIA WEITZMAN, *Warren Hastings and Philip Francis.*

SYDNEY C. GRIER, *The Letters of Warren Hastings to his Wife.*

H. H. DODWELL, *Warren Hastings' Letters to Sir John Macpherson.*

G. W. FORREST (ed.), *Selections from the Letters, Despatches and other State Papers preserved in the Foreign Dept. of the Govt. of India, 1772–1785.*

G. W. FORREST (ed.), *Selections from the State Papers of the Governors-General of India: Warren Hastings.*

R. B. RAMSBOTHAM, *Studies in the Land Revenue History of Bengal, 1769–1787.*

H. E. BUSTEED, *Echoes from Old Calcutta.*

ALFRED SPENCER (ed), *Memoirs of William Hickey.*

EDWARD THOMPSON and G. T. GARRATT, *The Rise and Fulfilment of British Rule in India.*
The Cambridge History of India, Vol. 5.

P. E. ROBERTS, *India* (Historical Geography of India, Vol. 7).

MACAULAY, *Historical Essays: Warren Hastings.*

Index

Adams, Major, 54
Ahmadabad, 216
Akbar, 74f., 95
Ali Ibrahim Khan, 269
Allahabad, 73f., 118, 120
Allahvardi Khan, 14–16, 19, 25f., 38, 40
Amini Office, 188–90
Anderson, 190
Anwar-ud-din, 15, 21–3, 25
Aras, battle of, 203
Arni, 227
Asaf Jah, 15, 22
Asaf-ud-daula, 108, 148f., 255–7, 269f., 272–6, 278f., 281f., 296, 301
Aurangzeb, 12f., 15, 103, 123

Baillie, Colonel, 223
Balaki Das, 161f., 165
Barker, General Sir Robert, 112, 118, 120, 124–6, 128
Barrington, Lord, 140f.
Barwell, 112, 138f., 145f., 149, 154, 158f., 170, 175f., 178, 183f., 192, 194, 207, 223, 242f., 246, 285
Basalat Jang, 221f., 225
Bassein, 202, 216, 218
Batson, 56
Becher, 106f., 348
Beerboom, Rajah of, 37
Benares, 145f., 148, 191, 254–83, 300
Benfield, Paul, 221, 284f., 293
Bengal, 2f., 5, 13f., 17, 19, 23, 27, 31, 36–8, 55, 68f., 72, 74, 79–84, 94, 107, 133f., 136, 157, 175, 202, 209f., 336
Bengal, Council of, 135–49,

151–76, 187, 189, 192f., 206f., 236–8
Berar, 13
Berar, Rajah of, 209–11, 213, 222, 225f., 234, 261, 270
Bhutanese, the, 105
Biha, 14, 33, 36, 44, 54, 74, 90, 136
Black Hole, 27f., 30
Bogle, 108f., 190
Bombay, 16, 202
Bombay, Council of, 202–7, 213, 215
Bristow, 149, 191, 274, 282f., 295f., 300
British Dominion in India, 1–4, 81, 86f., 134–6, 156, 197, 201–34, 304f., 324, 333–6, 343, 349, 353f.
Buchanan, Captain, 30
Bundelkhand, 208, 210f.
Burdwan, 34, 39, 80
Burgoyne, General, 208
Burke, 122, 257, 287, 294, 304, 309–11, 315, 322f., 328n., 343
Burney, Fanny, 309, 328
Bussy, 23f., 29, 221, 227
Buxar, 2, 54f., 57, 223, 262, 271

Calcutta, 11, 14, 16f., 26–30, 64, 86, 98, 105, 137
Calcutta, Council of, 34, 36, 39, 42f., 45, 48, 51–7, 215, 223f.
Carmac, Colonel, 217, 244, 249, 260
Carnatic, the, 3, 14, 21f., 25–8, 67, 202, 218, 220, 222f., 230, 251, 255, 292

Cartier, 43, 79–81, 85
Chait Singh, 5f., 148, 209, 244, 254–68, 289f., 313, 323
Champion, Colonel, 127, 130–2
Chanda Sahib, 22, 24
Chandernagore, 16, 208
Chatham, 9
Chitab Rai, 90f.
Chittagong, 39, 80
Clavering, General, 138–41, 150–3, 155, 157, 173, 175–7, 179, 182–93, 290
Clive, 24f., 29–35, 45, 47, 59f., 70, 72–4, 78f., 82–4, 117, 130, 155, 171, 215, 282
Coote, Sir Eyre, 223–8, 240, 242f., 252, 260
Cornwallis, Lord, 100, 300, 305n., 322–5
Cossijura, Rajah of, 237f.
Cowper, 10, 331
Creswicke, 11
Croftes, 190
Curzon, Lord, 336

Dacca, 18
Dacoity, 82, 105f.
Dacres, P. M., 170
Day, Sir John, 243, 245
Deccan, the, 22f., 251
Delhi, 13f., 117, 124
Diwani, the, 74–6, 89, 101f., 253
Drake, 27, 29, 31
Drought, 81f., 299f.
Dual System (Clive's), 76f., 80, 83, 142, 171, 196–8
Dundas, 312, 316–19
Dupleix, 21–5
Dupré, 66f., 114, 284
Dustuks, 26, 107f.
Dutch, the, 16, 27, 33, 171
Duties, customs, 46f., 52, 57, 107f.

East India Company, 2f., 6, 9, 11, 14–20, 32, 36f., 40f., 46, 54f., 59, 61, 71f., 106f., 109f., 134f., 171, 178–80, 328, 335
East India Company servants, 2f., 14, 17, 19f., 25, 27, 32, 36, 40–2, 46f., 50, 60f., 66, 72, 77–9, 81, 100, 107, 109, 111, 139, 146, 170, 191, 195, 197f., 220f., 301, 324f., 333, 346, 348, 351
East India Company wars, 68, 71f., 74–6, 79–82, 203–12, 216–30, 249–57. See also Rohilla war
Egerton, Colonel, 212
Elliott, Alexander, 209, 211
Ellis, 43f., 48, 50, 53, 55f.

Famine, 81f., 84, 96, 106, 299
Farakhsiyar, Emperor, 18f., 46
Fateh Singh, 216
Forde, Colonel, 71
Fort St. David, 15
Fort St. George, 15, 250f.
Fort William, 17, 19, 27, 184, 209
Fowke (Senior), 155, 158f.
Fowke, Francis, 191, 261
Fox, 287f., 303f., 309f., 313f., 316
Francis, Philip, 4, 65, 129, 138, 140–4, 148, 152f., 155, 166, 170f., 173, 175, 183–200, 205, 208–10, 213–15, 218, 223f., 231f., 235, 240–50, 258, 260, 286–8, 304, 315
French, the, 16, 21–9, 171, 201, 205f., 219, 221, 227, 231
Fulta, 27–30

Gaillaud, Colonel, 36
Ghulam Husain Khan, 332n.

Gleig, G. R., 63n.
Goddard, 211–18, 249
Gohad, Rana of, 216f., 340
Graham, 176
Gujarat, 13, 15, 216
Guntur, 221f., 225
Guru Das, 92f.
Gwalior, 217

Hafiz Rahmat, 127–9
Haidar Ali, 68, 209, 218–23, 226–8, 255
Halhed, 351
Hastings, Warren:
  as Company clerk, 11f., 18f.
  as Governor-General, 1, 10, 137f., 143, 283
  as Governor of Bengal, 85–116, 137f., 143, 340
  his ability, 5, 10, 20f., 61, 71, 94, 109, 114f., 139, 177, 189, 194, 231f.
  his attitude to British Rule, 1–4, 334–7, 342
  his birth, 7
  his career and policy, 14, 20, 31–5, 39–41, 43, 45f., 49–51, 58, 62, 66–9, 72, 82f., 85, 87–9, 94, 105, 191, 193f., 218, 256, 290, 297, 306, 334f.
  his character, 5–7, 9f., 19–21, 27f., 30, 43, 48–51, 55–62, 64, 71, 97, 109, 113–15, 128–30, 132, 138, 173–5, 185, 215f., 219, 231f., 242, 269–72, 298, 303, 309, 319f., 328–54
  his childhood and education, 8–11
  his death, 327
  his duel with Francis, 246–50
  his first marriage, 30
  his foreign policy, 117, 195, 199

  his impeachment and retirement, 10, 308–27
  his second marriage, 64f., 185f.
  his view of Christian virtues, 348
Hay, 43
Hindu bankers (Seths), 29, 31, 34
Hindu law, 103, 348, 351
Hinduism, 349–52
Hindus, execution of, 53
Holwell, 36–8, 42, 61
Hugli, 34
Hyderabad, 3f.
Hyderabad, Nizam of, 28, 67f., 221f., 224–6, 234
Hyde, 236

Imhof, Baroness (Mrs. Hastings), 63–6, 185, 297f.
Imperialism, see British Dominion in India
Impey, Sir Elijah, 10, 143, 158–61, 164f., 174, 235f., 238–42, 249, 254

Johnson, Dr., 58, 350f.
Johnstone, 43
Jones, Monckton, 81n.
Jones, Sir William, 351
Jumna, the, 208, 216

Kamal-ud-din, 158f.
Kasimbazar, 18, 20, 27, 30
Korah, 73f., 118, 120
Kuch-Behar, 105

Legislation, parliamentary, 135f., 178, 182, 242, 303–5, 324, 343
Lemaistre, 236
Leslie, Colonel, 133, 208, 210f.
Lucknow, 146, 191, 280, 296f.

Macartney, Lord, 228f., 292–4

Macaulay, 54, 122, 126, 128, 160, 165, 238, 241, 311f., 329–34, 345, 352

Macleane, Colonel, 156, 178–82

Macpherson, John, 284–6, 289–91, 298

Madras, 15f., 21, 23, 28, 62, 64, 66, 68, 220f., 223f., 227

Madras, Council of, 62, 66f., 209

Mahadaji Sindhia, 216–18, 226, 230, 234, 245, 270

Mahé, 16, 209, 222

Malwa, 13, 15

Mani Begum, the, 92

Mansfield, Lord, 61, 103, 348

Marathas, the, 12–15, 68, 73, 117–19, 123–5, 201–7, 210–13, 215–20, 230, 256

Markham, 249, 261, 264, 312

Middleton, Nathaniel, 121, 128, 130, 145–7, 191, 275–7, 294f.

Midnapur, 39, 80, 224

Mir Jafa, 31–40, 44–6, 57, 77, 130, 197

Mir Kasim Ali, 38–57, 72f., 80, 197

Miran, 33, 36, 38

Mogul Empire, 12–16, 23f., 54f., 75, 87, 123f., 342–4

Mohammedanism, 350

Mohan Pershad, 161–3

Monckton, General, 139

Monghyr, 49f., 52

Monson, Colonel, 138, 140f., 150–5, 157, 175f., 182, 187f.

Morgan, Colonel, 184

Mubarak-ud-daula, 91–4

Muhammad Ali, 25, 67f., 220, 284, 293f.

Muhammad Reza Khan, 77, 80, 89–92, 152, 171, 191

Muhammadan law, 101–3, 106, 149

Murshidabad, 20, 27–9, 32, 34–6, 39, 43, 48, 61, 76, 86, 98, 105, 154

Muslim rulers, 13f., 25, 55

Mutiny, the, 150

Mysore, 68, 209, 218, 220, 222

Nadir Shah, 13

Nadya, 34

Najm-ud-daula, 77f.

Nana Farnavis, 204, 206f., 210–13

Nandakumar, 5f., 34f., 90f., 150–67

Naryan Rao, 202

Nizamat, the, 75, 89, 102, 171

North, Lord, 61, 135, 138–41, 146f., 156f., 176–8, 180, 183, 185, 188, 235, 285, 287f., 303

Orissa, 14, 74, 136

Oudh, 3, 73, 108, 150, 281, 294, 301f.

Oudh, Begum of, 5f., 149, 152, 154, 274f., 277f., 280, 314, 323

Palmer, Major, 301

Panipat, 124

Patna, 18, 34, 36, 43f.

Patna, massacre of, 53–6, 72

Pearse, Colonel, 224, 226f., 247f.

Pigot, Lord, 221, 284

Pitt, the younger, 288, 304f., 309, 311–19

Plassey, 2, 4, 31, 41, 54f., 220, 223

Pondicherry, 16, 21, 209

Poona, 201–3, 205–7, 210, 212, 216, 218

Popham, Captain, 217, 244, 249, 267

Porto Novo, 227

Punjab, 97

Purandhar, Treaty of, 203–5, 210, 212, 216, 218

Raghoba, 202–7, 210, 212, 215, 218

Raj Ballabh, 38

Ramnarain, 45, 53

Roberts, P. E., 262n.

Robinson, 177, 180

Rohilkhand, 122–5, 201, 312

Rohilla war, 5, 117–33, 145f. 149f., 156, 172, 312, 317

Rumbold, Sir Thomas, 221f.

Ryots, 189, 199, 254

Sadar Diwani Adalat, 239–41, 254

Salbai, Treaty of, 218–20, 230, 292

St. Lubin, the Chevalier de, 201f., 204, 207

Salsette, 202f., 212, 215, 218

Sanyasis, the, 105f.

Satara, Rajah of, 123f.

Scott, Major, 286–8, 310, 318

Scrafton, 32, 71

Seven Years' War, 67, 140, 193, 200f., 221

Shah Alam, the Shahzada, 33, 36, 44f., 50, 54, 73, 75, 117, 124

Shore, John, 170

Shuja-ud-daula, 49f., 54f., 73, 118–32, 145–8, 171, 199, 274, 277f., 338

Siraj-ud-daula, 25–31, 34, 55

Sivaji, 123

Suffren, 229

Sukapan Bapu, 204–6

Sulivan, Lawrence, 70, 72, 113, 121, 232, 236, 244, 285, 337

Supervisors, 80f., 86, 88f., 98–101, 198, 253

Surat, 214

Surman, John, 19

Stables, John, 286, 290

Sykes, Francis, 61, 139

Thompson & Garratt, 165n., 339n.

Thurlow, Lord, 304, 309, 316, 318

Tipu Sultan, 228–30, 234, 292

Trusteeship, idea of, 3

Upton, Colonel, 203

Vansittart, 36, 38f., 42f., 45, 48, 52, 57, 59–62, 70f., 111, 143

Verelst, 72, 79–81, 155

Vernon, Sir Edward, 209

Vynett, 27

War of American Independence, 4, 201, 208, 235, 285

Wargaon, Convention of, 212–14, 219, 232

Watson, Admiral, 28, 30

Watson, Colonel, 247f.

Watts, 20, 32

Wheler, 192, 223f., 240, 242, 252, 256, 261, 266, 291f., 303

Whitehill, 225, 227

Wilkins, Sir Charles, 351f.

Zemindari, 17, 32, 94–7, 100f., 106, 148, 169f., 174, 189, 199, 237f., 254, 257f., 313

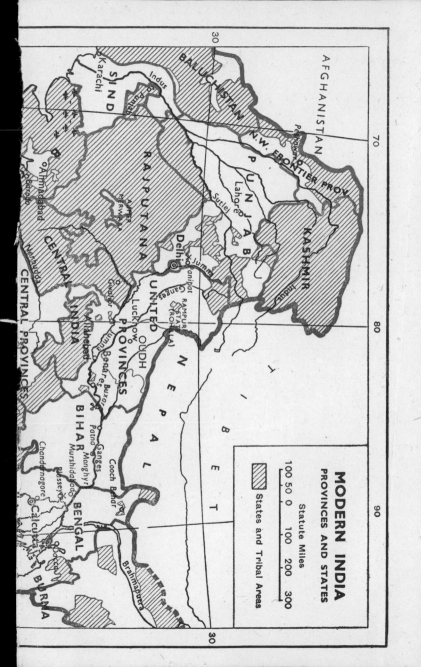